THE INDIVIDUAL IN THE ECONOMIC AND MONETARY UNION

A contribution to legal theories of accountability, this book offers pioneering research on the position of the individual in the EU's Economic and Monetary Union. Its premise is that the EU's response to the financial crisis placed undue emphasis on equality of Member States, to the detriment of political equality of citizens. As a remedy, this book reimagines legal accountability as the vehicle for achieving the common interest by presenting a novel understanding of the relationship between solidarity and equality. The author argues that, by carrying out an intensive review of the duty to state reasons, courts can ensure that decision-makers act in the common interest. The book explores judicial review in financial assistance, the monetary policy mechanisms of the European Central Bank, and the Single Supervisory Mechanism. Looking into the future, it tests its theoretical and normative propositions on the newly established Next Generation EU. This title is available as Open Access on Cambridge Core.

Ana Bobić is a référendaire at the Court of Justice of the EU in the cabinet of Advocate General Ćapeta. In 2022, she published her monograph *The Jurisprudence of Constitutional Conflict in the EU* (Oxford University Press). Previously, she worked at the Hertie School on questions of legal accountability in the Economic and Monetary Union (EMU).

The Individual in the Economic and Monetary Union

A STUDY OF LEGAL ACCOUNTABILITY

ANA BOBIĆ

Court of Justice of the European Union

CAMBRIDGE
UNIVERSITY PRESS

CAMBRIDGE
UNIVERSITY PRESS

Shaftesbury Road, Cambridge CB2 8EA, United Kingdom

One Liberty Plaza, 20th Floor, New York, NY 10006, USA

477 Williamstown Road, Port Melbourne, VIC 3207, Australia

314–321, 3rd Floor, Plot 3, Splendor Forum, Jasola District Centre, New Delhi – 110025, India

103 Penang Road, #05-06/07, Visioncrest Commercial, Singapore 238467

Cambridge University Press is part of Cambridge University Press & Assessment, a department of the University of Cambridge.

We share the University's mission to contribute to society through the pursuit of education, learning and research at the highest international levels of excellence.

www.cambridge.org
Information on this title: www.cambridge.org/9781009207973

DOI: 10.1017/9781009207942

When citing this work, please include a reference to the DOI 10.1017/9781009207942

First published 2024

A catalogue record for this publication is available from the British Library.

A Cataloging-in-Publication data record for this book is available from the Library of Congress

ISBN 978-1-009-20797-3 Hardback

Für Ole

Contents

Acknowledgements

When writing a book comes to an end, one is overwhelmed by looking back at the entire process and cannot help but think of all those who provided vital support and encouragement along the way. This book would not exist without the people I want to honour here.

The book is part of the wider research project LEVIATHAN – 'Legal and Political Accountability in "Post-Crisis" EU Economic Governance' (2017–2021) – funded by the European Research Council (ERC) within the framework of the Horizon 2020 research and innovation programme (grant agreement 716923). I am immensely grateful to Mark Dawson, the principal investigator of LEVIATHAN, for entrusting me with one of the work packages of the project. Working with Mark has been an incredible privilege: a brilliant EU law scholar, an encouraging mentor, and supportive beyond measure in the professional and the personal sphere. He has always had time to discuss my research, read my work, and provide constructive and helpful feedback. The four years I spent working with him on the project were some of the most enjoyable and academically enriching times of my career as an EU lawyer. I hope the future will bring many more opportunities for us to work together and I am so lucky to also be able to call Mark, and his husband Pierre, my dear friends. I am also extremely happy that Mark, in selecting his project team, brought Adina Akbik into my life. Her dedication to work, thorough approach to research, and unwavering support have helped me become a better researcher and shaped many of the ideas expressed in this book. She is my dear academic sister and I am grateful for all her support and inspiration. The Hertie School and its Jacques Delors Centre are a wonderful academic community that always challenged and pushed my thinking forward, and I am especially thankful for the multidisciplinary environment these institutions provided. My special thanks go to Markus Jachtenfuchs and Christian Freudlsperger for making political science indispensable in my work. I am also grateful for the help of the research assistants at the LEVIATHAN Project: Evgenija Kroeker, Rebecca Segall, Harry McNeill Adams, Elena Bertolini, and Francesco Lanzone. Writing this book has been less stressful thanks to Cambridge University Press, and in particular Tom Randall, Sharon McCann, and Gemma Smith.

I am incredibly grateful to Paul Dermine for taking the time to read large parts of this book and offering generous and useful feedback, raising important counterarguments, and generally helping me improve the text. It was wonderful having him as a colleague at the Court of Justice and discuss ongoing developments with our academic hats on. My thanks also go to Thomas Reyntjens, for reading parts of this book and challenging my arguments from a practical point of view. I have presented different parts of this book at numerous conferences, and the feedback and discussions that took place there shaped my thinking and significantly improved my work. I am particularly grateful to Anuscheh Farahat, Xabier Arzoz, Joana Mendes, Klaus Tuori, Julian Nowag, and Martijn van den Brink. I am also grateful to the anonymous reviewers who assessed the book proposal and gave valuable suggestions and feedback that made this book better. I am happy to be part of the EU law academic community, and I hope I will be able to pay the same favours forward in the future.

The last stretches of writing were done during my work in the Cabinet of Advocate General Tamara Ćapeta at the Court of Justice of the EU. I am beyond grateful to Tamara for her support and encouragement, for the intense and stimulating exchanges during our cabinet meetings, and for forcing me to think differently about pressing questions of EU law. From day one, working with my colleagues in the cabinet – Nicolaj, Franck, Kathleen, Antonia, Cian, Corinne, Benoît – has been an inspiring and enjoyable experience; the intellectual environment they create has allowed me to continue my academic research alongside my work on pending cases at the Court.

I am grateful to my friends and family for their love and care. Thank you, Jelena and Milan, Bruno and Grga, Lucija and Mislav. Thank you, Lilas, Josephine, Petra, Kristina, Tamara (P), Branka, Selçuk, Alice, and Ulrike und Albrecht.

This book is dedicated to Ole, my partner and my favourite person. He has been by my side since this book was only a proposal, when I had ample time to write it, and when it was most difficult to find the focus and strength to finish it. Thank you, Ole, for being in my life. 'That it now.'

Luxembourg, 21 March 2023

Table of Cases

EUROPEAN UNION

Court of Justice

Case 9/56 *Meroni* EU:C:1958:7
Case 26/62 *van Gend en Loos* EU:C:1963:1
Case 13/63 *Commission v Italy* EU:C:1963:20
Case 6/64 *Costa v ENEL* EU:C:1964:66
Case 22/70 *Commission v Council* EU:C:1971:32
Case 39/72 *Commission v Italy* EU:C:1973:13
Case 128/78 *Commission v United Kingdom* EU:C:1979:32
Case 804/79 *Commission v United Kingdom* EU:C:1981:93
Case 244/80 *Foglia v Novello* EU:C:1981:302
Case 60/81 *IBM v Commission* EU:C:1981:264
Case 283/81 *Cilfit* EU:C:1982:335
Case 294/83 *Les Verts* EU:C:1986:166
Case 34/86 *Council v Parliament* EU:C:1986:291
Case 314/85 *Foto-Frost* EU:C:1987:452
Case 151/88 *Italy v Commission* EU:C:1989:201
Joined Cases C-181/88, C-182/88 and C-218/88 *Deschamps* EU:C:1989:642
Case C-322/88 *Grimaldi* EU:C:1989:646
Case C-366/88 *France v Commission* EU:C:1990:348
Case C-128/89 *Commission v Italy* EU:C:1990:311
Case C-269/90 *Technische Universität München* EU:C:1991:438
Case C-303/90 *France v Commission* EU:C:1991:424
Case C-282/90 *Vreugdenhil v Commission* EU:C:1992:124

Case C-343/90 *Dias* EU:C:1992:327
Case C-97/91 *Borelli* EU:C:1992:491
Case C-325/91 *France v Commission* EU:C:1993:245
Case C-188/92 *TWD Textilwerke Deggendorf GmbH* EU:C:1994:90
Case C-415/93 *Bosman* EU:C:1995:463
Opinion 3/94 EU:C:1995:436
Case C-57/95 *France v Commission* EU:C:1997:164
Case C-147/96 *Netherlands v Commission* EU:C:2000:335
Case C-50/00 P *UPA* EU:C:2002:462
Case C-60/00 *Carpenter* EU:C:2002:434
Case C-491/01 *BAT and Imperial Tobacco* EU:C:2002:741
Case C-11/00 *Commission v ECB* EU:C:2003:395
Case C-27/04 *Commission v Council* EU:C:2004:436
Case C-392/02 *Commission v Denmark* EU:C:2005:683
Case C-12/03 P *Tetra Laval* EU:C:2005:87
Case C-301/03 *Italy v Commission* EU:C:2005:727
Case C-64/05 P *Sweden v Commission* EU:C:2007:802
Case C-521/06 P *Athinaïki Techniki v Commission* EU:C:2008:422
Case C-166/07 *Parliament v Council* EU:C:2009:499
Case C-362/08 P *Internationaler Hilfsfonds v Commission* EU:C:2010:40
Joined Cases C-188/10 and C-189/10 *Melki and Abdeli* EU:C:2010:363
Joined Cases C-78/08 to C-80/08 *Paint Graphos and Others* EU:C:2011:550
Opinion 1/09 EU:C:2011:123
Case C-34/09 *Ruiz Zambrano* EU:C:2011:124
Case C-14/10 *Nickel Institute* EU:C:2011:503
Joined Cases C-463/10 and C-475/10 *Deutsche Post and Germany v Commission* EU:C:2011:656
Case C-434/11 *Corpul National al Politistilor v MAI* EU:C:2011:830
Case C-462/11 *Cozman v Teatrul Municipal Targoviste* EU:C:2011:831
Case C-134/12 *MAI et al. v Corpul National al Politistilor* EU:C:2012:288
Case C-369/12 *Corpul National al Politistilor v MAI* EU:C:2012:725
Case C-370/12 *Pringle* EU:C:2012:756
Case C-399/11 *Melloni* EU:C:2013:107
Case C-583/11 P *Inuit Tapiriit Kanatami* EU:C:2013:625
Case C-128/12 *Sindicato dos Bancarios do Norte et al. v BPN* EU:C:2013:149
Opinion 2/13 EU:C:2014:2454
Case C-31/13 P *Hungary v Commission* EU:C:2014:70

Case C-264/12 *Sindicato Nacional dos Profissionais de Seguros e Afins v Fidelitate Mundial* EU:C:2014:2036
Case C-333/13 *Dano* EU:C:2014:2358
Case C-665/13 *Sindicato Nacional dos Profissionais de Seguros e Afins v Via Directa* EU:C:2014:2327
Case C-62/14 *Gauweiler* EU:C:2015:400
Case C-67/14 *Alimanovic* EU:C:2015:597
Case C-526/14 *Kotnik* EU:C:2016:570
Joined Cases C-8/15 P to C-10/15 P *Ledra Advertising and Others v Commission* EU:C:2016:701
Case C-41/15 *Dowling* EU:C:2016:836
Joined Cases C-105/15 P to C-109/15 P *Mallis* EU:C:2016:702
Case C-201/15 AGET *Iraklis* EU:C:2016:972
Case C-243/15 *Lesoochranáske zoskupenie* EU:C:2016:838
Case C-258/14 *Florescu* EU:C:2017:448
Case C-589/15 P *Anagnostakis* EU:C:2017:663
Joined cases C-643/15 and C-647/15 *Slovakia and Hungary v Council* EU:C:2017:631
Case C-16/16 P *Belgium v Commission* EU:C:2018:79
Case C-64/16 *Associação dos Juízes Portugueses* EU:C:2018:117
Case C-219/17 *Berlusconi* EU:C:2018:1023
Case C-493/17 *Weiss* EU:C:2018:1000
Case C-621/18 *Whigtman* EU:C:2018:999
Case C-450/17 P *Landeskreditbank* EU:C:2019:372
Joined Cases C-663/17 P, C-665/17 P and C-669/17 P *Trasta Komercbanka* EU:C:2019:923
Joined Cases C-152/18 P and C-153/18 P *Crédit Mutuel Arkéa* EU:C:2019:810
Joined Cases C-202/18 and C-238/18 *Rimšēvičs* EU:2019:139
Case C-35/19 *Belgian State (Indemnité pour personnes handicapées)* EU:C:2019:894
Case C-686/18 *OC and Others v Banca d'Italia and Others* EU:C:2020:567
Case C-575/18 P *Czech Republic v Commission* EU:C:2020:530
Joined Cases C-597/18 P, C-598/18 P, C-603/18 P and C-604/18 P *Chrysostomides* EU:C:2020:1028
Case C-785/18 *Jeanningross* EU:C:2020:46
Case C-148/19 P *BTB Holding Investments and Duferco Participations Holding* v *Commission* EU:C:2020:354
Joined Cases C-225/19 and C-226/19 *R.N.N.S. & K.A.* EU:C:2020:951
Case C-316/19 *Commission v Slovenia* EU:C:2020:1030

Case C-571/19 P *EMB Consulting SE v ECB* EU:C:2020:208
Case C-423/20 P(R) *Council v Sharpston* EU:C:2020:700
Case C-424/20 P(R) *Representatives of the Governments of the Member States v Sharpston* EU:C:2020:705
Case C-501/18 *Balgarska Narodna Banka* EU:C:2021:249
Case C-848/19 P *Germany v Poland* EU:C:2021:598
Joined Cases C-357/19, C-379/19, C-547/19, C-811/19 and C-840/19 *Asociaţia 'Forumul Judecătorilor din România'* EU:C:2021:1034
Case C-911/19 *Fédération bancaire française* EU:C:2021:599
Case C-408/20 P *Poggiolini* EU:C:2021:806
Case C-817/19 *Ligue des droits humains* EU:C:2022:491
Case C-616/20 *M2Beauté Cosmetics GmbH* EU:C:2022:781
Case C-673/20 *Préfet du Gers* EU:C:2022:449
Case C-45/21 *Banka Slovenije* EU:C:2022:670
Case C-156/21 *Hungary v Parliament and Council* EU:C:2022:97
Case C-157/21 *Poland v Parliament and Council* EU:C:2022:98
Case C-397/21 *HUMDA* EU:C:2022:790
Case C-430/21 *RS* EU:C:2022:99
Case C-443/21 *Avicarvil Farms* EU:C:2022:899

Advocate General Opinions

Opinion of Advocate General Maduro in Case C-141/02 P *Commission v max-mobil* EU:C:2004:646
Opinion of Advocate General Léger in Case C-40/03 P *Rica Foods* EU:C:2005:93
Opinion of Advocate General Maduro in Case C-411/06 *Commission v Parliament and Council* EU:C:2009:189
Opinion of Advocate General Kokott in Case C-13/07 *Commission v Council* EU:C:2009:190
Opinion of Advocate General Bot in Case C-166/07 *Parliament v Council* EU:C:2009:213
Opinion of Advocate General Sharpston in Case C-34/09 *Ruiz Zambrano* EU:C:2010:560
Opinion of Advocate General Mengozzi in Case C-401/09 P *Evropaïki Dynamiki v ECB* EU:C:2011:31
Opinion of Advocate General Trstenjak in Case C-539/09 *Commission v Germany* EU:C:2011:345

View of Advocate General Kokott in Case C-370/12 *Pringle* EU:C:2012:675
Opinion of Advocate General Szpunar in Case C-113/14 *Germany v Parliament and Council* EU:C:2016:279
Opinion of Advocate General Wahl in Case C-526/14 *Kotnik* EU:C:2016:102
Opinion of Advocate General Wahl in Joined Cases C-8/15 P to C-10/15 P *Ledra* EU:C:2016:290
Opinion of Advocate General Wathelet in Joined Cases C-105/15 P to C-109/15 P *Mallis* EU:C:2016:294
Opinion of Advocate General Szpunar in Joined Cases C-360/15 and C-31/16 *College van Burgemeester en Wethouders van de gemeente Amersfoort* EU:C:2017:397
Opinion of Advocate General Mengozzi in Case C-589/15 P *Anagnostakis* EU:C:2017:175
Opinion of Advocate General Bobek in Case C-16/16 P *Belgium v Commission* EU:C:2017:959
Opinion of Advocate General Campos Sánchez-Bordona in Case C-219/17 *Berlusconi* EU:C:2018:502
Opinion of Advocate General Hogan in Case C-450/17 P *Landeskreditbank Baden-Württemberg* EU:C:2018:982
Opinion of Advocate General Wathelet in Case C-493/17 *Weiss* EU:C:2018:815
Opinion of Advocate General Kokott in Joined Cases C-202/18 and C-238/18 *Rimšēvičs* EU:C:2018:1030
Opinion of Advocate General Kokott in Joined Cases C-663/17 P, C-665/17 P and C-669/17 P *Trasta Komercbanka* EU:C:2019:323
Opinion of Advocate General Pitruzzella in Joined Cases C-597/18 P, C-598/18 P, C-603/18 P and C-604/18 P *Chrysostomides* EU:C:2020:390
Opinion of Advocate General Campos Sanchez-Bordona in Case C-848/19 P *Germany v Poland* EU:C:2021:218
Opinion of Advocate General Bobek in Case C-911/19 *Fédération bancaire française* EU:C:2021:294
Opinion of Advocate General Ćapeta in Case C-500/20 *ÖBB-Infrastruktur Aktiengesellschaft* EU:C:2022:79
Opinion of Advocate General Richard de la Tour in Case C-624/20 *E.K. v Staatssecretaris van Justitie en Veiligheid* EU:C:2022:194
Opinion of Advocate General Ćapeta in Case C-721/20 *DB Station & Service* EU:C:2022:288

Opinion of Advocate General Ćapeta in Case C-268/21 *Norra Stockholm* EU:C:2022:755
Opinion of Advocate General Emiliou in Case C-389/21 P *ECB v Crédit Lyonnais* EU:C:2022:844

Court of First Instance/General Court

Case T-139/99 *AICS v Parliament* EU:T:2000:182
Case T-18/10 *Inuit* EU:T:2011:419
Case T-262/10 *Microban* EU:T:2011:623
Case T-450/12 *Anagnostakis v Commission* EU:T:2015:739
Case T-79/13 *Accorinti and Others v ECB* EU:T:2015:756
Case T-122/15 *Landeskreditbank* EU:T:2017:337
Case T-247/16 *Fursin and Others v ECB* EU:T:2017:623
Case T-680/13 *Chrysostomides* EU:T:2018:486
Case T-883/16 *Poland v Commission* EU:T:2019:567
Case T-107/17 *Steinhoff* EU:T:2019:353
Case T-504/19 *Crédit lyonnais v ECB* EU:T:2021:185
Case T-913/16 *Fininvest and Berlusconi v ECB* EU:T:2022:279
Case T-502/19 *Corneli v ECB* EU:T:2022:627
Case T-709/21 *WhatsApp Ireland Ltd* EU:T:2022:783

MEMBER STATES

Estonia

Supreme Court

Constitutional Judgment 3-4-1-6-12 (ESM Treaty), 12 July 2012

Germany

Federal Constitutional Court

2 BvR 2134/92 and 2159/92 *Maastricht Treaty* Judgment of 12 October 1993
2 BvR 2/08 *Lisbon Treaty* Judgment of 30 June 2009
2 BvR 2661/06 *Honeywell* Order of 06 July 2010
2 BvR 987/10 *ESM Treaty* Judgment of 07 September 2011
2 BvR 615/09 and 2 BvR 535/09 Judgment of 21 November 2011
2 BvR 1390/12 *ESM Treaty II* Judgment of 12 September 2012

2 BvR 2728/13 *Gauweiler* Order of 14 January 2014
2 BvR 2735/14 *Mr R.* Order of 15 December 2015
2 BvR 2728/13 *Gauweiler* Judgment of 21 June 2016
2 BvR 859/15, 2 BvR 980/16, 2 BvR 2006/15, 2 BvR 1651/15 *Weiss* Order of 18 July 2017
2 BvR 1685/14 and 2 BvR 2631/14 *Banking Union* Judgment of 30 July 2019
2 BvR 859/15, 2 BvR 980/16, 2 BvR 2006/15, 2 BvR 1651/15 *Weiss* Judgment of 5 May 2020
2 BvR 547/21 Decision of 26 March 2021
2 BvR 547/21 Order of 15 April 2021
2 BvR 1651/15 and 2 BvR 2006/15 Order of 29 April 2021
2 BvR 547/21 and 2 BvR 798/21 *Own Resources Decision* Judgment of 6 December 2022

Portugal

Constitutional Tribunal

Ruling N. 353/12 of 5 July 2012

The Netherlands

Hague Civil Court

Wilders and Others v the Dutch State, case no. 419556 / KG ZA 12-523, Judgment in summary proceedings of 1 June 2012

Other Jurisdictions

United Kingdom

Secretary of State for Education and Science v Tameside MBC [1976] UKHL 6
Miller & Anor, R (On the Application Of) v The Secretary of State for Exiting the European Union (Rev 1) [2016] EWHC 2768 (Admin)
Miller & Anor, R (on the application of) v Secretary of State for Exiting the European Union (Rev 3) [2017] UKSC 5

United States

James B. Beam Distilling Co. v Georgia 501 US 529 (1991), Concurring Opinion of Justice Scalia
Obergefell v Hodges 576 US 644 (2015), Dissenting Opinion of Justice Scalia

Table of Legislation

EUROPEAN UNION LAW

Primary Law

Treaty Establishing the European Community (TEC) [1992] OJ C224/1

Consolidated version of the Treaty on European Union [2016] OJ C202/13

Consolidated version of the Treaty on the Functioning of the European Union [2016] OJ C202/47

Charter of Fundamental Rights of the European Union [2016] OJ C202/389

Statute of the European System of Central Banks and of the European Central Bank. Protocol No 4 to the Lisbon Treaty (OJ 2016 C202/230)

Secondary Law

Act of 20 September 1976 concerning the election of the representatives of the Assembly by direct universal suffrage (OJ 1976 L278/5)

Second Council Directive 77/91/EEC of 13 December 1976 on coordination of safeguards which, for the protection of the interests of members and others, are required by Member States of companies within the meaning of the second paragraph of Article 58 of the Treaty, in respect of the formation of public limited liability companies and the maintenance and alteration of their capital, with a view to making such safeguards equivalent (OJ 1977 L26/1)

Council Regulation (EU) No 407/2010 of 11 May 2010 establishing a European financial stabilisation mechanism (OJ 2010 L118/1)

Council Regulation (EU) 1177/2011 of 8 November 2011 amending Regulation (EC) No 1467/97 on speeding up and clarifying the implementation of the excessive deficit procedure (OJ 2011 L306/33)
Council Directive 2011/85/EU of the Council of 8 November 2011 on the requirements for budgetary frameworks of the Member States (OJ 2011 L306/41)
Regulation (EU) 1173/2011 of the European Parliament and of the Council of 16 November 2011 on the effective enforcement of budgetary surveillance in the euro area (OJ 2011 L306/1)
Regulation (EU) 1174/2011 of the European Parliament and of the Council of 16 November 2011 on enforcement measures to correct excessive macroeconomic imbalances in the euro area (OJ 2011 L306/8)
Regulation (EU) 1175/2011 of the European Parliament and of the Council of 16 November 2011 amending Council Regulation (EC) No 1466/97 on the strengthening of the surveillance of budgetary positions and the surveillance and coordination of economic policies (OJ 2011 L306/12)
Regulation (EU) 1176/2011 of the European Parliament and of the Council of 16 November 2011 on the prevention and correction of macroeconomic imbalances (OJ 2011 L306/25)
Regulation (EU) 472/2013 of the European Parliament and of the Council of 21 May 2013 on the strengthening of economic and budgetary surveillance of Member States in the euro area experiencing or threatened with serious difficulties with respect to their financial stability (OJ 2013 L140/1)
Regulation (EU) 473/2013 of the European Parliament and of the Council of 21 May 2013 on common provisions for monitoring and assessing draft budgetary plans and ensuring the correction of excessive deficit of the Member States in the euro area (OJ 2013 L140/11)
Regulation (EU) No 575/2013 of the European Parliament and of the Council of 26 June 2013 on prudential requirements for credit institutions and investment firms and amending Regulation (EU) No 648/2012 (OJ 2013 L176/1)
Directive 2013/36/EU of the European Parliament and of the Council of 26 June 2013 on access to the activity of credit institutions and the prudential supervision of credit institutions and investment firms, amending Directive 2002/87/EC and repealing Directives 2006/48/EC and 2006/49/EC (OJ 2013 L176/338)
Council Regulation (EU) No 1024/2013 of 15 October 2013 conferring specific tasks on the European Central Bank concerning policies relating to the prudential supervision of credit institutions (OJ 2013 L287/63)

Regulation (EU) No 468/2014 of the European Central Bank of 16 April 2014 establishing the framework for cooperation within the Single Supervisory Mechanism between the European Central Bank and national competent authorities and with national designated authorities (ECB/2014/17) (OJ 2014 L141/1)

Directive 2014/59/EU of the European Parliament and of the Council of 15 May 2014 establishing a framework for the recovery and resolution of credit institutions and investment firms and amending Council Directive 82/891/EEC, and Directives 2001/24/EC, 2002/47/EC, 2004/25/EC, 2005/56/EC, 2007/36/EC, 2011/35/EU, 2012/30/EU and 2013/36/EU, and Regulations (EU) No 1093/2010 and (EU) No 648/2012, of the European Parliament and of the Council, (OJ 2014 L173/190)

ECB Decision 2015/774 of 4 March 2015 on a secondary markets public sector asset purchase programme (OJ 2015 L121/20)

Decision 2015/2101 of 5 November 2015 amending Decision (EU) 2015/774 on a secondary markets public sector asset purchase programme (OJ 2015 L303/106)

Decision 2015/2464 of 16 December 2015 amending Decision (EU) 2015/774 on a secondary markets public sector asset purchase programme (OJ 2015 L344/1)

Decision 2016/702 of 18 April 2016 amending Decision (EU) 2015/774 on a secondary markets public sector asset purchase programme (OJ 2016 L121/24)

Decision (EU) 2017/100 of 11 January 2017 amending Decision (EU) 2015/774 on a secondary markets public sector asset purchase programme (OJ 2017 L16/51)

Council Decision (EU, Euratom) 2018/994 of 13 July 2018 (OJ 2018 L 178/1)

Regulation (EU, Euratom) 2018/1046 of the European Parliament and of the Council of 18 July 2018 on the financial rules applicable to the general budget of the Union (OJ L193/1)

Decision 2020/440 of the ECB of 24 March 2020 on a temporary pandemic emergency purchase programme (OJ 2020 L91/1)

Council Regulation (EU) 2020/2094 of 14 December 2020 establishing a European Union Recovery Instrument to support the recovery in the aftermath of the COVID-19 crisis (OJ L433 I/23)

Council Decision (EU, Euratom) 2020/2053 of 14 December 2020 on the system of own resources of the European Union and repealing Decision 2014/335/EU, Euratom (OJ L424/1)

Regulation (EU, Euratom) 2020/2092 of the European Parliament and of the Council of 16 December 2020 on a general regime of conditionality for the protection of the Union budget (OJ L433I/1)

Interinstitutional Agreement (IIA) of 16 December 2020 between the EP, the Council and the Commission on budgetary discipline, on cooperation in budgetary matters and on sound financial management, as well as on new own resources, including a roadmap towards the introduction of new own resources, (OJ L433I/28)

Regulation (EU) 2021/241 of the European Parliament and of the council of 12 February 2021 establishing the Recovery and Resilience Facility (OJ L57/17)

Other Documents

Technical features of Outright Monetary Transactions, 6 September 2012, <www.ecb.europa.eu/press/pr/date/2012/html/pr120906_1.en.html>

European Parliament's Committee on Constitutional Affairs 'Article 136 TFEU, ESM, Fiscal Stability Treaty Ratification requirements and present situation in the Member States', June 2013, available at <www.europarl.europa.eu/meetdocs/2009_2014/documents/afco/dv/2013-06-12_pe462455-v16_/2013-06-12_pe462455-v16_en.pdf>

Communication from the Commission on the application, from 1 August 2013, of State aid rules to support measures in favour of banks in the context of the financial crisis (OJ 2013 C 216/1)

Communication from the Commission to the European Parliament, the Council, the European Central Bank, the Economic and Social Committee, the Committee of Regions and the European Investment Bank, 'Making the Best Use of the Flexibility within the Existing Rules of the Stability and Growth Pact' COM (2015) 12 final

Conclusions of the Special meeting of the European Council (17 to 21 July 2020) <www.consilium.europa.eu/media/45109/210720-euco-final-conclusions-en.pdf>

Court of Auditors, Opinion No 6/2020 concerning the proposal for a regulation of the European Parliament and of the Council establishing a Recovery and Resilience Facility (COM(2020) 408) (OJ C 350/1)

Presentation by Commissioner Hahn of the NextGenerationEU, 14 April 2021 <https://ec.europa.eu/commission/presscorner/detail/en/speech_21_1743>

European Parliament legislative resolution of 3 May 2022 on the proposal for a Council Regulation on the election of the members of the European Parliament by direct universal suffrage, repealing Council Decision (76/787/ECSC, EEC, Euratom) and the Act concerning the election of the members of the European Parliament by direct universal suffrage annexed to that Decision (2020/2220(INL) – 2022/0902(APP))

'SRB, EBA and ECB Banking Supervision statement on the announcement on 19 March 2023 by Swiss authorities'. Press Release of 20 March 2023. Available at <www.srb.europa.eu/en/content/srb-eba-and-ecb-banking-supervision-statement-announcement-19-march-2023-swiss-authorities#:~:text=The%20Single%20Resolution%20Board%2C%20the,order%20to%20ensure%20financial%20stability>

International Law

Charter of the United Nations, 24 October 1945, 1 UNTS XVI

Treaty Establishing the European Stability Mechanism T/ESM 2012-LT/en 1

Abbreviations

ABoR	Administrative Board of Review
ABSSP	Asset-Backed Securities Purchase Programme
APP	Asset Purchase Programme
CBPP3	Bond Purchase Programme
CJEU	Court of Justice of the European Union
EBA	European Banking Authority
EC	European Community
ECB	European Central Bank
EEA	European Economic Area
EFSF	European Financial Stability Facility
EFSM	European Financial Stabilisation Mechanism
EMU	Economic and Monetary Union
ESCB	European System of Central Banks
ESM	European Stability Mechanism
EU	European Union
EURI	European Union Recovery Instrument
IMF	International Monetary Fund
MoU	Memorandum of Understanding
NCA	National Competent Authority
NGEU	Next Generation EU
OMT	Outright Monetary Transaction Mechanism
ORD	Own Resources Decision
PEPP	Pandemic Emergency Purchase Programme
PSPP	Public Sector Purchase Programme
RRF	Recovery and Resilience Facility

SRM	Single Resolution Mechanism
SSM	Single Supervisory Mechanism
TEU	Treaty of the European Union
TFEU	Treaty on the Functioning of the European Union

Introduction

I.1 THE PROBLEM

The European Union 'places the individual at the heart of its activities'.[1] So begins the Charter of Fundamental Rights of the European Union. Likewise, the old story of integration through law[2] tells us that law pushed forward the integration programme, the individual being its main enforcer and beneficiary. The European legal landscape has, on this view, evolved into a unique[3] supranational system that empowered primarily the individual through legal principles such as primacy and direct effect,[4] but also through the case law of the Court of Justice concerning the internal market, EU citizenship, and the protection of fundamental rights. The EU's response to the Euro crisis challenged that convention, with the focus instead shifting to the Member States. In this book, I reconceptualise legal accountability in a way that replaces the individual at the heart of all activities in the Economic and Monetary Union (EMU).

Introduced in the Maastricht Treaty,[5] the EMU symbolised a step of unprecedented integration, while also witnessing a sharp decline in public

1 Charter of Fundamental Rights of the European Union [2016] OJ C202/389, Preamble.

2 M Cappelletti, M Seccombe and J H H Weiler (eds), *Integration through Law: Europe and the American Federal Experience*, Book 1 (de Gruyter 1986).

3 J H H Weiler, 'Prologue: Global and Pluralist Constitutionalism – Some Doubts' in G de Búrca and J H H Weiler (eds), *The Worlds of European Constitutionalism* (Cambridge University Press 2012) 11–12. For a criticism of this view of European law, see S R Larsen, 'European Public Law after Empires' (2022) 1(1) *European Law Open* 6.

4 Case 26/62 *van Gend en Loos* EU:C:1963:1; Case 6/64 *Costa v ENEL* EU:C:1964:66.

5 Treaty Establishing the European Community (TEC) [1992] OJ C224/1.

support, unlike any previous Treaty revision.[6] The reason for this may be found in the fact that European integration expanded into areas traditionally considered core state powers,[7] resulting in new intergovernmental modes of governance,[8] such as differentiation through opt-outs and the establishment of regulatory agencies.[9] The Euro crisis displayed serious accountability deficiencies, exacerbating these concerns further.[10] The emphasis on authority derived from regulatory effectiveness and market prosperity[11] over democratic accountability has been particularly visible in the ad hoc creation of EU's economic governance mechanisms[12] and in the activities of the European Central Bank (ECB).[13]

A common denominator behind these solutions is that they bypass the individual and limit her influence in economic governance decision-making. Judicial review by national and EU courts relied heavily on the principle of equality of sovereign Member States, by protecting the budgetary autonomy of national parliaments through an emphasis on conditionality in financial assistance.[14] Yet, these conditions, imposed by the Troika outside the framework of EU law proper, left little to no wiggle room for parliamentary

6 J H H Weiler, *The Constitution of Europe: 'Do the New Clothes Have an Emperor?' and Other Essays on European Integration* (Cambridge University Press 1999) 4; N MacCormick, *Questioning Sovereignty* (Oxford University Press 1999) 98–99.

7 P Genschel and M Jachtenfuchs, 'More Integration, Less Federation: The European Integration of Core State Powers' (2016) 23(1) *Journal of European Public Policy* 42.

8 C J Bickerton, D Hodson and U Puetter, 'The New Intergovernmentalism: European Integration in the Post-Maastricht Era' (2015) 53(4) *Journal of Common Market Studies* 703.

9 Genschel and Jachtenfuchs (n 7) 46–48. For an overview of the literature, see A Maricut-Akbik, 'EU Politicization beyond the Euro Crisis: Immigration Crises and the Politicization of Free Movement of People' (2019) 17 *Comparative European Politics* 380, 382–383.

10 C Fasone, 'European Economic Governance and Parliamentary Representation: What Place for the European Parliament?' (2014) 20(2) *European Law Journal* 164; M Dawson, 'The Legal and Political Accountability Structure of "Post-crisis" EU Economic Governance' (2015) 53(5) *Journal of Common Market Studies* 976, 983; J Pisani-Ferry, 'Rebalancing the Governance of the Euro Area' in M Dawson, H Enderlein and C Joerges (eds), *Beyond the Crisis: The Governance of Europe's Economic, Political, and Legal Transformation* (Oxford University Press 2015) 72; A Maatsch, *Parliaments and the Economic Governance of the European Union: Talking Shops or Deliberative Bodies?* (Routledge 2016).

11 B Crum and S Merlo, 'Democratic Legitimacy in the Post-crisis EMU' (2020) 42(3) *Journal of European Integration* 399; T Isiksel, *Europe's Functional Constitution* (Oxford University Press 2016) 6, 13.

12 Isiksel (n 11) 224 onwards. See also J Habermas, 'Democracy, Solidarity and the European Crisis' in A-M Grozelier, B Hacker, W Kowalsky, J Machnig, H Meyer and B Unger (eds), *Roadmap to a Social Europe* (Social Europe Report 2013).

13 For an argument that the ECB has become a constitutional organ surpassing its role as an independent agency, see M Goldoni, 'The Limits of Legal Accountability of the European Central Bank' (2017) 24 *George Mason Law Review* 595.

14 Case C-370/12 *Pringle* EU:2012:756 [136].

deliberations in debtor Member States.[15] Beyond financial assistance, the ECB, through its quantitative easing programmes, became the largest creditor of the eurozone and significantly affected asset prices across different interest groups. Similar to financial assistance, the ECB operates without outside input due to its high level of independence. Consequently, we know very little about how the ECB balances the interests of various socioeconomic groups across the eurozone and the normative considerations that guide its activities.[16]

Departing from the well-established EU law routes of regulation, these developments were characterised by 'legal experimentalism'.[17] This can, in part, be attributed to the lack of a more coordinated approach to the possibility of a crisis in the Maastricht Treaty and its amendments.[18] In essence, as Chiti and Teixeira underline, risk-sharing did not feature in the initial EMU logic, which instead only focused on the mutual benefits of the shared currency area.[19] Regarding the EMU as a solidarity area was not present in its original design.[20] The underlying principle of the EMU framework relies on the equality of Member States,[21] embedded in the protection of national sovereignty in budgetary matters.[22] This concerns specifically the no-bailout clause in Article 125(1) TFEU, intended to incentivise Member States to follow a sound budgetary policy, which would be jeopardised should the euro area transform into a transfer union.[23] Such a focus influenced the division of competences between the EU and the national level in a way that reduced emphasis on solidarity, which I argue ultimately led to a decreased ability of all EU citizens equally to hold EMU decision-makers to account.

15 See also A Guazzarotti, '"It's the (Asymmetric) Economy, Stupid!" Some Remarks on the Weiss Case of the Bundesverfassungsgericht' (2020) 6 *Italian Law Journal* 655, 666.

16 For a recent criticism, see M Sandbu, 'A Political Backlash against Monetary Policy Is Looming' *Financial Times*, 23 October 2022. Available at <www.ft.com/content/6f70bbcd-72b7-4518-be6b-401adba7cc34>.

17 K Tuori and K Tuori, *The Eurozone Crisis: A Constitutional Analysis* (Cambridge University Press 2014) 90.

18 ibid 89.

19 E Chiti and P G Teixeira, 'The Constitutional Implications of the European Responses to the Financial and Public Debt Crisis' (2013) 50 *Common Market Law Review* 683, 697.

20 ibid 697–700.

21 F Losada, 'Institutional Implications of the Rise of a Debt-Based Monetary Regime in Europe' (2016) 22(6) *European Law Journal* 822, 828; A Mody, *EuroTragedy: A Drama in Nine Acts* (Oxford University Press 2018) 320.

22 Chiti and Teixeira (n 19) 698–699.

23 2 BvR 1390/12 *ESM Treaty II* Judgment of the Second Senate of 12 September 2012 [153].

At the same time, existing accountability mechanisms in the Treaties were no longer appropriate for such novel legal developments. For example, political accountability of the Council and Parliament was overshadowed by the dominance of the Euro Group and the Commission in the decision-making processes concerning financial assistance.[24] Furthermore, legal accountability as the task of the Court of Justice was reduced in effect as it could not extend the responsibility of the Euro Group beyond the letter of the Treaties.[25] The idiosyncrasies of the regulatory approach to the financial crisis were further strongly reflected in the review of financial assistance measures and the European Stability Mechanism (ESM), which the Court of Justice initially did not assess against the standards of the Charter of Fundamental Rights.[26] In monetary policy, the ECB's constitutionally entrenched independence removed it from the traditional routes of political and administrative accountability found in national contexts. It was likewise shielded from legal accountability, as the Court of Justice applied a lax standard of review of its monetary policy decisions.[27] In effect, accountability structures originally devised in the Treaties were not efficient in the EMU and brought about a diminished capacity of EU citizens to hold decision-makers to account after the financial crisis.[28]

National constitutional courts, except for the Portuguese Constitutional Court,[29] have not called into question the austerity measures that formed part of the conditionality requirements attached to financial assistance. Both EU and national courts focused on conditionality as a way of protecting creditors and ensuring the sound budgetary policy of debtor states. In that sense, the

[24] P Craig, 'The Eurogroup, Power and Accountability' (2017) 23 *European Law Journal* 234.

[25] Most evident in Joined Cases C-597/18 P, C-598/18 P, C-603/18 P and C-604/18 P *Chrysostomides* EU:C:2020:1028, where the Court of Justice overturned the finding of the General Court that the Euro Group may be considered a body for the purposes of establishing non-contractual liability of the Union. For a further analysis, see Chapter 3, Section 3.4.1.

[26] Case C-370/12 *Pringle* (n 14).

[27] M Dawson, A Maricut-Akbik and A Bobić, 'Reconciling Independence and Accountability at the European Central Bank: The False Promise of Proceduralism' (2019) 25(1) *European Law Journal* 75; N de Boer and J van 't Klooster, 'The ECB, the Courts and the Issue of Democratic Legitimacy after Weiss' (2020) 57(6) *Common Market Law Review* 1689.

[28] See also M Hildebrand, 'Unravelling the Politicisation – Depoliticisation Nexus of Decontestatory Politics during the Euro-Crisis' in A Farahat and X Arzoz (eds), *Contesting Austerity: A Socio-Legal Inquiry* (Hart 2021) 59.

[29] Even so, the Portuguese Constitutional Court limited the temporal effects of its judgment in which it struck down austerity measures it found contrary to the Constitution. See Ruling N. 353/12 of 5 July 2012, English summary available at <www.tribunalconstitucional.pt/tc/en/acordaos/20120353s.html>. See further in Chapter 3, Section 3.3.1.

principle of equality of Member States has taken centre stage. Solidarity was acknowledged solely to the extent that it does not intrude on the budgetary prerogative of national parliaments,[30] causing a disregard of the major redistributive effects that financial assistance,[31] as well as monetary policy measures,[32] have had in the eurozone, in particular by increasing wealth inequality. Such effects do not follow Member State lines, but rather socio-economic ones, and have so far not been accounted for by the relevant decision-makers on the supranational level.[33] Solidarity, although a common soundbite in political discourse of that time, made no impact in regulatory design or judicial review.

At the end of this story comes the Next Generation EU (NGEU): a package of instruments allowing the EU, for the very first time, to borrow money on capital markets in unprecedented amounts and use portions of it for transfers to Member States in the form of non-refundable grants. Thus, 'in a spirit of solidarity between Member States, in particular for those Member States that have been particularly hard hit',[34] coherent and unified measures are exceptionally necessary to address the 'significant disturbances to economic activity which are reflected in a steep decline in gross domestic product and have a significant impact on employment, social conditions, poverty and inequalities'.[35] The constitutional justification of the NGEU framework laid bare debates, old and new, on the flexibility of Treaty rules as well as the accountability mechanisms embedded in this exceptional, and at present temporary, experiment. These developments, then, inevitably invite us to consider how best to ensure that decision-makers meet their duty to deliver the common interest, ensuring that all EU citizens can demand so under equal conditions.

30 The German Bundesverfassungsgericht, for example, stated that every individual measure taken in the spirit of solidarity must be explicitly approved by the Bundestag and it must not in any event lose the decisive influence on budgetary matters. See Case 2 BvR 987/10 *Aids for Greece and EFSF* Judgment of 7 September 2011 [128].

31 M P A Schneider, S Kinsella and A Godin, 'Redistribution in the Age of Austerity: Evidence from Europe 2006–2013' (2017) 24(1) *Applied Economics Letters* 672.

32 K Adam and P Tzamourani, 'Distributional Consequences of Asset Price Inflation in the Euro Area' (2016) 89 *European Economic Review* 172.

33 For an argument that the EU should re-orient itself as the arena for resolving these new types of conflict, see D Chalmers, 'The European Redistributive State and a European Law of Struggle' (2012) 18(5) *European Law Journal* 667.

34 Council Regulation (EU) 2020/2094 of 14 December 2020 establishing a European Union Recovery Instrument to support the recovery in the aftermath of the COVID-19 crisis (OJ L 433 I/23) Recital 5.

35 ibid Recital 2.

I.2 THE ARGUMENT

Accountability has been the object of legal and political science research alike. In both, accountability was conceptualised predominantly as a procedural mechanism, relying on the principal–agent model.[36] This model takes different shapes. First, political accountability relies on representative institutions that are obliged to deliver the mandate given by their constituents and suffer political loss in the next election cycle should they fail to make good on their promises. Legal accountability rests, by contrast, on the ability of citizens to seek courts to review the actions of the legislator, the administration, and the executive in the exercise of their tasks. Finally, it is important to add administrative accountability, whereby specialist bodies, through their knowledge, authority, and publicity, exert other types of pressure on the actor to deliver sound policy within the exercise of its mandate.[37] These varieties of accountability can be exercised either on procedural or substantive grounds.

Most famously expressed by Bovens,[38] a procedural concept of accountability leaves out any reference to normative content but rather focuses on a procedural checklist. Once met, it means that the agent has been held accountable in one way or another by the principal. While useful in terms of generalisability, Bovens's and similar procedural frameworks may be misused by decision-makers and reduced to a box ticking exercise.[39] They fail to capture conceptually and structurally diverse relationships of any given polity and cannot be used as a Procrustean bed to accommodate the diverse world of supranational governance. Substantive accountability, by contrast, surpasses a mere evaluation of the process that led to a certain decision, focusing instead on its content and compliance with the mandate conferred by the principal on the agent.[40] Attempts at substantive conceptualisations of accountability, however, focus predominantly on the nation-state as the role model. For

[36] G J Brandsma and J Adriaensen, 'The Principal–Agent Model, Accountability and Democratic Legitimacy' in T Delreux and J Adriaensen (eds), *The Principal Agent Model and the European Union* (Palgrave 2017) 37–38, 42; A Lupia, 'Delegation and Its Perils' in K Strøm, W C Müller and T Bergman (eds), *Parliamentary Democracy: Promise and Problems* (Oxford University Press 2006) 33.

[37] For a useful account, see M Krajewski, *Relative Authority of Judicial and Extra-Judicial Review: EU Courts, Boards of Appeal, Ombudsman* (Hart 2021).

[38] M Bovens, 'Analysing and Assessing Accountability: A Conceptual Framework' (2007) 13(4) *European Law Journal* 447; M Bovens, D Curtin and P 't Hart (eds), *The Real World of EU Accountability: What Deficit?* (Oxford University Press 2010).

[39] For a useful overview of the weaknesses of Bovens' framework, see R L Heidelberg, 'Political Accountability and Spaces of Contestation' (2017) 49(10) *Administration & Society* 1379.

[40] Dawson, Maricut-Akbik and Bobić (n 27) 76.

example, legal accountability introduced by Oliver[41] has been used as a basis for further research of accountability and legitimacy in the EU.[42] Yet, the EU has famously created an institutional system that often sits uneasily with these categories.[43] For example, it is difficult to locate the principal of the ECB, given that its Treaty-granted mandate and independence escape any meaningful control.

In an attempt to address this gap in the study of legal accountability beyond the state, this book brings together works from sociology and philosophy in order to move beyond the principal–agent relationship as the determinant characteristic[44] of approaches that theorise accountability across the social sciences.[45] In addition, I argue that we should abandon the formal reading of equality of states that pervades the intergovernmental logic of supranational polities by arguing instead for a substantive reading of equality. To achieve this, adding solidarity to the mix is indispensable. The two principles will then be brought together to offer a theory of accountability beyond the state, where instead of being marked by a clear representational relationship between the principal and the agent,[46] accountability is achieved by decision-makers acting in the common interest of all citizens. Such a normative approach regards accountability as a virtue in itself, rather than as a pure responsiveness mechanism.[47]

An attempt to conceptualise legal accountability through political equality of citizens will provide a basis for further study into legal accountability in transnational contexts. I will approach this under-researched topic from a more general perspective of constitutionalism beyond the state.[48] At the

41 D Oliver, *Government in the United Kingdom: The Search for Accountability, Effectiveness and Citizenship* (Open University Press 1991).

42 See, for example, C Harlow, *Accountability in the European Union* (Oxford University Press 2002); Bovens, Curtin and 't Hart (n 38); A Arnull and D Wincott, *Accountability and Legitimacy in the European Union* (Oxford University Press 2013). Addressing these issues in the context of multilevel polities, see Y Papadopoulos, 'Accountability and Multi-level Governance: More Accountability, Less Democracy?' (2010) 33(5) *West European Politics* 1030.

43 R Dehousse, 'Delegation of Powers in the European Union: The Need for a Multi-principals Model' (2008) 31(4) *West European Politics* 789.

44 Bovens (n 38).

45 D Braun and D H Guston, 'Principal–Agent Theory and Research Policy: An Introduction' (2003) 30(5) *Science and Public Policy* 302.

46 See also J Black, 'Constructing and Contesting Legitimacy and Accountability in Polycentric Regulatory Regimes' (2008) 2 *Regulation & Governance* 137, 138.

47 M Bovens, 'Two Concepts of Accountability: Accountability as a Virtue and as a Mechanism' (2010) 33(5) *West European Politics* 946.

48 For a significant contribution to this discussion, see G Teubner, *Constitutional Fragments: Societal Constitutionalism and Globalization* (Oxford University Press 2012); N Krisch,

moment, legal accounts of post-crisis EMU governance focus on the institutional context and analyse accountability as imagined in the nation-state.[49] This book will offer an original conceptualisation of legal accountability, while addressing the idiosyncrasies of EU post-crisis economic governance. My emphasis on legal accountability will shed new light on the individual, an approach currently missing in the literature.

What about other forms of accountability? I do not argue that legal accountability is the *only* route that would guarantee that decision-makers act towards achieving the common interest. I also do not consider that courts are the platform for democratic deliberation and participation, and they cannot provide legitimacy to decisions taken in democratically deficient procedures. Instead, focusing on courts is based on two ideas. First, by focusing on the common interest that underpins all Union action, they are able to provide remedies to affected individuals through the award of damages or annulment of decisions that depart from values underpinning the common interest. Their second important function is creating legitimate expectations not only for individuals but also for decision-makers. By insisting on a high duty of care and an extensive obligation of giving reasons in line with the common interest, courts can, to a certain extent, shape the behaviour of decision-makers in the future.

While political and administrative mechanisms constitute essential components of accountability, they remain outside the scope of this book for two reasons. First, political accountability in the EMU post-crisis has been extensively researched and yielded important contributions that pertain more generally to research on the empowerment of the European Parliament and national parliaments.[50] By contrast, the literature on legal accountability in the EMU, in particular post-crisis, is less about theorising accountability in a

Beyond Constitutionalism: The Pluralist Structure of Postnational Law (Oxford University Press 2013); K Tuori, *European Constitutionalism* (Cambridge University Press 2015).

49 M Markakis, *Accountability in the Economic and Monetary Union: Foundations, Policy, and Governance* (Oxford University Press 2020).

50 A Akbik, *The European Parliament as an Accountability Forum: Overseeing the Economic and Monetary Union* (Cambridge University Press 2022); B Crum, 'Parliamentary Accountability in Multilevel Governance: What Role for Parliaments in Post-crisis EU Economic Governance?' (2018) 25(2) *Journal of European Public Policy* 268; D Fromage, 'The European Parliament in the Post-crisis Era: An Institution Empowered on Paper Only?' (2018) 40(3) *Journal of European Integration* 281; D Jančić (ed), *National Parliaments after the Lisbon Treaty and the Euro Crisis: Resilience or Resignation?* (Oxford University Press 2017); K Auel and O Höing, 'National Parliaments and the Eurozone Crisis: Taking Ownership in Difficult Times?' (2015) 38(2) *West European Politics* 375; F Amtenbrink and K van Duin, 'The European Central Bank before the European Parliament: Theory and Practice after Ten Years of Monetary Dialogue' (2009) 34(3) *European Law Review* 561.

supranational context and more about analysing the quality of judicial involvement using traditional nation-state benchmarks of accountability.[51] This book thus aims to contribute to our understanding of legal accountability from a novel perspective.

The second reason for narrowing the focus to legal accountability is the exceptionally court-centred nature of the EU's functioning. The central role of the Court of Justice in the development of the EU's constitution and the contestation of that authority by national courts[52] makes courts crucial accountability actors, especially given that they are the only institution that provides direct access to individuals. Coupled with the low democratic legitimacy of EMU decisions in the political sphere, where the individual lacks space for expressing her preferences, courts are the institutions capable of providing that space. Having said that, whenever other forms of accountability intersect with legal accountability, this will be acknowledged and addressed.

With this starting position, my aim will be to determine the position of the individual and her ability to make use of existing routes of legal accountability in the EMU post-crisis through a novel approach to legal accountability. I argue that the current institutional set-up of EU economic governance, and specifically the idiosyncratic legal nature of anti-crisis mechanisms, caused political inequality between EU citizens. The design of anti-crisis mechanisms is premised on the principle of equality of Member States and is heavily anchored in conditionality. However, this creates disparities among EU citizens in terms of their influence on the decision-making process and access to accountability mechanisms: first, given the decreased ability to use accountability mechanisms at the EU level, and second, due to the variety of accountability mechanisms at the national level. In that sense, the book will answer the question: what is the influence of the individual in holding decision-makers in EU economic governance to account through judicial review?

In addition, the book aims to propose a framework of legal accountability for EU's economic governance that reasserts the centrality of the individual in its institutional framework. As will be argued, the equal ability of all EU citizens to access mechanisms of legal accountability and hold decision-makers in the EMU accountable can be achieved through a balanced application of the principles of equality and solidarity. On this view, accountability is the glue that ties the public institution to the common interest. To achieve

[51] Markakis (n 49); Tuori and Tuori (n 17).

[52] A Bobić, *The Jurisprudence of Constitutional Conflict in the European Union* (Oxford University Press 2022).

it, these institutions have a duty to maintain a balance between the principles of equality and solidarity. Seen in this way, all institutions are under an obligation to consider the interests involved and balance them in a way that best serves the common interest. This approach moves beyond the constraints of the nation-state and lends itself to multilevel polities beyond the state, where traditional routes of legitimation are more difficult to identify in a straightforward manner. To reimagine legal accountability in this way, I put forward a normative proposal concerning the relationship between equality and solidarity of political units, with the aim of achieving the equality of every person in pursuing the common interest.

I further argue that courts are and should be the institutions where individuals enforce the duty of policymakers to act in the common interest. The EMU is an area characterised by high redistributive effects coupled with a wide discretion on the part of decision-makers. Under these conditions, courts are, unlike political institutions, in the perfect position to ensure that such decisions meet the Treaty-entrenched objectives in the common interest.[53] To do so successfully, I claim that judicial review of decisions in the EMU entails two duties. First, the starting point for courts must be an assumption of a full review, which is an expression of their duty to safeguard the common interest, as expressed in the Treaties and in the norm granting competence to the decision-maker in question. Second, the decision-makers for their part have an extensive duty of giving reasons for their decisions and thus put to the court the arguments on the nature of their discretion and how they used it. In this way, courts become the public platform for discussing the extent of the power given to an institution and deciding on the way it has contributed to the common interest.

In every case that comes before a court, the presumption should be that it is to perform a high standard of review. This includes an intensive examination of all the factual, legal, and political considerations that went into reaching the decision under review. Decisions in the EMU carry high redistributive effects, which should be an important concern in judicial scrutiny. By the same token, the legitimacy structure behind the granting of discretion to the decision-making body is relevant: what limitations and conditions are attached to the granting of discretion and what accountability duties in other spheres (e.g., political and administrative) were or are in store for the decision-maker. The burden then shifts to the parties to demonstrate not only who should win the case, but also, preliminarily, what the appropriate standard of review and

[53] These are presented and analysed in detail in Chapter 1, Section 1.3.5.

all the necessary evidence should be. I propose that the parties in the litigation carry the responsibility to present a rich evidentiary basis that is to serve as ammunition aimed at endorsing or rebutting the presumption of full judicial review. This judicial activity should be shared between national and EU courts, as is done in other areas of EU law. How this book will reach these conclusions is what I turn to next.

I.3 STRUCTURE OF THE BOOK

The central concern of this book is determining how individuals can hold decision-makers in the EMU to account before EU and national courts. In addressing the problems presented in this introduction, the analysis in this book will embark on an expedition across theory (Chapters 1 and 2), practice (Chapters 3–5), and back – to reach its destination with conclusions on what sort of legal accountability is necessary to achieve political equality of citizens in the EMU (Conclusion and Epilogue). To achieve this, the book will look at three case studies in EU economic governance during and after the crisis: the financial assistance mechanisms; the monetary policy mechanisms of the ECB; and the Single Supervisory Mechanism (SSM). These case studies capture diverse contexts of post-crisis economic governance: the ESM operates outside the legal framework of EU law and operates on the basis of strict conditionality; monetary policy, on the one hand, and the SSM, on the other, represent distinct roles of the ECB. In the following passages, I will present how this journey will play out.

In Chapter 1, I present the theoretical framework of legal accountability grounded in the common interest, ensuring the political equality of citizens in their ability to hold decision-makers to account. This framework will draw on sociological and philosophical approaches to solidarity and the cosmopolitan literature on equality, to present a conceptual understanding of political equality of citizens. The framework put forward is based on an equilibrium between the principles of solidarity and equality that better provides for the political equality of citizens. I then apply this normative framework to the EMU, addressing more specifically the ways in which courts can contribute to the political equality of citizens through procedural and substantive routes.

Chapter 2 zooms in on theorising judicial review in the EMU. I first turn to the most problematic examples of non-accountable decision-making that recently took place in the EMU. The purpose here is to offer a sneak-peek preview of what went wrong, how (the lack of) judicial review contributed to this problem, and why traditional arguments against judicial review do not work in this context. Next, I theorise the role of courts in respect of executive discretion more generally, to move away from seeing courts as undemocratic institutions, most notably drawing on the work of Dworkin and Ely. On this basis, I present a framework of judicial review, placed in the context of the EMU. This chapter also proposes a division of labour between national and EU courts by advancing an argument for their closer cooperation and the management of their possible conflict.

Moving to the empirical part of the book, Chapter 3 analyses in detail the practice of legal accountability in respect of financial assistance mechanisms during the Euro crisis. After a brief description of financial assistance measures, I present how judicial review of the ESM and the resulting Memoranda of Understanding took place before national and EU courts. In both these levels of analysis, I focus on the procedural (access and remedies) and substantive aspects (interpretation of equality and solidarity) of the existing case law. This chapter closes with a reflection upon the influence that judicial interactions between EU and national courts have on the improvement of legal accountability in financial assistance.

Chapter 4 turns to the ECB in its conduct of monetary policy. In the first step, I present the legal framework of monetary policy within the system of the European System of Central Banks and explain in more detail the quantitative easing programmes of the ECB. Here, I also provide a summary of the back-and-forth litigation on the limits to monetary policy between the Court of Justice and the Bundesverfassungsgericht (in *Gauweiler* and *Weiss*). Against this backdrop, I conduct a further in-depth analysis of these decisions. Both these sections follow the same structure: they focus, first, on access to courts and remedies, and second, on the ways in which the courts under analysis approached the principles of equality and solidarity for the purposes of achieving the common interest. The last section is concerned with judicial interactions between EU and national courts and the role these play in the legal accountability of the ECB.

Chapter 5, the last one with an empirical approach, deals with the SSM. It presents the legal framework of the SSM and the solutions chosen for its organisation and operation. This exercise both aids our reading of the case law to come and highlights several accountability distortions that are problematic for the political equality of citizens. I then focus on judicial review concerning the SSM before EU courts and repeat this exercise in respect of national courts. I follow the approach taken in the previous two case studies by looking at how the courts have approached questions of access, remedies, and any possible interpretation of the principles of equality and solidarity. This chapter closes by again reflecting upon the role that judicial interactions play in delivering accountability within the SSM.

The Conclusion of the book then joins the theoretical propositions from the first two chapters with the empirical findings in Chapters 3–5. It is here that an assessment is made of how legal accountability has so far been able to ensure that decision-makers in the EMU are held to account by politically equal citizens. Turning to the future, the Conclusion makes proposals on how the theory of legal accountability from Chapters 1 and 2 can be meaningfully achieved. The book ends with an Epilogue that looks into the future: still in its infancy, the NGEU is the perfect guinea pig for testing my theoretical propositions, taking into account the lessons learned throughout the case studies. The Epilogue starts by presenting the legal framework of the NGEU and the way it has been grounded in the Treaties. I then turn to the used and possible avenues of judicial review before national and EU courts, to close the book with some final thoughts on what awaits individuals when holding the decision-makers in the EMU to account before courts.

1

The Normative Framework of Legal Accountability

1.1 INTRODUCTION

The developments described in the Introduction to this book loom large on the political equality of citizens. For example, the European Stability Mechanism (ESM) has been established by way of an international treaty, with a set-up designed to ensure that the voting rights reflect the respective contributions of Member States.[1] Using economic criteria in order to determine political rights is problematic: inequalities between creditor and debtor Member States are necessarily prolonged, as the latter are inevitably in the position of accepting the conditions attached to financial assistance measures.[2] Furthermore, the role of the citizen is reduced to national elections, leaving her without any influence with regard to creating, designing, and ultimately implementing the obligations stemming from the ESM. Pernice argues that the insistence of Member States on remaining the Masters of the Treaties[3] and the ESM being concluded in the realm of public international law results in a reliance on national procedures (meaning national parliaments and governments) as the only possible source of EU's legitimation, which ultimately enables the bypassing of citizens in decision-making.[4]

1 Article 4(7) of the Treaty Establishing the European Stability Mechanism T/ESM 2012-LT/en 1 (ESM Treaty).

2 F Fabbrini, *Economic Governance in Europe: Comparative Paradoxes and Constitutional Challenges* (Oxford University Press 2016) 15. See also F Losada, 'Institutional Implications of the Rise of a Debt-Based Monetary Regime in Europe' (2016) 22(6) *European Law Journal* 822, 833.

3 See, for example, German Bundesverfassungsgericht Case 2 BvR 2728/13 *Gauweiler*, Order of 14 January 2014 [26]. On the novelty of the same rhetoric being used by the Court of Justice, see Section 1.3.1.

4 I Pernice, 'Multilevel Constitutionalism and the Crisis of Democracy in Europe' (2015) 11(3) *European Constitutional Law Review* 541, 543. See also M Dawson and F de Witte, 'From

Against this background, the aim of this chapter is to introduce a framework of legal accountability applicable to supranational multilevel polities, and thus to the EMU. As a first step, the chapter will offer a normative proposal of legal accountability that seeks to see it as a mechanism for achieving the political equality of citizens. On this view, accountability is the glue that binds the public institution to the common interest, in that it allows for a rebalancing of the principles underpinning it. Seen in this way, all decision-makers are under an obligation to take into account the interests involved and balance them in a way that best serves the common interest. This approach moves beyond the constraints of the nation-state structure of accountability and lends itself in particular to multilevel polities beyond the state, where traditional routes of legitimation can no longer be straightforwardly identified. This will include a normative proposal concerning the relationship between equality and solidarity of political units, with the aim of achieving the equality of every person in pursuing the common interest.

That framework is then applied to the EMU, while considering its specific features. The chapter will thus continue by looking at the position of the individual, and the principles of equality and solidarity. I will also zoom further into the Treaties in search of objectives and principles of the common interest that should guide public policy in the EMU. Taking into account the redistributive effects that EMU policies and measures have on EU citizens, I will argue that the EMU's legal framework allows courts to reinterpret these objectives in a way that overcomes the current lack of citizens' ability to influence decision-makers.

In that sense, I will first present the theoretical framework ensuring the political equality of citizens, resulting in their ability to hold decision-makers to account (Section 1.2). This framework will draw on sociological and philosophical approaches to solidarity and the cosmopolitan literature on equality in order to present a conceptual understanding of political equality of citizens. The framework put forward is based on an equilibrium between the principles of solidarity and equality that better provides for the political equality of citizens. I will then apply this normative framework to the EMU (Section 1.3), addressing also more specifically the ways in which courts can contribute to the political equality of citizens through procedural and

Balance to Conflict: A New Constitution for the EU' (2016) 22(2) *European Law Journal* 204, 206; J Pisani-Ferry, 'Rebalancing the Governance of the Euro Area' in M Dawson, H Enderlein and C Joerges (eds), *Beyond the Crisis: The Governance of Europe's Economic, Political, and Legal Transformation* (Oxford University Press 2015) 79.

substantive routes. Section 1.4 will summarise these findings and present the way the same analysis will be carried out in more depth in relation to individual case studies in Chapters 3–5.

1.2 A NORMATIVE PROPOSAL OF LEGAL ACCOUNTABILITY

We have seen in the Introduction how the dominance of the principal–agent theory shaped approaches to accountability studies, with the aim of transcending the constraints that the state as the default polity set to this theoretical inquiry. In that analysis, I have also shown the limited bite of the principal–agent theory[5] when it meets conditions of convoluted representation coupled with increased executive discretion:[6] it results in the political inequality of citizens. Legal accountability beyond the state requires taking a different approach. Achieving political equality of citizens in a supranational polity focuses on ways to ensure that institutions conduct public policy in the common interest. Accountability is in that construct central. However, instead of seeing accountability merely as a vehicle for ensuring the responsiveness of institutions, accountability should be seen as a value in itself,[7] a normative good to be achieved. In this context, accountability itself is seen as a good in the common interest. It is a value that leads to political equality of citizens. How though?

Accountability should be seen as the glue that binds the public institution to the common interest, a mechanism that allows for a rebalancing of the principles underpinning it. Seen in this way, all decision-makers are under an obligation to take into account the interests involved and balance them in a way that best serves the common interest. Through this approach, I want to emphasise that a dichotomy between institutions who make political decisions (the actor) and those who hold those decision-makers to account (the forum) is a misleading one. Instead, all public institutions make decisions of a

[5] M Bovens, 'Analysing and Assessing Accountability: A Conceptual Framework' (2007) 13(4) *European Law Journal* 447. For exceptions, see M Dawson and A Maricut-Akbik, 'Procedural vs Substantive Accountability in EMU Governance: Between Payoffs and Trade-offs' (2021) 28 (11) *Journal of European Public Policy* 1707; M Goodhart, 'Democratic Accountability in Global Politics: Norms, Not Agents' (2011) 73(1) *The Journal of Politics* 45.

[6] Exemplified clearly in the context of the EMU.

[7] See, for example, the argument of Bovens on accountability as a virtue. M Bovens, 'Two Concepts of Accountability: Accountability as a Virtue and as a Mechanism' (2010) 33(5) *West European Politics* 946.

political nature[8] inasmuch as these carry consequences for the achievement of the common interest. This outlook also helps us set aside the approach to accountability that regards it mainly as a process, one where we should be looking for chains of responsiveness and the resulting sanctions. In other words, accountability is not a process of some institutions controlling others in a set procedure, but rather a normative value that all institutions achieve in their own ways.

In the supranational context, my accountability framework seeks to overcome the formal reading of equality of states pervading the intergovernmental logic of polities beyond the state, which hampers the achievement of the common interest of citizens. Shifting from the perspective of states to that of the individual in my opinion needs a substantive reading of equality. To achieve this, adding solidarity to the mix is indispensable. The two are then brought together to offer an abstraction of accountability beyond the state for the benefit of the individual. Here, instead of being marked by a clear representational relationship between the principal and the agent, accountability is characterised by decision-makers acting in the common interest of all citizens. The abstract common interest takes concrete shape in a specific polity, in constitutional foundations that determine the common interest to be pursued equally for all citizens.[9] In the following sections, I will further specify my approach to equality and to solidarity and conclude by showing how I see them operating in an equilibrium.

1.2.1 *Equality*

Turning to the interpretation of equality, the starting point of this inquiry is based on the argument that accountability in multilevel polities beyond the state demands taking into account the common interest of all citizens of the states that are members of such a polity. This requires a rethink of the necessary routes of legitimation in multilevel supranational polities, with the aim of moving past the classic elections–ratification spectrum. In that sense, a cosmopolitan understanding of equality will be used to support the argument that accountability means delivering public policy in the common interest.

8 For this argument made specifically as regards judicial activity, see J Rawls, *A Theory of Justice* (Harvard University Press 1971) 107–111.

9 In Section 1.3, I will present the foundations determining the common interest in the EMU context.

This also means abandoning the formal equality of states participating in the supranational organisation.

Any initial search of the term equality of states yields results from the area of public international law and the principle of sovereign equality of states. Article 2 of the UN Charter[10] tells us that sovereign equality is the basic principle guiding states' interactions in the international arena. Sovereign equality also means that once states sign up to a legal obligation in the international sphere, they are all equally bound to abide by it.[11] The cosmopolitan literature emphasises the drawbacks that equality of states inflicts upon the equality of individuals.[12] In the words of Buchanan:

> ... political equality among states is of value *only* so far as it contributes to justice as goal or as process. Political equality among states is not valuable for its own sake, and certainly cannot be regarded as a necessary condition in its own right for system legitimacy.[13]

In fact, sovereign equality of states in the international arena serves the purpose of non-domination[14] or non-interference: each state is equal and can only be bound by an international obligation through consent.[15] This rings particularly true for single-purpose international treaties that lead to none or a very limited extent of political connection between the contracting states. However, states' consent is in that respect unable to ensure equality under conditions of increased interdependence that follows from the multiplication of areas of international cooperation, coordination, and ultimately, integration.[16] When international treaties create complex duties and obligations between its members, insistence on formal equality can also become an instrument of domination. Sharing resources and mutually deciding on ways in which to redistribute them, in pursuit of multiple commonly pursued

[10] United Nations, Charter of the United Nations, 24 October 1945, 1 UNTS XVI.

[11] S R Ratner, *The Thin Justice of International Law* (Oxford University Press 2015) 194.

[12] D Chandler, 'New Rights for Old: Cosmopolitan Citizenship and the Critique of State Sovereignty' (2003) 51 *Political Studies* 332, 343.

[13] A Buchanan, *Justice, Legitimacy, and Self-Determination: Moral Foundations for International Law* (Oxford University Press 2004) 321.

[14] I am grateful to Mark Dawson for raising this point.

[15] M Lister, 'The Legitimating Role of Consent in International Law' (2011) 11(2) *Chicago Journal of International Law* 663.

[16] I am aware of the risk of coming across as a neo-functionalist here. The argument here is, however, much narrower.

objectives, paves the way for actual inequality.[17] In that sense, insistence on formal equality of states in supranational organisations for its own sake may be counterproductive.

As argued by Rossi, with the increase in the ability of international (and arguably, supranational) organisations to assume responsibility for carrying out the common interest of its members, it is likelier that those members will decrease their insistence on their 'sovereign status and, correlatively, to equality'.[18] Thus, the principle of equality of states is merely an indicator of membership, whereas the normative aim should be one of partnership.[19] Admittedly, this demands a higher level of engagement by states in the multilevel polity in question, and at times, the possibility of accepting varying outcomes for different members. This higher standard of responsibility stems from mutual obligations taken up by partnering states, who then work for the common interest of all citizens, rather than just their own. This reading of equality of states provides the possibility of moving beyond formal equality, meaning that decision-makers in the supranational sphere may at times detract from it, in order to serve the common interest of all citizens of partnering states.

1.2.2 *Solidarity*

In the quest for determining the role of solidarity in delivering public policy in the common interest, a brief theoretical examination of the concept of solidarity is due. The purpose of this theoretical exploration is to conceptualise the conditions under which citizens, rather than states, can become the primary focus in multilevel polities beyond the state. In other words, solidarity is the principle that allows for a move towards a cosmopolitan understanding of equality in the supranational context. This will allow us ultimately to reconceptualise legal accountability from account being owed through indirect routes of democratic legitimation (first by way of elections and then by supranational participation of elected representatives), to one where the

[17] For a discussion on the normative argument concerning the established contractual norms in international law, see N Krisch, 'The Decay of Consent: International Law in an Age of Global Public Goods' (2014) 108(1) *The American Journal of International Law* 1 and the references cited.

[18] L S Rossi, 'The Principle of Equality among Member States of the European Union' in L S Rossi and F Casolari (eds), *The Principle of Equality in EU Law* (Springer 2017) 10.

[19] ibid 39.

recognition of equality of each citizen creates a demand for the decision-makers to conduct public policy in the common interest.[20] Durkheim found that the danger for solidarity lies in selfish individualism, but importantly also in the nationalism of states, which he claimed can be countered by supranational integration.[21]

I therefore argue that solidarity provides the basis for a connection between citizens beyond the indirect route of democratic legitimation through elections on the national level and ratification on the supranational level. We will see that the literature demonstrates the existence of roughly three stages of understanding of solidarity in societies, each of which represents a conceptually tighter bond between citizens than the previous one. Accordingly, the third stage will be used as the blueprint for the type of accountability relationship necessary in multilevel polities beyond the state.

The first two stages of solidarity can be found in the well-known work of Durkheim, who differentiates between mechanic and organic solidarity.[22] First, mechanic solidarity is present in traditionally small and homogeneous societies and assumes help is provided on the premise that it will also be received if and when necessary as an act of altruism. Second, organic solidarity exists in modern and heterogeneous societies with a multitude of interests and interdependence, where help is provided based on 'enlightened self-interest' that guides the smooth operation of the system.[23]

The third understanding of solidarity in the work of Forst and Honneth is, however, of most relevance to the re-conceptualisation of accountability in supranational multilevel polities. For Forst, solidarity has an important social cohesive as well as political role. As a consequence, citizenship is the necessary condition for the expression of equality in terms of rights and taking part in a common project.[24] In this respect, he underlines that 'a political community is a community of the recognition *and* realisation of equal rights and duties'.[25] In other words, recognition is due to the other as ethical and legal

[20] See also Dawson and Maricut-Akbik (n 5) 1719.

[21] E Durkheim, *The Division of Labour in Society* (1893; New York Free Press 1997) 405.

[22] ibid. Durkheim's contributions are also prevalent in the existing literature concerning solidarity and the EU. See, for example, F de Witte, *Justice in the EU: The Emergence of Transnational Solidarity* (Oxford University Press 2015); V Borger, *The Currency of Solidarity: Constitutional Transformation during the Euro Crisis* (Cambridge University Press 2020).

[23] S Fernandes and E Rubio, 'Solidarity within the Eurozone: How Much, What For, For How Long?' Notre Europe Policy Paper 51 (2012) 3–4.

[24] R Forst, *Contexts of Justice: Political Philosophy beyond Liberalism and Communitarianism* (University of California Press 2002) 116.

[25] ibid 136.

persons, and as fellow citizens both in their difference and their sameness.[26] Similarly, Honneth introduced the concept of social solidarity, defining it as 'a felt concern for what is individual and particular about the other person', implying the recognition of 'one another in light of values that allow the abilities and traits of the other to appear significant for shared praxis'[27] based on mutual and unconditional respect.[28]

Crucially, then, solidarity is a necessary tool for organising society according to standards which ensure equal opportunities of recognition for everyone[29] and where the relationship between individuals and groups allow for 'collective interest to be served'.[30] A solidarity obligation is therefore one owed in the common interest.[31] As put by Cohen and Sabel:

> Solidarity here rests neither on a sentiment of identity nor on a complementarity rooted in the division of labor. Rather it is both moral and practical. Moral, in that individuals recognize one another as moral agents entitled to be treated as equals; practical, in that they are bound to each other by the recognition that each is better able to learn what he or she needs to master problems through collaboration with the others whose experiences, orientations and even most general goals differ from his or her own – a recognition that both expresses and reinforces a sense of human commonality that extends beyond existing solidarities.[32]

In the language of democratic theory, such an understanding of solidarity can be translated to political equality of all citizens.[33] Solidarity should thus serve the function of recognition of each citizen in the social sphere, in the

[26] ibid 137.

[27] A Honneth, *The Struggle for Recognition: The Moral Grammar of Social Conflicts* (MIT Press 1996) 129.

[28] N Fraser and A Honneth, *Redistribution or Recognition? A Political-Philosophical Exchange* (Verso 2003) 188. With great thanks to Wayne V Walton for inspiring conversations on these concepts.

[29] S Juul, 'Solidarity and Social Cohesion in Late Modernity: A Question of Recognition, Justice and Judgement in Situation' (2010) 13(2) *European Journal of Social Theory* 253, 256. See also H Brunkhorst, *Solidarity: From Civic Friendship to a Global Legal Community* (MIT Press 2005).

[30] W van Oorschot and A Komter, 'What is it that ties . . .? Theoretical Perspectives on Social Bond' (1998) 41(3) *Sociale Wetenschappen* 4, 11.

[31] Borger (n 22) 52.

[32] J Cohen and C F Sabel, 'Sovereignty and Solidarity: EU and US' in K H Ladeur (ed), *Public Governance in the Age of Globalization* (Routledge 2004) 721–722.

[33] R A Dahl, *Polyarchy: Participation and Opposition* (Yale University Press 1971) 1.

language of Honneth. Importantly for the context of multilevel polities beyond the state, solidarity should be used to extend, rather than narrow down, membership[34] and the resulting public policy duties towards the common interest. This in turn means that accountability must be organised in a way that ensures the recognition, by the institutions holding public powers, of the individual in the design, implementation, and consequences of public policy. Specifically, they must show how this inclusion figured in the decision-making process and how the decision itself will serve the common interest.[35]

1.2.3 *The Equilibrium*

Taking into account these considerations, the application of an equilibrium between equality and solidarity in a multilevel polity with different layers of membership (state and individual) has the purpose of ensuring the political equality among all its citizens (their ability to 'determine politically their destiny').[36] The idea behind connecting equality and solidarity seeks to overcome the use of traditional concepts, such as nationality, to connect citizens to commitments of justice[37] in the supranational sphere. The need for this equilibrium stems precisely from the nature of supranational polities, where we can observe different sources of membership overlapping and potentially inhibiting each other.[38] This may lead to undesirable results: a public policy conducted by decision-makers with input from one level of membership (for example, national) with consequences for the other level (individual), or vice versa. Traditional accountability routes in that context are increasingly unable to ensure that public policy is delivered in a way that serves the common interest.

A possible solution to this problem is, I argue, to rethink what role pertains to the principles of equality (of political units on the one hand, and of citizens,

[34] In the words of Steinvorth: 'Solidarity is understood as a bond that makes up a "we".' U Steinvorth, 'Applying the Idea of Solidarity to Europe' in A Grimmel and S My Giang (eds), *Solidarity in the European Union: A Fundamental Value in Crisis* (Springer 2017) 10.

[35] See also Dawson and Maricut-Akbik (n 5).

[36] E O Eriksen, 'Structural Injustice: The Eurozone Crisis and the Duty of Solidarity' ARENA Working Paper 4/2017, 13.

[37] de Witte (n 22) 60.

[38] See also Dawson and de Witte (n 4) 218–219; M van den Brink, 'The Promises and Drawbacks of European Union Citizenship for a Polycentric Union' in J van Zeben and A Bobić, *Polycentricity in the European Union* (Cambridge University Press 2019) 164.

on the other) and that of solidarity in conceiving and ensuring the common interest. In the above theorisation of solidarity, Honneth's work was used as an inspiration to imagine a society connected through the respect of the other as an individual. This requires that decision-makers are guided by the common interest in the conduct of supranational public policy that accounts for preferences of individuals, rather than those of states. Equality between states was, in turn, theorised not as a value in itself but as instrumental for achieving justice among all citizens of a supranational polity. In that sense, the two principles read together create conditions of achieving the common interest. Accountability in this context is the process which allows for the rebalancing of the two principles to take place. Specifically, it is through the activity of giving account in all the different stages of the decision-making process that the principles are identified and given specific weight.

This approach promotes accountability, but in a different manner than that employed in the nation-state context. Dahl defines the key characteristic of democracy as 'the continuing responsiveness of the government to the preferences of its citizens, considered as political equals'.[39] Returning to the proposed understanding of the principle of solidarity as a concept where the recognition of the individual is central for delivering public policy in the common interest, creating conditions for democratic discourse equally for all is imperative. Accountability is in this context the necessary condition of political equality, given that it guarantees that the institutions pursue public policy in the common interest. Solidarity adjusts the attention of decision-makers from states to citizens, and their equality thus becomes the normative focus of public policy. In that sense, accountability is the mechanism ensuring that decision-makers achieve that equilibrium between the two principles. Specifically, they are to use a wide array of contributions (by shifting the focus from states to citizens) in the fact-finding process and the expected outcomes of public policy.[40]

This conceptualisation of supranational accountability necessarily results in a changed relationship between different types of accountability mechanisms found in the national setting,[41] where political accountability dominates the system through electoral legitimation. The very temporal

[39] Dahl (n 33) 1. See also G de Búrca, 'Developing Democracy beyond the State' (2008) 46(2) *Columbia Journal of Transnational Law* 101, 130.

[40] See also, in this sense, the accountability good of publicness discussed by Dawson and Maricut-Akbik (n 5) 8.

[41] J Black, 'Constructing and Contesting Legitimacy and Accountability in Polycentric Regulatory Regimes' (2008) 2 *Regulation & Governance* 137, 141.

relationship of the *ex ante* political and *ex post* legal control at the national level does not recognise the diminished control capacity of the traditional principal on the supranational level.[42] In addition, the conventional role of legal accountability as a corrective to the majoritarian set-up of political accountability,[43] in particular vis-à-vis the executive,[44] is facing legitimacy and enforcement issues at the supranational level.[45] Processes of accountability therefore need to provide a space for connection between all citizens,[46] where solidarity represents the act of defining the shared goal through the recognition of the citizen as the central normative concern for public policy, while equality ensures mutual respect among partners on the path of achieving that goal. In that sense, accountability structures need to ensure that the institutions are in fact making decisions towards the fulfilment of that common goal.

1.3 APPLYING THE FRAMEWORK TO THE EMU

In this section, my aim is to assess the correspondence between accountability in the EMU with the normative proposal of accountability from the previous section. The starting point for this task is that problematically, the design of EMU decision-making placed an emphasis on giving voice to Member States and ensuring their formal equality. As I explained in the Introduction, political forms of accountability in the Treaties have proven deficient in the realities of the financial crisis, specifically in the operation of different institutions that worked on addressing it.[47] Dawson and de Witte convincingly showed that reliance on legitimation through the national level deprived citizens of the ability to be meaningfully represented at the EU level, due to

42 C Scott, 'Accountability in the Regulatory State' (2000) 27(1) *Journal of Law and Society* 38, 39.

43 C Harlow, *Accountability in the European Union* (Oxford University Press 2002) 17.

44 ibid 146; C Harlow and R Rawlings, 'Promoting Accountability in Multi-Level Governance: A Network Approach' (2006) *European Governance Papers* No. C-06-02, 8.

45 A von Bogdandy, 'The Democratic Legitimacy of International Courts: A Conceptual Framework' (2013) 14(2) *Theoretical Inquiries in Law* 361, 364; N Grossman, 'Legitimacy and International Adjudicative Bodies' (2009) 41 *George Washington International Law Review* 107.

46 In the context of legal accountability, see Harlow (n 43) 148–149.

47 P Craig, 'The Eurogroup, Power and Accountability' (2017) 23 *European Law Journal* 234, 248.

the domination of Member State preferences clashing against each other at the EU level.[48] In that constellation, citizens were unable to connect based on their social or economic preferences but only through the preferences of the political majority in their Member State.[49]

For example, routes of national democratic legitimation were not sufficient to control the Troika in devising financial assistance mechanisms and the conditions imposed on the Member States receiving such assistance.[50] Legal accountability, although traditionally dominant in EU law, has in the financial crisis not been used to its full potential, given the refusal of the Court of Justice to place a more serious hold over the decision-makers within the European Financial Stabilisation Mechanism[51] and the ESM,[52] or in respect of the unconventional monetary policies of the ECB.[53] To achieve this, we must rethink the position of legal accountability and its possible contribution within existing rules on the EMU and the ESM Treaty. To do so, legal accountability needs to ensure the equilibrium between the principles of equality and solidarity in the conduct of public policy in the EMU.

I will show that this is a normative aim that is possible to achieve within the current constitutional framework, although it requires a shift in the conduct of judicial review. In so doing, I will first conceptualise the terminology relevant for guiding my argument. I will then set out the working definition of the individual in the EMU as the citizen that requires recognition in the conduct of public policy in the common interest. Next, I will present how EU law currently treats the principle of equality of Member States, on the one hand, and the principle of solidarity, on the other. This will make visible the deficiencies as well as space for progress towards the normative framework of accountability proposed in the previous section. The last part of this section will then bring these findings together to conceptualise the common interest in the EMU that strives towards the recognition of the individual and the achievement of political equality.

48 Dawson and de Witte (n 4) 212. See also C Harlow, 'Citizen Access to Political Power in the European Union' (1999) EUI Working Paper RSC No. 99/2, 32.

49 Dawson and de Witte (n 4) 209.

50 M Markakis, *Accountability in the Economic and Monetary Union: Foundations, Policy, and Governance* (Oxford University Press 2020) 55–57.

51 Council Regulation (EU) No 407/2010 of 11 May 2010 establishing a European financial stabilisation mechanism (OJ 2010 L 118) 1.

52 For example, explicitly constrained in terms of the applicability of the Charter in Case C-370/12 *Pringle* EU:2012:756.

53 For example, in Case C-62/14 *Gauweiler* EU:C:2015:400.

1.3.1 *On Concepts*

For the purposes of applying the proposed accountability framework to the EMU context, the aim here is to determine the relevant level of analysis and the terminology that I will use throughout the book. Both equality and solidarity are principles, the meaning of which spans several dimensions and refers to different actors. In EU law, different provisions of the Treaties refer to the two principles addressing relationships between states and between citizens. For example, Article 3(3) of the Treaty of the European Union (TEU) refers to solidarity among generations and among Member States,[54] whereas Article 2 TEU lists solidarity between men and women as one of the founding values of the EU. The same is the case with the principle of equality: Article 2 TEU mentions equality of Member States (also reinforced in Article 4(2) TEU); Articles 9 and 10(3) TEU refer to the political equality of EU citizens who have the right to participate in the democratic life of the Union; whereas equality between men and women, referred to in Article 3(3) TEU and in Articles 8 and 10 of the Treaty on the Functioning of the European Union (TFEU), is also among the founding values.

Keeping this variety in mind, this book takes the following approach: in revisiting the way in which the principle of equality *between Member States* is interpreted, the normative proposal concerning their interpretation seeks to achieve political equality *between citizens*. I argue that achieving political equality of citizens in the EU cannot be achieved by retaking the nation-state path. In the words of Walker, the '[t]ouch of stateness – so familiar as to be often invisible – affects our understanding of key ideas and institutional possibilities as diverse as democracy, fundamental rights, equality [...]'.[55] While the current realities of EU integration make it impossible to disregard the sovereignty discourse and the central role that the Member States still occupy in its institutional structure, this does not mean there is no space for the principle of solidarity to change our understanding of equality of Member States, in particular if such a change is capable of improving the political equality of citizens.

54 Solidarity between Member States is further used in the context of the Area of freedom, security and justice (Articles 67(2) and 80 TFEU), in economic policy (Article 122(1) TFEU), energy policy (Article 194(1) TFEU) and in the general solidarity clause (Article 222 TFEU).

55 N Walker, 'Late Sovereignty in the European Union' in N Walker (ed), *Sovereignty in Transition* (Hart 2003) 5.

Legal accountability is one mechanism that can contribute to the transformation of how the principle of equality of Member States, on the one hand, and the principle of solidarity, on the other, may be applied in the EMU. My aim here is not to propose a Treaty change but to offer ways in which legal accountability in specific can serve as a mechanism that shifts the relationship between these principles. In my view, the Treaties already offer the possibility of reimagining the common interest, which would place the political equality of citizens at the centre of public policy. The dominant position of courts in the EU means they are able to act as a corrective to other forms of accountability, as they hold the interpretative powers necessary for ensuring the conduct of public policy in the common interest. Courts can and should, the argument goes, act as promoters of the recognition of the citizen, which should be the central concern if decision-makers are to act in the common interest.

1.3.2 *The Individual*

This book's focus is on the position of the individual in her quest for political equality. But who exactly is this individual? The answer to this question is by no means simple: one natural or legal person, under EU law, may have several defining characteristics, depending on the EU law situation she finds herself in (e.g., worker, provider and/or receiver of services, dependent family member, to name a few).[56] Two directions present themselves in defining the individual: first, our intuition may take us to the rules on EU citizenship that focus on addressees of the EU's economic constitution and its four freedoms. The second option is to look further into the political dimension of who is in fact the EU citizen with a legitimate demand to seek recognition in shaping and enforcing the common interest. I will first show how the first direction does not lead to satisfactory political equality outcomes. After this, I will present my approach to the concept of the individual.

The EU's economic constitution has, at least until the Maastricht Treaty's inclusion of EU citizenship in primary law, been the dominant source of and rationale for granting and expanding the rights of individuals. Free movement rights have been elevated to the status of fundamental rights, placing

[56] See L Azoulai, S Barbou des Places and E Pataut, 'Being a Person in the European Union' in L Azoulai, S Barbou des Places and E Pataut (eds), *Constructing the Person in EU Law: Rights, Roles, Identities*. (Hart 2016) 3.

cross-border economic activity at the centre of individual rights discourse.[57] On this view, individuals are instrumental to the greater aim of legitimising the EU as an autonomous system of law and governance,[58] rendering the EU itself as 'functional and not ontological'.[59] With the formal introduction of EU citizenship and subsequent decisions of the Court of Justice,[60] EU citizenship has arguably acquired a self-standing quality moving beyond its original economic mover paradigm.[61]

The critique directed to the Court of Justice in this phase revolves around its superficial appropriation of the proportionality discourse that national constitutional courts traditionally employ in the fundamental rights discourse. On this view, the balance is primarily skewed in favour of economic rights, whereas fundamental rights come into play merely as a possible counterargument.[62] In consequence, the economic element remains dominant[63] and cannot, in my view, produce conditions for political equality of all citizens. More importantly, the dominance of the economic element does not provide space for the exercise of political rights at a transnational level. At the same time, it provides only a limited exercise of political rights of those moving across national borders (e.g., the active and passive right to vote in local elections in the host Member State).[64]

57 A J Menéndez, 'Whose Citizenship? Whose Europe? – The Many Paradoxes of European Citizenship' (2014) 15(5) *German Law Journal* 907, 908. For a comprehensive overview of this law and its critique, see Opinion of Advocate General Sharpston in Case C-34/09 *Ruiz Zambrano* EU:C:2010:560 [67]–[89].

58 M Dani, 'The Subjectification of the European Citizen' in Azoulai, Barbou des Places and Pataut (n 56) 61; J H H Weiler, 'Van Gend en Loos: The Individual as Subject and Object and the Dilemma of European Legitimacy' (2014) 12(1) *International Journal of Constitutional law* 93, 102.

59 Azoulai, Barbou des Places and Pataut (n 56) 9.

60 For example, Case C-60/00 *Carpenter* EU:C:2002:434; Case C-34/09 *Ruiz Zambrano* EU:C:2011:124. However, the Court has arguably backtracked from this progressive trend in Case C-333/13 *Dano* EU:C:2014:2358 and Case C-67/14 *Alimanovic* EU:C:2015:597. A similar trend is proposed to the Court in the Opinion of Advocate General Richard de la Tour in Case C-624/20 *E.K. v Staatssecretaris van Justitie en Veiligheid* EU:C:2022:194. See also R Lanceiro, '*Dano* and *Alimanovic*: The Recent Evolution of CJEU Caselaw on EU Citizenship and Cross-border Access to Social Benefits' (2017) 3(1) *UNIO – EU Law Journal* 63.

61 E Spaventa, 'From Gebhard to Carpenter: Towards a (Non-)economic Constitution' (2004) 41 (3) *Common Market Law Review* 743, 744.

62 Menéndez (n 57) 925.

63 F de Witte, 'Emancipation through Law?' in Azoulai, Barbou des Places and Pataut (n 56) 24, 29–30.

64 Article 20(2)(b) TFEU, Article 22 TFEU, and Article 40 of the Charter. See also Case C-673/20 *Préfet du Gers* EU:C:2022:449 [49]–[51]. For an elaboration of the deficiencies attached to

The second way of envisioning the individual entails a greater level of political autonomy for EU citizens. Their role in the European project is not merely to use and benefit from the internal market and its (many and diverse) by-products. It is possible to envisage a role for the EU citizen that is more than a self-interested agent in the internal market:[65] that of political citizenship.[66] As the integration project expands, so does the space for the citizen to take part in these political and institutional transformations. Harlow argues that cultural identity and bonds of solidarity are both the necessary condition *and* the consequence of input into political decision-making.[67] Habermas highlights the same mutual reinforcement of solidarity and the sovereignty of EU citizens at a transnational level.[68] The literature emphasises that the position of the EU citizen in the EU's constitutional frame does not yet amount to a true political role (or in the words of de Witte, offer emancipation on the transnational level).[69]

This is certainly also due to the lack of a proper political stage for such participation, exemplified most clearly by the representation in the European Parliament, which is still based on national voting lists.[70] It is also the result of multiple memberships that EU citizens hold: at a minimum, a national and

this set-up and an argument for a more local focus on the exercise of political rights of EU citizens, see van den Brink (n 38) 180–184.

65 Azoulai, Barbou des Places and Pataut (n 56) 5; F de Witte, 'Sex, Drugs and EU Law: The Recognition of Moral and Ethical Diversity in EU Law' (2013) 50(6) *Common Market Law Review* 1545.

66 See also Harlow (n 48) 1.

67 She explicitly emphasises the circularity of this position as embedded in political citizenship. ibid.

68 J Habermas, *The Crisis of the European Union: A Response* (Polity 2012) 45–47; J Habermas, *Between Facts and Norms: Contributions to a Discourse Theory of Law and Democracy* (MIT Press 1996) 269.

69 de Witte (n 56) 31; Menéndez (n 57) 933; P C Schmitter, *How to Democratize the European Union ... and Why Bother?* (Lanham, Rowman & Littlefield 2000) 33–34.

70 See Articles 1 to 4 of the Act of 20 September 1976 concerning the election of the representatives of the Assembly by direct universal suffrage (OJ 1976 L 278, p. 5), last amended by Council Decision (EU, Euratom) 2018/994 of 13 July 2018 (OJ 2018 L 178, p. 1). For a proposal of the European Parliament on the creation of transnational lists, see European Parliament legislative resolution of 3 May 2022 on the proposal for a Council Regulation on the election of the members of the European Parliament by direct universal suffrage, repealing Council Decision (76/787/ECSC, EEC, Euratom) and the Act concerning the election of the members of the European Parliament by direct universal suffrage annexed to that Decision (2020/2220(INL) – 2022/0902(APP)). See also a Study conducted by the European Parliamentary Research Service, 'Transnational Electoral Lists: Ways to Europeanise Elections to the European Parliament' (February 2021), available at <www.europarl.europa.eu/RegData/etudes/STUD/2021/679084/EPRS_STU(2021)679084_EN.pdf>.

supranational one (with the possibility of autonomous regions and local self-government adding political rights and obligations to the spectrum).[71] While a full transnational political membership in the EU is still incipient,[72] it creates an important momentum: the sovereign power of citizens at the supranational level now exists alongside and is a competitor to Member State sovereignty.[73]

It is here that the principle of solidarity comes into play and offers space for recognition that may result in genuine political citizenship. And this is where the courts can step in: the institutional set-up does not explicitly recognise but allows for an interpretation of transnational membership of citizens as a demand of recognition and the exercise of public power in their common interest. The courts can demand that decision-makers recognise such transnational interests in their conduct of public policy precisely through the tool of accountability. Primacy and autonomy of EU law are specifically the glue that binds EU citizens, allowing them to circumvent the laws of Member States,[74] also, or particularly, when EU law is constructed to stress the common interest. In the same vein, the political exercise of citizenship takes shape through the actions of individuals accessing courts and seeking that they impose common interest demands on the exercise of public policy.[75]

I therefore argue for a move towards an approach that sees the individual as capable of shaping and enforcing the common interest in the public space of a supranational polity such as the EU. Specifically in the context of legal accountability, this means that individuals enforce the common interest before national and EU courts. This, in any event, has been the main logic of enforcing EU law due to political fragmentation within Member States and a strong focus on judicial enforcement led by individuals.[76] For lack of a treaty change that would create a genuine public sphere for 'unconstrained deliberation among equals',[77] courts under this view provide the arena for public debate and deliberation. I am not suggesting that citizens suddenly abandon

71 van den Brink (n 38) 163.

72 But nevertheless, unprecedented and a powerful counterforce to the traditional nation-state monopoly of force through its constituting powers on the EU level. Habermas, *The Crisis of the European Union* (n 68) 30.

73 ibid 13, 35.

74 ibid 26.

75 On a principled level, the same argument is taken up by R D Kelemen, 'Suing for Europe: Adversarial Legalism and European Governance' (2006) 39(1) *Comparative Political Studies* 101, 103. See also Cohen and Sabel (n 32) 731.

76 Kelemen (n 75) 107–114.

77 Cohen and Sabel (n 32) 718–719.

the membership of the nation-state they belong to, and they indeed may have different interests and preferences vis-à-vis that constituency.[78] However, the powers granted to the supranational level in the creation of the EMU conferred upon that level redistributive powers not explicitly spelled out in the treaties and without appropriate mechanisms to account for them.[79] The EU citizen is at the moment able to fill that gap through the demand of a reinterpretation of solidarity and equality by courts.

Throughout this book, I will look at national and EU case law where applicants will be those privileged by the EU or national procedural rules (such as the EU institutions and Member States at the EU level, and political actors such as presidents or groups of members of parliament before national courts). In addition, I will also include non-privileged applicants: natural and legal persons who either find themselves in concrete cases of enforcing their rights or who challenge national or EU legislation and thus must meet high standing thresholds, most commonly demonstrating a certain interest in the action. My broader argument is that all these actors, not only natural persons, can and do, in direct or indirect ways, enforce the common interest.[80]

What of the argument that access to courts is an elitist exercise accessible only to some[81] and therefore in practice of only a limited contribution to the achievement of genuine political equality? The Single Supervisory Mechanism (SSM) provides fertile ground for this criticism: litigation in this area before the Court of Justice by non-privileged applicants is dominated by banks and other types of credit institution as they are the ones directly and individually concerned by the decisions of the ECB or national supervisors.[82] In my view, notwithstanding the fact that it is these arguably more powerful actors who have the ability to raise issues related to banking supervision, the result of their activity is to bring matters of common interest before EU courts. In that sense, we will see that in the SSM, EU courts can contribute to ensuring prudential requirements upon banks and credit institutions, thereby increasing their overall responsibility also towards citizens

78 Habermas, *The Crisis of the European Union* (n 68) 37.

79 Dawson and de Witte (n 4) 214.

80 For a comprehensive analysis of using litigation as an enforcement tool of EU law on the EU, national, and litigant-type level, see L Conant, A Hofmann, D Soennecken and L Vanhala, 'Mobilizing European Law' (2018) 25(9) *Journal of European Public Policy* 1376.

81 Menéndez (n 57) 921.

82 For more detailed information on these trends, see Chapter 5, Section 5.3.1.

who have not directly taken part in a specific litigation. Powerful actors are, in that sense, inadvertent promoters of legal accountability under the condition that the courts use their powers to enforce the common interest.

At the national level, the picture is more nuanced and may allow for a greater variety of applicants to access justice. For example, class actions, interest group litigation,[83] and differing standing rules before national courts allow citizens to surpass the national prism of representation at the EU level and organise themselves instead based on social and economic interests, and ultimately bring these issues, along different conflict lines, also before the Court of Justice through the preliminary reference procedure. Even when national courts refrain from submitting a reference, it is important to keep in mind that they too are, regardless, courts with an EU law mandate and take part in the enforcement of the common interest.[84] Access to national courts is furthermore not confined solely to nationals and residents of a Member State, as are voting rights. Consequently, national courts are powerful enough actors[85] to impose on decision-makers within their jurisdiction requirements that the conduct of public policy in the common interest demands.

1.3.3 *Equality*

In EU law more generally, Article 4(2) TEU provides for the equality of Member States, whereas Article 9 TEU places the equality of citizens as the underlying obligation for all Union's activities. Under Article 8 TFEU, the Union shall in all its activities aim to eliminate inequalities. The balance between the two perspectives of the principle of equality (of states and of individuals) has originally been tilted towards EU citizens, when the Court of Justice established the so-called Simmenthal mandate, according to which national courts must apply EU law to cases within their jurisdiction and protect the resulting citizens' rights.[86]

In economic governance, equality of Member States in my view acquired a novel quality through the application of conditionality. Judicial review of

83 For an interesting analysis of interest group litigation in Belgium, Lithuania, the Netherlands, Slovenia and Sweden, see A Hofmann and D Naurin, 'Explaining Interest Group Litigation in Europe: Evidence from the Comparative Interest Group Survey' (2021) 34 *Governance* 1235.

84 For an example of this trend in the securities regulation and enforcement, see Kelemen (n 75) 117–118.

85 Conant et al argue that the bulk of EU law litigation happens before national courts and never reaches EU courts. Conant et al (n 80) 1384.

86 M Claes, *The National Courts' Mandate in the European Constitution* (Hart 2006) 108.

measures of economic governance at both the national and EU level[87] endorsed that logic, to the detriment of equality between citizens. Specifically, the logic of conditionality is at its core an insurance that the Member States receiving assistance will continue to pursue a sound budgetary policy. It would thus not become necessary for Member States to cover the liabilities of others in contravention of the prohibition of monetary financing under Article 125 TFEU.[88] As a result, strict conditionality that features in Article 136(3) TFEU, endorsed both in financial assistance and as a relevant consideration in the quantitative easing programmes of the ECB, had rather different outcomes across the EU, with little ability for the affected citizens to contest them. Take the example of the conditionality attached to financial assistance: debtor states implemented severe cuts to their social security systems and citizens affected by these changes only had recourse against the national decision-makers implementing them. Yet, because these changes were the result of the conditions set out in Memoranda of Understanding, there was no possibility for a challenge at the national level to succeed. In creditor states, the same financial assistance mechanisms were subject to legal challenge for fears that this would incentivise debtor states to shirk their responsibility of a sound budgetary policy. Inevitably, macroeconomic surveillance was also conducted differently for the two groups of states.[89]

In the context of the litigation concerning the Public Sector Purchase Programme (PSPP) of the ECB, equality of Member States was emphasised yet again as the normative priority: the Bundesverfassungsgericht insisted that a risk-sharing programme could not find its place under the Treaties as it would breach the prohibition of monetary financing, whereas the ECB must be bound by the principle of proportionality in designing and implementing its monetary policy decisions. This, because it would otherwise remove from the Member States their equal sovereign right to determine their budgetary policy. However, such an approach disregards the fact that debtor Member States already, through conditionality, lost a significant part of their budgetary sovereignty by the need to abide by specific reforms that usually remain within their powers.[90] The Bundesverfassungsgericht's focus on the PSPP's effects on different social groups in Germany equally misses the bigger picture that

87 Analysed in detail in Chapters 3–5.

88 See, for example, Case C-370/12 *Pringle* (n 52) [143]–[147].

89 For a detailed comparison of macroeconomic surveillance between Germany and Greece, see Markakis (n 50) 76–102.

90 Markakis (n 50) 66–67.

monetary policy is supposed to achieve: that of ensuring the stability of the euro for all eurozone members, which entails a much broader consideration of the policy's effects.[91]

It is equally lamentable that the Court of Justice employed the equality of Member States logic in its press release following the *Weiss* judgment of the Bundesverfassungsgericht, where it restated the jurisprudence concerning the primacy of EU law, concluding: 'That is the only way of ensuring the equality of Member States in the Union they created.'[92] In the context of the EU's economic governance, this results in an emphasis on conditionality and less on the major redistributive effects of such decisions for citizens across different socioeconomic groups across the EU.

Yet, it was not always like this. The way that the Court of Justice previously applied and interpreted the principle of equality of Member States departs from formal equality and is relevant for the present discussion in at least three ways. First, equality of Member States ensures uniform and effective application of EU law across its territory and to all its citizens.[93] In *Commission v Italy*,[94] the Court stated that national interests are not a justification to depart from an obligation imposed by EU law, as this would jeopardise the effective application of EU law throughout the Member States and would result in an undue advantage over those Member States that have given proper effect to the same obligation.[95] The Court also stressed that Member States' equality before EU law ensures the equal treatment of their citizens.[96] Second, the Court stated that equal treatment of Member States does not apply where differentiated circumstances exist. In consequence, the Court separated formal and substantive equality: '[an] appearance of discrimination in form may therefore correspond in fact to an absence of discrimination in substance.'[97] Third, the principle of equality may be overridden if concerns of

91 P Dermine, 'The Ruling of the Bundesverfassungsgericht in *PSPP* – An Inquiry into Its Repercussions on the Economic and Monetary Union' (2020) 16 *European Constitutional Law Review* 525, 538.

92 Available at <https://curia.europa.eu/jcms/upload/docs/application/pdf/2020-05/cp200058en.pdf>. For a rebuke of the logic of the Press Release, see J Lindeboom, 'Is the Primacy of EU Law Based on the Equality of the Member States? A Comment on the CJEU's Press Release Following the PSPP Judgment' (2020) 21(5) *German Law Journal* 1032.

93 See also Rossi (n 18) 15–16. For an argument that an unconditional application of the principle of supremacy ensures the equality of Member States, see F Fabbrini, 'After the OMT Case: The Supremacy of EU Law as the Guarantee of the Equality of Member States' (2015) 16 *German Law Journal* 1003.

94 Case 39/72 *Commission v Italy* EU:C:1973:13.

95 ibid [21].

96 ibid [24].

97 Case 13/63 *Commission v Italy* EU:C:1963:20 [4].

market unity so require.[98] The rationale is simple: the application of differentiated measures will ultimately result in homogeneous conditions across the market. All these considerations ring true particularly loudly for the EMU context.

The architecture of the EMU as set out in the Maastricht Treaty sought to preserve the balance between large and small states.[99] Despite this ideal, the EMU was in its very creation not an optimal currency area, meaning that the economic conditions across members varied significantly.[100] Formal equality was therefore a shield against the EMU turning into a transfer union, resulting in the introduction of the no-bailout clause and the prohibition of direct transfers from the ECB.[101] The strong focus on the sovereignty of Member States influenced the division of competences between the EU and the Member States in a way that necessarily decreased the emphasis on solidarity.[102] The deficiencies of this design became obvious in the management of the EMU after the crisis, dominated by the European Council, and within it, Germany and France. The actions undertaken demonstrated the limits of formal equality of Member States,[103] to paraphrase the Court of Justice.[104] The guise of equality allowed for an ideological domination of some Member States over others (the well-known German ordoliberal approach, for example).[105] To this, we may also add the unified voice of Member States in the institutions which does not allow for spaces of recognition for diverse socioeconomic preferences of citizens.[106]

Equality of Member States has, since the conflict between the Court of Justice and the Bundesverfassungsgericht in respect of quantitative easing programmes of the ECB,[107] gained renewed attention in the former's

98 Joined Cases C-181/88, C-182/88 and C-218/88 *Deschamps* EU:C:1989:642 [21].
99 Fabbrini (n 2) 8.
100 Losada (n 2) 828.
101 ibid.
102 Domurath (n 122) 466. See also M Ekengren, N Matzén, M Rhinard and M Svantesson, 'Solidarity or Sovereignty? EU Cooperation in Civil Protection' (2006) 28(5) *Journal of European Integration* 457, 470.
103 Fabbrini (n 2) 13–15. See also S Fabbrini, 'Intergovernmentalism and Its Limits' (2013) 46(9) *Comparative Political Studies* 1003, 1018.
104 See n 98 in this chapter.
105 Dermine (n 91) 538.
106 Dawson and de Witte (n 4) 212–213.
107 See Chapter 4 for more detail.

jurisprudence concerning primacy of EU law. Arguably echoing the argument put forward by Fabbrini,[108] the Court's response to national challenges to primacy has now turned into a standardised formula: primacy is a tool for ensuring equality of Member States.[109] In other words, primacy requires that all Member States always disregard conflicting national legislation of any possible type.

What is more, the Court has even begun referring to the Member States as 'Masters of the Treaties'.[110] Of course, I am not suggesting that Member States do not have a decisive influence on the creation of and amendments to the treaties. However, the Court of Justice has worked long and hard to push the EU's constitutional identity outside and beyond this public international law logic. For example, the Court rejected the original version of the European Economic Area (EEA) Treaty despite the possibility for the Member States to afterwards entirely abandon and amend the system in which the Court of Justice can reject an international treaty.[111] This is even more so in the internal realm. A brief glance over the case law concerning general principles

108 Fabbrini (n 93). I have strongly criticised Fabbrini's argument elsewhere. See A Bobić, 'Constitutional Pluralism Is Not Dead: An Analysis of Interactions between Constitutional Courts of Member States and the European Court of Justice' (2017) 18(6) *German Law Journal* 1395.

109 Case C-430/21 *RS* EU:C:2022:99 [55]; Joined Cases C-357/19, C-379/19, C-547/19, C-811/19 and C-840/19 *Asociația 'Forumul Judecătorilor din România'* EU:C:2021:1034 [249].

110 Case C-423/20 P(R) *Council v Sharpston* EU:C:2020:700 [17] and Case C-424/20 P(R) *Representatives of the Governments of the Member States v Sharpston* EU:C:2020:705 [17]. Prior to this, the phrase was mentioned only by Advocates General of the Court, in only a handful of occasions. Opinion of Advocate General Kokott in Case C-13/07 *Commission v Council* EU:C:2009:190 [60]; Opinion of Advocate General Szpunar in Case C-113/14 *Germany v Parliament and Council* EU:C:2016:279 [93]; Opinion of Advocate General Szpunar in Joined Cases C-360/15 and C-31/16 *College van Burgemeester en Wethouders van de gemeente Amersfoort* EU:C:2017:397 [3], footnote 9.

111 While this is certainly politically true, legally the Court has, starting with its Opinion concerning the Uruguay round of negotiations, drawn red lines that Member States would not be able to cross when concluding international treaties without 'rise to adverse consequences for all interested parties, including third countries'. See Opinion 3/94 EU:C:1995:436 [17]; Opinion 1/09 EU:C:2011:123 [48]; Opinion 2/13 EU:C:2014:2454 [146]. The Court stated in 1971 that 'each time the Community [...] adopts provisions laying down common rules ... the Member States no longer have the right [...] to undertake obligations with third countries which affect those rules'. Case 22/70 *Commission v Council* EU:C:1971:32 [17]. For a comprehensive overview of how EU law affects Member States' competences in the international sphere, see Opinion of Advocate General Ćapeta in Case C-500/20 *ÖBB-Infrastruktur Aktiengesellschaft* EU:C:2022:79 [59]–[86]; A Arena, 'Exercise of EU Competences and Pre-emption of Member States' Powers in the Internal and the External Sphere: Towards "Grand Unification"?' (2016) 35(1) *Yearbook of European Law* 28, 64–98.

of EU law that now have horizontal effect[112] demonstrates that Member States can hardly be considered Masters of the Treaties. Finally, in affirming the validity of the Rule of Law Conditionality Regulation, the Court emphasised that the identity of the European Union, expressed in Article 2 TEU, is shared by and cannot be detracted from by the Member States.[113] In sum, the approach of the Court of Justice is regrettably moving towards a formal reading of equality of Member States, paradoxically using a public international law logic to advance a more federalist result: one where the Member States are equal in their subordination to the legal order of the EU.[114] It will be one of the main aims of the case studies in Chapters 3–5 to point to possible changes to this approach in improving the political equality of citizens.

Thus, we have seen that the principle of equality of Member States and recourse to national sovereignty dominated the discourse employed in judicial review of anti-crisis mechanisms, consequently distancing the decision-makers from the influence of citizens. At the same time, the redistributive consequences of anti-crisis mechanisms were felt with different intensities across the Member States,[115] without a proper avenue for the EU citizens to have a say on the creation or the aftermath of such disparities.

1.3.4 *Solidarity*

Solidarity, in contrast to the principle of equality, is a principle of an unclear legal nature in the EU legal system.[116] The Treaties refer to solidarity in multiple places,[117] but do not offer clarity in respect of the principle's different scopes and legal nature. The Court of Justice, in the above-mentioned decision in *Commission v Italy*, stated that the principle of solidarity underpins the

[112] For an analysis, see A Bobić, *The Jurisprudence of Constitutional Conflict in the European Union* (Oxford University Press 2022) chapter 5.

[113] Case C-156/21 *Hungary v Parliament and Council* EU:C:2022:97 [127]; Case C-157/21 *Poland v Parliament and Council* EU:C:2022:98 [145].

[114] With thanks to Mark Dawson for pointing this out.

[115] Markakis (n 50) 67.

[116] A Ott, 'A Flexible Future for the European Union: The Way Forward or a Way Out?' in S Blockmans and S Prechal (eds), *Reconciling the Deepening and Widening of the European Union* (TMC Asser Press 2007) 153. This is particularly the case in relation to the rights stemming from EU citizenship and the consequences for national social welfare systems. C Barnard, 'EU Citizenship and the Principle of Solidarity' in E Spaventa and M Dougan (eds), *Social Welfare and EU Law* (Hart 2005) 161–165.

[117] See Section 1.3.1.

entire EU legal system.[118] In theorising solidarity in the EU context, the literature differentiates between three levels of solidarity: between Member States, between generations, and between peoples.[119] All three find expression in different places in the Treaties, albeit without defining precisely its position as a principle. However, as McDonnell argues, solidarity should be regarded as a fundamental principle of the EU legal framework and guide interpretation even where it is not explicitly mentioned.[120] The literature on solidarity in the EU echoes its unclear legal nature by most extensively addressing it in the context of social rights and social policy contrasted to the imperatives of the internal market.[121]

Nevertheless, it is possible to discern several types of solidarity mechanisms in EU law. Durkheim's mechanic solidarity is evident in the law on EU citizenship, where the Court of Justice gradually expanded solidarity obligations of the host Member State, albeit solely after a certain period of integration, or in the words of Domurath, of 'acquired sameness'.[122] Solidarity here is premised at a certain level of integration of free movers into the host Member State, thus still not departing from identity as the glue for membership. Conversely, we can find the elements of solidarity formation based on the pursuit of a shared goal in Cohesion Policy, the aim of which is 'reducing disparities between the various regions and the backwardness of the least-favoured regions'.[123] Solidarity in that sense means recognising the high level of interdependence and a shared sense of advancing European integration to everyone's benefit.[124] Yet, solidarity in the EU legal framework has still not reached the cohesive status where its central purpose is creating conditions for achieving the political equality of all EU citizens.

[118] Case 39/72 *Commission v Italy* (n 94) [25]. See also Case 128/78 *Commission v United Kingdom* EU:C:1979:32 [12].

[119] V Borger, 'How the Debt Crisis Exposes the Development of Solidarity in the Euro Area' (2013) 9 *European Constitutional Law Review* 7, 8.

[120] A McDonnell, 'Solidarity, Flexibility and the Euro-Crisis: Where Do Principles Fit In?' in L S Rossi and F Casolari (eds), *The EU after Lisbon Amending or Coping with the Existing Treaties?* (Springer 2014) 61. See also M Kotzur, 'Solidarity as a Legal Concept' in Grimmel and My Giang (n 34) 43–44.

[121] See, for example, Barnard (n 116); A J Menéndez, 'The Sinews of Peace: Rights to Solidarity in the Charter of Fundamental Rights of the European Union' (2003) 16(3) *Ratio Juris* 374.

[122] I Domurath, 'The Three Dimensions of Solidarity in the EU Legal Order: Limits of the Judicial and Legal Approach' (2013) 35(4) *Journal of European Integration* 459, 463.

[123] <http://ec.europa.eu/regional_policy/en/faq/#1>.

[124] In that sense, see M Ross, 'Solidarity – A New Constitutional Paradigm for the EU?' in M Ross and Y Borgmann-Prebil (eds), *Promoting Solidarity in the European Union* (Oxford University Press 2010) 30–31.

Recently, the Court of Justice has added further flesh to the bone of the principle of solidarity in its decision in the field of energy. Germany appealed against the decision of the General Court in which the latter annulled a Commission decision concerning the OPAL pipeline.[125] Originally, the OPAL pipeline was to be used exclusively for gas supplied through the Nord Stream by the Russian Gazprom.[126] However, Gazprom never used more than 50 per cent of the pipeline's capacity. As a consequence, following Germany's request, the Commission amended the conditions of use and allowed that 50 per cent of the pipeline use be bid for by an undertaking having a dominant position on the Czech market (given that the exit point of the pipeline is in Czechia).[127]

Poland initiated an action for annulment of this decision, among others, based on the breach of the principle of energy solidarity, which the General Court upheld.[128] In its appeal to the Court of Justice,[129] Germany argued that the principle of solidarity has but a political significance and cannot be relied on to annul a decision of the Commission.[130] This, in turn, prompted both the Advocate General and the Court of Justice explicitly to address the legal status of the principle of solidarity. The Advocate General found that, although the principle of solidarity appears throughout the Treaties, it has many forms and purposes and does not always operate at the same level (between Member States, between citizens, between generations). Nevertheless, the Advocate General found that the principle 'is such that it may be regarded as significant enough to create legal consequences'.[131]

[125] As usefully explained by Advocate General Campos Sanchez-Bordona: 'OPAL stands for Ostseepipeline-Anbindungsleitung. The OPAL pipeline is the onshore section, to the west, of the Nord Stream gas pipeline, the point of entry to which is located close to the municipality of Lubmin, near Greifswald, in Germany, and the point of exit from which is in the municipality of Brandov in the Czech Republic. The Nord Stream pipeline transports gas from Russian fields across the Baltic Sea to Germany. Nord Stream has another onshore extension, the NEL (Nordeuropäische Erdgasleitung) pipeline, which has a capacity of 20 million cubic metres and runs from Greifswald to the Netherlands and the rest of North-West Europe.' See Opinion of Advocate General Campos Sanchez-Bordona in Case C-848/19 P *Germany v Poland* EU:C:2021:218 [1], footnote 3.

[126] Case C-848/19 P *Germany v Poland* EU:C:2021:598 [10].

[127] ibid [14].

[128] Case T-883/16 *Poland v Commission* EU:T:2019:567.

[129] Poland's original action before the General Court and the appeal were supported by Latvia and Lithuania, whereas Germany supported the Commission. Interestingly, before the Court of Justice, the Commission did not submit an appeal against the General Court's decision in support of Germany.

[130] Case C-848/19 P *Germany v Poland* (n 126) [28]–[29].

[131] Opinion of Advocate General Campos Sanchez-Bordona in Case C-848/19 P *Germany v Poland* (n 125) [70].

The Advocate General also explicitly emphasised that the application of the principle of solidarity in the area of asylum, immigration and external border control[132] is transferrable to the area of energy.[133] By the same token, I argue it is transferrable to the EMU.

In the presentation of the normative framework in Section 1.2, I have argued that legal accountability specifically is able to change the way decision-makers balance the principles of equality and solidarity by demanding that they show how these principles figured in the decision-making process and how the decision itself will serve the common interest. Advocate General Campos Sanchez-Bordona set out exactly the type of obligations that befall accountable decision-makers and are subject to judicial review:[134]

> A judicial review of such decisions must, first and foremost, establish whether the EU institutions have conducted an analysis of the interests involved which is compatible with energy solidarity and takes into account, as I have said, the interests of both the Member States and the European Union as a whole (...).[135]

The Court of Justice followed the Advocate General's approach. It stated that the principle of energy solidarity is a specific expression of the principle of solidarity, one of the fundamental principles of EU law and closely linked to the principle of sincere cooperation.[136] The Court continued, agreeing with the Advocate General, that solidarity has in fact been justiciable before, in the area of asylum, immigration, and external border control, and there is no reason for it not to form the legal basis for reviewing the decisions of EU institutions.[137]

[132] For an endorsement of differentiated measures issued by the Council on the basis of solidarity in this area, see Joined cases C-643/15 and C-647/15 *Slovakia and Hungary v Council* EU:C:2017:631 [251]–[253].

[133] Opinion of Advocate General Campos Sanchez-Bordona in Case C-848/19 P *Germany v Poland* (n 125) [73].

[134] Although the Advocate General refers to obligations pertaining specifically to the area of energy, as is already established, the principle of solidarity and the obligations it imposes are transferrable across areas of EU law.

[135] Opinion of Advocate General Campos Sanchez-Bordona in Case C-848/19 P *Germany v Poland* (n 125) [116]. Endorsed explicitly by the Court in Case C-848/19 P *Germany v Poland* (n 126) [53].

[136] Case C-848/19 P *Germany v Poland* (n 126) [41].

[137] ibid [42]–[45].

Perhaps addressing the concern expressed by the Advocate General on the lack of an express definition of the principle of solidarity, the Court set out an important interpretation of the principle:

> [...] the principle of solidarity entails rights and obligations both for the European Union and for the Member States, the European Union being bound by an obligation of solidarity towards the Member States and the Member States being bound by an obligation of solidarity between themselves and with regard to the common interest of the European Union and the policies pursued by it.[138]

Solidarity is therefore the glue connecting the Member States and the European Union in all their interactions. The common interest, in turn, is contingent upon Member States and the EU acting in respect of the principle of solidarity. In carrying out that commitment, it may well happen that equality of Member States is at times reduced. The Court of Justice's explicit approach in setting out the scope and content of solidarity obligations importantly also tells us that courts indeed can be one forum for protecting the political equality of citizens. In their work, they are able to impose on decision-makers solidarity considerations, which in turn may hinder the equality of Member States. In so doing, the courts can ensure that decision-makers balance the interests of citizens over those of the Member States, or, if they do not do so, they may impose on them a higher burden of justification for the balance of interests they carried out. My argument here is that such an approach is beneficial for achieving the political equality of citizens.

1.3.5 *The Common Interest*

Conceptualising the common interest seems a deceptively straightforward exercise at first glance. It appears in the TFEU and the case law of the Court of Justice[139] at several places, albeit without further specification as to its content. For example, Article 107(3)(c)–(d) TFEU determines that State aid shall be considered compatible with the internal market 'to facilitate the development of certain economic activities or of certain economic areas, where such aid does not adversely affect trading conditions to an extent

[138] ibid [49]. Confirmed also by the Court most recently in the two decisions concerning the Rule of Law Conditionality Mechanism. See Case C-156/21 *Hungary v Parliament and Council* (n 113) [129]; Case C-157/21 *Poland v Parliament and Council* (n 113) [147].

[139] For example, cited above in Case C-848/19 P *Germany v Poland* (n 126) [49].

contrary to the common interest' and 'to promote culture and heritage conservation where such aid does not affect trading conditions and competition in the Union to an extent that is contrary to the common interest'.

One can infer from this that the common interest is the limit to individual decisions of Member States to selectively support certain policy areas, contrary to a unified approach of the EU as a whole. Following this logic, Article 197 (1) TFEU provides that 'effective implementation of Union law by the Member States, which is essential for the proper functioning of the Union, shall be regarded as a matter of common interest'. In addition, in areas where the EU has exclusive competence, Member States can only act as 'trustees of the common interest'.[140] Across the board, the common interest is implicitly achieved through more integration and harmonisation.

Beyond express references to the common interest, it is worth looking closer at the Treaty rules relevant for the EMU. To begin with, there are minimum standards in national and EU constitutional spheres that have achieved a universal level of agreement,[141] codified[142] in Article 2 TEU. Values listed in this provision may be seen as the underlying common interest of all activities of the Union and the Member States. As already mentioned, these values have recently been proclaimed by the Court of Justice to represent the constitutional identity of the EU.[143] To this must be added the principle of sincere cooperation from Article 4(3) TEU.[144]

We have also already seen that Article 3 TEU lists the EU's aims, many of which are relevant for discerning the common interest behind the EMU's operation. Such is in specific Article 3(3) TEU, focusing on balanced economic growth and price stability, a highly competitive social market economy, aiming at full employment and social progress. The same provision also refers

[140] Case 804/79 *Commission v United Kingdom* EU:C:1981:93 [30]; Opinion of Advocate General Maduro in Case C-411/06 *Commission v Parliament and Council* EU:C:2009:189 [12].

[141] Although the universality of this agreement might have been taken for granted, as we are currently witnessing the grave deterioration of Article 2 TEU values in a number of Member States. For an overview of the numerous judgments of the Court of Justice in response to these issues, see L Pech and D Kochenov, 'Respect for the Rule of Law in the Case Law of the European Court of Justice: A Casebook Overview of Key Judgments since the *Portuguese Judges* Case' SIEPS Report 2021. Available at <www.sieps.se/globalassets/publikationer/2021/sieps-2021_3-eng-web.pdf?>.

[142] But by no means sourcing its original authority exclusively in Article 2 TEU, but rather in the constitutional foundations of all the Member States and the EU.

[143] See n 113 in this chapter.

[144] We have seen above that when Member States act in line with the principle of solidarity, they do so also as an expression of the principle of sincere cooperation. Case C-848/19 P *Germany v Poland* (n 126) [41].

to economic, social, and territorial cohesion, alongside solidarity between Member States. In the TFEU, the elimination of inequalities is an aim underpinning all Union activities under its Article 8. Article 9 TFEU adds to these the promotion of a high level of employment, the guarantee of adequate social protection, as well as the fight against social exclusion.[145] These are all considerations directly or indirectly influenced by the decisions taken within the EMU. They should without a doubt contribute to our understanding of the common interest in the EMU,[146] which provides space for these interests to be taken into account when making redistributive choices.

Moving next to the EMU section of the TFEU, Article 119 TFEU sets the principle of an open market economy with free competition as a guidance for setting common objectives in economic policy. It sets further guiding principles: stable prices, sound public finances and monetary conditions, and a sustainable balance of payments. Under Article 120 TFEU, Member States are obliged to conduct economic policy with a view to contributing to the achievement of the objectives of the EU, keeping to an efficient allocation of resources. The conduct of economic policies is for the Member States under Article 121(1) TFEU a matter of common concern and to be coordinated with the Council. All these provisions always explicitly connect EMU action with the aims in Article 3 TEU.

In the interpretation of the common interest in the EMU, of relevance is also Article 122 TFEU, something we might call an emergency solidarity clause: it allows, in the spirit of solidarity between Member States, to introduce measures appropriate to the economic situation of severe difficulties (paragraph 1), and to provide, in the same spirit, financial aid to an individual Member State experiencing 'severe difficulties caused by natural disasters or exceptional occurrences beyond its control' (paragraph 2). We will see in the Epilogue that this article used as one of the legal bases for Next Generation EU,[147] which allows the Commission to borrow on capital markets for the purposes of providing loans, but also non-refundable grants, to the Member States as a response to the COVID-19 crisis. The generous nature of this

[145] See also on the role of Article 9 TEU, E Muir, 'Drawing Positive Lessons from the Presence of "The Social" outside of EU Social Policy *Stricto Sensu*' (2018) 14(1) *European Constitutional Law Review* 81.

[146] For an example of Article 3 TEU being used as an overarching objective in the public interest, see Case C-201/15 *AGET Iraklis* EU:C:2016:972 [76].

[147] Specifically of Council Regulation (EU) 2020/2094 of 14 December 2020 establishing a European Union Recovery Instrument to support the recovery in the aftermath of the COVID-19 crisis (OJ 2020 L 433 I) p. 23.

provision is arguably there to offset it against the no-bailout clause (Article 125 TFEU).[148] That latter provision, as well as the prohibition of monetary financing from Article 123(1) TFEU, offer a contrasting spirit of the Treaties: that of a tight set of rules for national fiscal policy revolving around strict responsibility.[149]

Lastly of relevance for the common interest in the EMU is monetary policy, with Article 127(1) TFEU at the centre. The primary objective of monetary policy is to maintain price stability. We will see in Chapter 4 that this primary objective provided the ECB with unprecedented constitutive powers,[150] which is to be read alongside Article 130 TFEU, which grants it independence 'from Union institutions, bodies, offices or agencies, from any government of a Member State or from any other body'. Subordinate to that primary objective of price stability, the ECB also supports economic policies of Member States (again in line with the objectives of Article 3 TEU). Its activities should further be in line with the principle of an open market economy, free competition, and the efficient allocation of resources. The objectives of Article 119 TFEU that were mentioned above are also referred to here.

We have therefore seen that the common interest in the EMU is a category of broadly defined aims, and it is possible to imagine their interpretation in multiple ways. The idea is that the common interest can only loosely be defined in the Treaties,[151] with Article 3 TEU operating as a horizontal provision, providing a normative anchor to all EMU activities. This is exactly its main strength in a polity that lacks proper spaces for the citizen in the political sphere. Another advantage of broad objectives is that they provide an interpretative margin when they come into conflict with one another, which is not at all seldom. For example, the exercise of the price stability mandate of the ECB necessarily entails value choices that materialise in the redistribution field. It is impossible to say that its decisions, although aiming at price stability, do not also have consequences for income inequality, to take one example. The

[148] B de Witte, 'Guest Editorial: EU Emergency Law and Its Impact on the EU Legal Order' (2022) 59(1) *Common Market Law Review* 3, 9.

[149] This in itself was arguably a counterweight granted to Germany for its acceptance of a monetary union without a high level of macroeconomic convergence as the necessary starting position. See P Dermine, *The New Economic Governance of the Eurozone: A Rule of Law Analysis* (Cambridge University Press 2022) 28–32.

[150] J Mendes, 'Constitutive Powers and Justification: The Duty to Give Reasons in EU Monetary Policy' in M Dawson (ed), *Towards Substantive Accountability in EU Economic Governance* (Cambridge University Press, forthcoming 2023); and more generally J Mendes, 'Constitutive Powers of Executive Bodies: A Functional Analysis of the Single Resolution Board' (2021) 84 (6) *Modern Law Review* 1330, 1339–1342.

[151] See also Dawson and de Witte (n 4) 212–213.

pursuit of sound budgetary policy, to take another, can exacerbate social exclusion, as the implementation of austerity measures in Greece demonstrated.[152]

The interpretation of these different objectives by courts should ensure that decision-makers have made a sufficient effort to understand, within the current institutional structure, what is the common interest in pursuing public policy. We have seen above that solidarity, as interpreted by the Court of Justice, demands a shift in the approach of decision-makers, accepting deviations from equality of Member States as an expression of sincere cooperation. If in so doing, the aims from Article 3 TEU and Article 9 TFEU, for example, are taken seriously, they may, at times, demand a different balance against the principles set out in Article 119 TFEU. Specifically, solidarity concerns between citizens may lead to an interpretation according to which price stability can only be pursued so long as it does not hamper income inequality within and between Member States. In such a situation, courts can demand of the ECB, for example, to demonstrate that, while working on achieving price stability, it also sought to prevent income inequality or similar redistributive outcomes that hinder aims from Article 3 TEU and Article 9 TFEU.

1.4 CONCLUDING REMARKS

The expression and enforcement of the common interest in the EMU thus needs renewed attention, in particular by reconsidering the possible mechanisms available to citizens in the design and subsequently access to accountability mechanisms. Without attempting to conceive of new fora for political participation of individuals in the creation of EMU policies and instruments in the common interest, my analysis will be confined to proposing ways in which access to legal accountability can be reimagined. As already presented in the previous section, substantively the focus will be placed on the relationship between the principles of solidarity and equality in legal accountability. Precisely because the individual is unable to express her preferences in the political sphere, courts are capable of providing space for that expression. There are at least three main areas of judicial action through which courts can act on behalf of citizens in holding decision-makers to account through a

[152] For some striking examples, see Markakis (n 50) 86–93; M E Salomon, 'Of Austerity, Human Rights and International Institutions' (2015) 21(4) *European Law Journal* 521, 523–527; M Matsaganis, 'The Greek Crisis: Social Impact and Policy Responses' Friedrich Ebert Stiftung (November 2013) 12–13; A Koukiadaki and L Kretsos, 'Opening Pandora's Box: The Sovereign Debt Crisis and Labour Market Regulation in Greece' (2012) 41(3) *Industrial Law Journal* 276.

reinterpretation of the common interest, thereby shifting the current balance between the principles of solidarity and equality.

First, through a teleological interpretation of the relevant legal framework, the courts are able to control the scope of access. For example, Article 263 TFEU, regulating access for direct action, requires that the applicant be directly and individually concerned, or directly concerned when the act in question does not require further implementing measures.[153] The issue of standing is a topic where a well-established pessimism pervades the literature.[154] If we understand the EMU as a solidarity area where decision-makers act in the interest of all citizens, and where the effects of these decisions (for example, resulting in austerity measures at the national level) lead to more immediate effects to a broad group of citizens, there is space for the concept of 'direct concern' to be interpreted more broadly when interpreting access conditions. For example, the effects-based review that courts employed in the financial crisis[155] may well be used to interpret more broadly the direct concern requirement necessary to trigger access to justice.

Second, judicial remedies are not static legal instruments withstanding the demands created by societal realities. In its decision in *Rimšēvičs*,[156] the Court of Justice invalidated a national measure when applying the Statutes of the European System of Central Banks and of the ECB.[157] The Court justified the decision by underlining the independence of the ECB and entered for the first time an unchartered territory by annulling a national measure. The relevant provision of the Statutes provides for a referral to the Court of Justice, but nowhere explicitly allows annulling a national measure. Yet, it is through the interpretation of the purpose of this provision that the Court found the legal justification for its action.[158] In addition, the Bundesverfassungsgericht in *Weiss* employed a novel temporary remedy,

[153] See Case T-18/10 *Inuit* EU:T:2011:419 and Case T-262/10 *Microban* EU:T:2011:623.

[154] On this more generally, see A Arnull, 'Private Applicants and the Action for Annulment under Article 173 of the EC Treaty' (1995) 32(1) *Common Market Law Review* 7; C F Bergstrom, 'Defending Restricted Standing for Individuals to Bring Direct Actions against Legislative Measures: Court of Justice of the European Union Decision of 3 October 2013 in Case C-583/11 P' (2014) 10 *European Constitutional Law Review* 481; L Carmosino, 'Direct Concern in State Aid Direct Actions: A Review of the Scuola Montessori Case' (2019) 2019 *European State Aid Law Quarterly* 71.

[155] A Steinbach, 'Effect-Based Analysis in the Court's Jurisprudence on the Euro Crisis' (2017) 42 (2) *European Law Review* 254, 254.

[156] Joined Cases C-202/18 and C-238/18 *Rimšēvičs* EU:2019:139.

[157] For a comment on the novelties of the case, see A Hinarejos, 'The Court of Justice Annuls a National Measure Directly to Protect ECB Independence: *Rimšēvičs*' (2019) 56 *Common Market Law Review* 1649.

[158] Joined Cases C-202/18 and C-238/18 *Rimšēvičs* (n 156) [45]–[48].

providing the Bundesbank with a three-month period to ensure that the ECB had, in fact, taken a plurality of interests into account when rolling out its PSPP programme.[159]

Finally, even without interfering into the structure of remedies formally prescribed, the courts are still able to enforce the obligation of decision-makers to act in the interest of the entire interdependent euro area. The grounds for reviewing administrative action, such as the duty to state reasons or legality, may be used to ascertain the interests pursued by the decision under review, as well as to determine standards of necessity in proportionality review. I turn to explore these possibilities in more detail in Chapter 2. Without reforming the Treaties, courts are able to control the access, remedies, and interpretation of the obligations of decision-makers towards the common interest of all EU citizens. This forms the basis for a more detailed inquiry into the three areas of economic governance that are the object of the case studies in Chapters 3–5: the law on financial assistance mechanisms, monetary policy mechanisms, and the single supervisory mechanism.

[159] Cases 2 BvR 859/15, 2 BvR 980/16, 2 BvR 2006/15, 2 BvR 1651/15 *Weiss* Judgment of 5 May 2020 [235].

2

Theorising Judicial Review in the Economic and Monetary Union

2.1 INTRODUCTION

'Enemies of the People', cried the cover of the UK's *Daily Mail* on 4 November 2016.[1] This was in response to the decision of the High Court of England and Wales in *Miller* that the Government needs the approval of the Parliament to notify its withdrawal from the EU.[2] Boiled down to its less extreme form, the argument goes: judges are unelected and cannot review legislation enacted by the democratically elected representatives of citizens.[3]

[1] The *Daily Telegraph* in the same vein ran the title 'The Judges versus the People'. In a somewhat more sophisticated form, see also Justice Scalia of the US Supreme Court: 'A system of government that makes the People subordinate to a committee of nine unelected lawyers does not deserve to be called a democracy.' *Obergefell v Hodges* 576 US 644 (2015), Dissenting Opinion of Justice Scalia, 5. Still, note Scalia himself twenty-four years prior: 'I am not so naive (nor do I think our forebears were) as to be unaware that judges in a real sense "make" law.' *James B. Beam Distilling Co. v Georgia* 501 US 529 (1991), Concurring Opinion of Justice Scalia, 549.

[2] The irony of protesting against parliamentary approval as an affront to the will of the people is a different can of worms that will not be addressed here. Suffice it to say that the UK Government argued that it is within its royal prerogative pertaining to foreign affairs to submit the withdrawal notification, without the oversight of the Parliament. The latter is competent to decide by primary legislation on matters of constitutional significance, and the High Court found the withdrawal notification to meet that standard. See *Miller & Anor, R (On the Application of) v The Secretary of State for Exiting the European Union* (Rev 1) [2016] EWHC 2768 (Admin) (3 November 2016). The judgment of the High Court was upheld by the Supreme Court in *Miller & Anor, R (On the Application of) v Secretary of State for Exiting the European Union* (Rev 3) [2017] UKSC 5 (24 January 2017).

[3] For a seminal piece, see J Waldron, 'The Core of the Case against Judicial Review' (2006) 115 *Yale Law Journal* 1346. In the US literature, this critique also developed into what is called the counter-majoritarian difficulty, according to which judicial review distorts majoritarian decision-making in democratically elected institutions. See A M Bickel, *The Least Dangerous Branch: The Supreme Court at the Bar of Politics* (Yale University Press 1986); M Tushnet, 'Policy Distortion and Democratic Debilitation: Comparative Illumination of the Counter-

In the camp opposite,[4] judicial review is seen as a corrective to the will of the majority, ensuring the protection of fundamental rights[5] and thus necessary in a democratic society that values equality, non-discrimination, and liberty.[6] The two opposing views of the role of courts concern the review of legislation, that is, acts of general application enacted by the representative body of a state.

I should also like to add a second layer to this story. Unlike that of legislation, judicial review of administrative action is widely accepted.[7] This is so given that the administration also lacks the democratic pedigree enjoyed by representative institutions and thus needs to be legally constrained.[8] But things get complicated also in this area, because the administration has a specific way of doing what it does: to implement and apply general (legislative) acts or to discharge of the roles delegated to it by the legislator,[9] it necessarily needs to make use of discretion.

There are at least three degrees of uses of discretion by an administrative body. First, it might be that the administrative body has specific technical knowledge necessary for the application of a certain act. For example, granting safety permits to building projects: here, technical knowledge will likely constrain, but not entirely limit, the ability to interpret safety in a variety of ways. Second, it is also possible that the body in question operates in an area where technical knowledge is a necessary precondition for dealing with situations of future uncertainty. For example, a body deciding whether one or another infrastructural project will have adverse environmental effects. The discretion in this case will manifest itself in predicting outcomes and deciding on the best course of action. Finally, the body in question may be granted the power to decide based on efficiency[10] or another similarly elusive criterion

Majoritarian Difficulty' (1995) 94(2) *Michigan Law Review* 245; J Waldron, *Law and Disagreement* (Oxford University Press 1999).

4 J H Ely, *Democracy and Distrust* (Harvard University Press 1981); R Dworkin, *Freedom's Law: The Moral Reading of the American Constitution* (Harvard University Press 1996).

5 This view is also central to the theory of liberal constitutionalism, whereby courts act as a limitation to the power of the legislature and the executive. See F A Hayek, *Law, Legislation and Liberty, Vol. 1 Rules and Order* (University Chicago Press 1978); M Warren, 'Liberal Constitutionalism as Ideology: Marx and Habermas' (1989) 17 *Political Theory* 511.

6 J Shaw, 'Process and Constitutional Discourse in the European Union' (2000) 27 *Journal of Law & Society* 4, 16.

7 Waldron (n 3) 1354.

8 For an excellent account, see R Baldwin, *Rules and Government* (Clarendon Press 1995), in particular chapter 3.

9 To name but a few roles of the administration.

10 For a useful discussion on the problem of efficiency or effectiveness as a standard in administrative decision-making, see D J Galligan, *Discretionary Powers: A Legal Study of Official Discretion* (Clarendon Press 1986, reprinted 2011) 129–132.

(for example, when deciding whether an application for a public demonstration threatens public safety).

In even these three ideal-type examples, the administrative body will dispose of different degrees of discretion[11] that courts typically control against the standards set out in legislation and, as the case may be, against constitutional standards and principles (such as good administration, the protection of legitimate expectations, or proportionality, to name a few). In general, the role of courts in controlling the administration should not be such that the judge puts herself in the position of the administrative body and *ex novo* decides the issue.[12] This is often supported by the argument of maintaining the separation of powers and preventing courts from stepping into the role of the executive.[13] Rather, what courts should review is the decision-making process: ensuring that the body in question properly used its expertise, coherently reached its decision in line with procedural requirements, and generally did not go beyond what is necessary in respect of achieving the tasks granted to it.[14] On the opposite end stands the use of discretion and it is generally argued that the courts are not to control the latitude given to the administration, lest they take up the mandate of the administrative body.[15]

Transposed to the context of EU economic governance, these considerations acquire an additional layer of complexity. Traditionally, the Court of Justice is perceived as one of the dominant actors among EU institutions, pushing the integration agenda forward when political institutions fall short of such action.[16] In addition, through the preliminary reference procedure, judicial review gradually acquired prominent status in the Member States as well.[17] EU's economic governance breaks away from this paradigm, in particular due to a greater prominence of direct actions as opposed to the

[11] C Hilson, 'Judicial Review, Policies and the Fettering of Discretion' (2002) *Public Law* 111, 112–113; Galligan (n 10) 10–11.

[12] See in that respect the Opinion of Advocate General Emiliou in Case C-389/21 P *ECB v Crédit Lyonnais* EU:C:2022:844 [60]–[62].

[13] D Ritleng, 'Judicial Review of EU Administration Discretion: How Far Does the Separation of Powers Matter?' in J Mendes and I Venzke (eds), *Allocating Authority: Who Should Do What in European and International Law?* (Hart 2018) 185 and the literature cited in footnote 13.

[14] This is but a general list of principles of judicial review of administrative action. Certainly, each national system has its own specific rules, as does the EU legal order. The latter will be dealt with in the coming sections.

[15] For a discussion, see J Mendes, 'Bounded Discretion in EU Law: A Limited Judicial Paradigm in a Changing EU' (2017) 80 *Modern Law Review* 443, 451–459.

[16] For an important account, see K Alter, *Establishing the Supremacy of European Law: The Making of an International Rule of Law in Europe* (Oxford University Press 2003).

[17] A Bobić, *The Jurisprudence of Constitutional Conflict in the European Union* (Oxford University Press 2022) 5–7.

preliminary reference procedure. While the powers of judicial review are clearly spelled out in the Treaties,[18] as are the bases for such review,[19] less obvious is which acts have 'binding legal effects'[20] to be susceptible to challenge at the EU level. Equally elusive is what standard EU courts use in reviewing decisions that involve a degree of discretion.[21]

Thus, we have before us a difficult constitutional structure: judicial review of legislation, and to some extent of administrative action, is in itself a disputed activity that continues to raise eyebrows of those demanding legitimation in the form of democratic elections. This is marred in addition by a multilevel operation of rules of economic governance and a central bank with an impervious screen of independence. My task in this chapter is to show why and how courts, despite all this, may contribute to legal accountability for decision-makers in EU's economic governance.[22]

Courts are and should be the institutions where individuals enforce the duty of policymakers to act in the common interest. The EMU is an area characterised by high redistributive effects coupled with a wide discretion on the part of decision-makers. Under these conditions, courts are, unlike political institutions, in a perfect position to ensure that such decisions meet the Treaty objectives of the common interest. To do so successfully, any review of decisions in the EMU entails two duties. First, the starting point for courts must be an assumption of a full review, which is an expression of their duty to

[18] Article 263(1) TFEU provides: 'The Court of Justice of the European Union shall review the legality of legislative acts, of acts of the Council, of the Commission and of the European Central Bank, other than recommendations and opinions, and of acts of the European Parliament and of the European Council intended to produce legal effects vis-à-vis third parties. It shall also review the legality of acts of bodies, offices or agencies of the Union intended to produce legal effects vis-à-vis third parties.'

[19] Article 263(2)–(3) TFEU states: 'It shall for this purpose have jurisdiction in actions brought by a Member State, the European Parliament, the Council or the Commission on grounds of lack of competence, infringement of an essential procedural requirement, infringement of the Treaties or of any rule of law relating to their application, or misuse of powers. The Court shall have jurisdiction under the same conditions in actions brought by the Court of Auditors, by the European Central Bank and by the Committee of the Regions for the purpose of protecting their prerogatives.'

[20] Joined Cases C-463/10 and C-475/10 *Deutsche Post and Germany v Commission* EU:C:2011:656 [36]; Case C-31/13 P *Hungary v Commission* EU:C:2014:70 [54]; Case C-16/16 P *Belgium v Commission* EU:C:2018:79 [30]. See further Section 2.2.3.

[21] For a useful overview, see M Krajewski, *Relative Authority of Judicial and Extra-Judicial Review: EU Courts, Boards of Appeal, Ombudsman* (Hart 2021) chapter 2.

[22] By way of a disclaimer, as also mentioned in the Introduction, my argument is not that courts are the sole locus of accountability in EU's economic governance, given that political and administrative institutions are operating in delivering other forms of accountability. Yet, the focus of my book is exclusively on courts and legal accountability.

safeguard the common interest as expressed in the Treaties and in the norm granting competence to the decision-maker in question. Second, decision-makers, for their part, have an extensive duty of giving reasons for their decisions and thus put to the court the arguments on the nature of their discretion and how they used it. The burden is in essence on the parties to demonstrate not only who should win the case, but also, preliminarily, what the appropriate standard of review should be. I propose that the parties carry the responsibility to present a rich evidentiary basis serving as ammunition for endorsing or rebutting the presumption of full judicial review. This judicial activity should be shared between national and EU courts, as is done in other areas of EU law. In this way, courts become the platform for discussing the extent of a power given to an institution and deciding whether it has contributed to the common interest.

Before detailing this proposal further in Section 2.3, I first turn to the most problematic examples of non-accountable decision-making that recently took place in the EMU (Section 2.2), causing problems for individuals accessing fora of legal accountability, most visibly in the reduction of the protection of fundamental rights.[23] The purpose of this section will be to offer a sneak-peek preview of what went wrong, how (the lack of) judicial review contributed to this problem, and why traditional arguments against judicial review do not work in this context. The chapter will close (Section 2.4) with conclusions as to how the proposed framework of judicial review will be used in the chapters to come.

2.2 PROBLEMS WITH JUDICIAL REVIEW IN THE EMU

In this section, my aim is to underline three specificities of the EU's economic governance law against which traditional anti-judicial review arguments do not bite, but instead exacerbate the problems associated with executive discretion. First, in response to the Euro crisis, many of the measures employed directly to aid debtor Member States did not have a source in EU law proper, but were formulated in novel legal constructions such as the powers of the Troika and the establishment of the European Stability Mechanism (ESM). Traditional channels of judicial review were consequently not available at the EU level and were of limited significance at the national level, given the economic urgency of accepting financial aid and the

[23] K H Ragnarsson, 'The Counter-Majoritarian Difficulty in a Neoliberal World: Socio-Economic Rights and Deference in Post-2008 Austerity Cases' (2019) 8 *Global Constitutionalism* 605, 611–615.

conditions attached. Second, in monetary policy, the ECB's independence (and by extension discretion) is constitutionally protected. This resulted in the ECB being de facto shielded from any meaningful judicial review, in particular given its expertise and mandate to define and conduct monetary policy. Finally, a third problem results from the legal nature of EU's economic governance, whereby the Commission and the ECB increasingly use soft law instruments and operate in composite institutional arrangements, making judicial review difficult.

These three areas will be explored as a broad-brush presentation of the issues transversally pervading the EMU's legal set-up: a high level of executive discretion, poor deliberative processes that produce strong redistributive effects, and a lack of acknowledgement of the structural inequalities that result from its rules. I will thus briefly turn to each of these problems in preparation of my argument on the proper role of judicial review in Section 2.3. This also serves as a primer for a more detailed exploration of judicial review and its weaknesses in Chapters 3–5, which will explore the areas of financial assistance, monetary policy, and the Single Supervisory Mechanism (SSM).

2.2.1 *Financial Assistance*

The area of financial assistance uncovered new ways of decision-making, specifically, by using public international law and deciding through Memoranda of Understanding concluded by the Troika and the Member State receiving financial assistance. Consequently, judicial review in this area became negligible given that the Court of Justice could only marginally control what has been decided (reviewing only the Treaty-compliance of the amendment to Article 136 TFEU for the purposes of creating the ESM in *Pringle*). In addition, some national constitutional courts had the opportunity to test the ESM against constitutional standards. Otherwise, outcomes for individuals stemming from financial assistance did not feature prominently before EU courts. Memoranda of Understanding only eventually crossed the admissibility threshold before the Court of Justice, which found that EU institutions are bound by the Charter in all their activities, within or without the Treaties.[24] Nevertheless, measures impacting the property rights of deposit

[24] Joined Cases C-8/15 P to C-10/15 P *Ledra Advertising and Others v Commission* EU:C:2016:701 [67].

holders have to this day not resulted in the finding of a sufficiently serious breach to trigger the non-contractual liability of the Union.[25]

There is but one decision of the Court of Justice in financial assistance significantly impacting the constitutional framework of EU law. Alas, little changed in terms of legal accountability of the Troika. Instead, it reshaped the way the principle of judicial independence (protected by Article 19(1) TEU) operates: it became justiciable, by happenstance in the context of financial assistance. In *Juizes Portugueses*, the Court found that although the reduction of salaries of judges resulted from the conditionality attached to financial assistance to Portugal,[26] the situation did not concern 'an implementation of Union law' necessary for the applicability of the Charter.[27] However, Article 19(1) TEU refers to 'fields covered by Union law' and the independence of the judiciary is one such field. Ground-breaking in terms of elevating the status of judicial independence in EU law, the decision ultimately had little effect on the possibility to challenge the measures stemming from financial assistance (spoiler alert: the Court found the salary reduction as not interfering with judicial independence).[28] In conclusion, the area of financial assistance is a showcase of a deferential approach by the Court of Justice,[29] where changes that took place did so in small and rather unsatisfactory steps for those affected by the seismic changes that the conditionality-induced austerity brought about.

Against this brief illustration, the argument according to which judicial review is undemocratic and decisions taken by representative bodies should be judicial review-proof greatly misses the mark. The power of the Troika to impose conditionality requirements on debtor Member States greatly diminished the level of democratic deliberation in their representative institutions.[30] In fact, Salomon shows in great detail how the Greek government relied on its international obligations to the Troika to justify its lack of consideration for the

[25] Joined Cases C-597/18 P, C-598/18 P, C-603/18 P and C-604/18 P *Chrysostomides* EU:C:2020:1028. For a more detailed analysis of this case, see Chapter 3, Section 3.4.1.

[26] The Court refers to the national measures at issue as 'linked to requirements to eliminate an excessive budget deficit and to an EU financial assistance programme'. Case C-64/16 *Juizes Portugueses* EU:C:2018:117 [27].

[27] ibid [29].

[28] ibid [51].

[29] For the same conclusion following an analysis of the relevant jurisprudence of other European national courts, see Ragnarsson (n 23) 611.

[30] C Kilpatrick, 'Constitutions, Social Rights and Sovereign Debt' in T Beukers, B de Witte and C Kilpatrick (eds), *Constitutional Change through Euro-Crisis Law* (Cambridge University Press 2017) 279; A Poulou, 'Austerity and European Social Rights: How Can Courts Protect Europe's Lost Generation?' (2014) 15 *German Law Journal* 1145.

effects of austerity measures in the social sphere and human rights.[31] Requests for a referendum on the conditionality measures were rejected, whereas the spread of poverty did not come up in discussions between the Greek government and the Troika at all.[32] Yet, the urgency of the situation should in no way justify a disregard of deliberative processes, but instead speaks in favour of an increased judicial protection of human rights.[33]

In such a context, judicial deference to the political process aggravates what Ragnarsson calls a representation failure (given that states had no choice but to respond to the market, instead of to their political constituents).[34] In this scenario, national legislators and governments were not controlled by courts but by the Troika, who in turn was controlled by no one.[35] As already mentioned, the Court of Justice did eventually expand the applicability of the Charter to the Commission and the ECB for their activities in the Troika. Nevertheless, we have yet to witness a situation in which the Court finds that this obligation was not complied with and led to a breach of individual rights.

This has grave consequences for the political equality of citizens. It is undisputed that conditionality distorted the way political institutions at the national level usually balance various interests when making budgetary decisions. Rather than following the usual procedures of deliberation in a parliamentary setting, preceded possibly by factual examinations, risk and impact assessments by the executive, the debtor states were presented with a very concrete set of targets to be implemented and were left with little to no choice but to accept them, given the urgency of their dire economic situation.[36] On this view, market interests entered into and guided the choice of interests to be balanced. Thus, the Troika-led financial assistance caused political inequality of citizens at a more fundamental level: in their own Member

[31] M E Salomon, 'Of Austerity, Human Rights and International Institutions' (2015) 21(4) *European Law Journal* 521, 527–532.

[32] ibid 529–530.

[33] See also A Poulou, 'Human Rights Accountability in European Financial Assistance' in M Dawson (ed), *Substantive Accountability in Europe's New Economic Governance* (Cambridge University Press, forthcoming 2023).

[34] Ragnarsson (n 23) 620. He therefore promotes a view whereby a stronger role for courts in the austerity era could have acted as 'an enforcer of socio-economic rights as "destabilisation rights" that allow citizens to disrupt structures that are unresponsive to democratic challenge', at 623.

[35] This resembles also the general logic of the regulatory state, whereby regulation does not occur in the public interest, but is rather fomented by and benefits a certain industry. G J Stigler, 'The Theory of Economic Regulation' (1971) 6(2) *Bell Journal of Economics and Management Science* 114.

[36] See M Markakis, *Accountability in the Economic and Monetary Union: Foundations, Policy, and Governance* (Oxford University Press 2020) 55–57; Salomon (n 31).

State. The next (EU) level amplified this, as conditionality targeted the debtor Member States.[37] Judicial review is therefore crucial firstly to recuperate the position of the individual at the national level, in respect of her own government and parliament, by ensuring that the existing democratic procedures in place are in fact observed. This includes not only the parliamentary process but also all the relevant executive and administrative actors taking part in decision-making. As a result, it would be reasonable to expect that at the national level, the deliberative process allows for recognition of a variety of socioeconomic interests. EU courts then have a second important function, to assuage the discrepancies between debtor and creditor states, by levelling the playing field among all EU citizens, thereby enhancing their political equality. This, with a view of ensuring that deliberative processes exist, are visible to those they concern, and are subject to accountability processes.

2.2.2 *The European Central Bank*

Turning next to one of the central actors in the EMU, the European Central Bank holds under the Treaties a privileged position in several respects. First, under Article 127(1) TFEU, the European System of Central Banks is to conduct a single monetary policy with the aim of ensuring price stability in the euro area (further explained in Article 132 TFEU).[38] Second, under Article 130 TFEU, the ECB shall not take instructions from 'Union institutions, bodies, offices or agencies, from any government of a Member State or from any other body', who are to respect its independence.[39] Under this legal construct, the ECB has wide discretion in the exercise of monetary policy and holds a constitutionally protected independent status. This position has arguably been further cemented[40] during the crisis, where the ECB employed

[37] This can be contrasted to the lenient approach of the Council to excessive deficits when it comes to creditor states, such as France and Germany, most clearly in Case C-27/04 *Commission v Council* EU:C:2004:436.

[38] Monetary policy is an exclusive competence of the EU under Article 3(1)(c) TFEU.

[39] See also Article 282(3) TFEU and Article 7 of the Statute of the European System of Central Banks and of the European Central Bank. Protocol No 4 to the Lisbon Treaty (OJ 2016 C 202) 230.

[40] F Amtenbrink, 'The European Central Bank's Intricate Independence versus Accountability Conundrum in the Post-crisis Governance Framework' (2019) 26(1) *Maastricht Journal of European and Comparative Law* 165, 167; M Dawson, A Maricut-Akbik and A Bobić, 'Reconciling Independence and Accountability at the European Central Bank: The False Promise of Proceduralism' (2019) 25 *European Law Journal* 75, 79.

unconventional[41] monetary policy measures under its mandate to maintain price stability (a mandate the ECB itself is to interpret).[42] It will become painfully clear in Chapter 4 how shielded that makes it from mechanisms of accountability.

In making conclusions on why the traditional 'courts cannot control discretion' paradigm exacerbates accountability deficiencies of the ECB, it suffices to look at the standards against which EU and national courts have so far reviewed decisions made in such a context. The ECB's ability to carry out its monetary policy mandate independently was initially protected by the Court of Justice in relation to its operational independence.[43] The approach of the Court later turned into an almost blanket check for the ECB's goal independence, according to which the latter enjoys a broad discretion in determining how to achieve its monetary policy objectives.[44] This is all the more so given that the Court seems to accord the ECB with unquestionable expertise in this area,[45] thus qualifying further its deferential standard of review of its discretion.[46]

The division between political assessments and technical expertise made by the Court in determining the relevant standard of review of discretionary decisions did not develop specifically for the context in which the ECB operates. The approach of the Court is as follows: grounds for review, determining its scope, are those listed in the Treaties.[47] The scope remaining always the same, the nature of the power granted to the decision-maker holding discretion in turn determines the intensity of judicial review.[48] Specifically, when the power is of a technical nature involving complex

[41] The ECB and national central banks later on changed the term in the discourse to 'nonconventional' or 'nonstandard' and/or 'accommodative' monetary policies. See M Chang, D Howarth and L Pierret, 'Unconventional Monetary Policies and Moral Hazard: Constructing or Deconstructing the Legitimacy of the European Central Bank's New Instruments?' Manuscript on file with author, cited with the authors' permission.

[42] J Mendes, 'Constitutive Powers and Justification: The Duty to Give Reasons in EU Monetary Policy' in M Dawson (n 33); M Dawson and A Bobić, 'Quantitative Easing at the Court of Justice – Doing Whatever It Takes to Save the Euro: *Weiss and Others*' (2019) 56(4) *Common Market Law Review* 1005, 1027.

[43] Case C-11/00 *Commission v ECB* EU:C:2003:395 [127].

[44] Case C-62/14 *Gauweiler* EU:C:2015:400 [68]; Case C-493/17 *Weiss* EU:C:2018:1000 [49]–[52]. See also Amtenbrink (n 40) 168.

[45] For an example of blind trust in the ECB's expertise, see Opinion of Advocate General Wathelet in Case C-493/17 *Weiss* EU:C:2018:815 [126]–[139].

[46] For example, in Case C-62/14 *Gauweiler* (n 44) [68]. See also Amtenbrink (n 40) 169.

[47] See n 19 in this chapter.

[48] See Opinion of Advocate General Maduro in Case C-141/02 P *Commission v max-mobil* EU:C:2004:646 [77]–[78], who refers to intensity as 'depth'. See also, with a reference to intensity, Opinion of Advocate General Léger in Case C-40/03 P *Rica Foods* EU:C:2005:93 [48],

assessments (cognition), the discretion is wide and the Court examines whether a manifest error of assessment occurred.[49] This assessment of the Court refers to 'the duty of the competent institution to examine carefully and impartially all the relevant aspects of the individual case, the right of the person concerned to make his views known and to have an adequately reasoned decision'.[50] The Court confirmed the ECB had such discretion in *Gauweiler* and *Weiss*.[51]

As opposed to this, if the nature of the power granted entails discretion, that is, political (volition), the intensity of the review is even lower,[52] albeit still focused on finding a manifest error. For the ECB in specific, the Court of Justice confirmed in *Gauweiler* and *Weiss* that monetary policy decisions are usually of a controversial nature.[53] The General Court in *Accorinti* provided further detail on the political nature of ECB's discretion:

> [A]ny sufficiently serious breach of the legal rules at issue must be based on a manifest and serious failure to have regard for the limits of the broad discretion enjoyed by the ECB when exercising its powers in monetary policy matters. That is even more true because the exercise of that discretion implies the need for the ECB (…) also to make political, economic and social choices in which it is required to weigh up and decide between the different objectives referred to in Article 127(1) TFEU, the main objective of which is the maintenance of price stability.[54]

The reticence towards reviewing ECB action may then be due to the Court considering that ECB powers embody both these types of discretion. Instead of seeing this as a warning sign that a single institution might be holding too much unchecked power in its hands, the Court saw this as a reason to double down on providing the ECB with all the leeway the latter itself claimed it needed.[55] In simple terms, the political discretion granted to the ECB is grounded in its highly complex expertise. That expertise may be used widely by the ECB to help it decide on the use of its political discretion in making

Opinion of Advocate General Emiliou in Case C-389/21 P *ECB v Crédit Lyonnais* (n 12) [41]–[42].

49 Case C-14/10 *Nickel Institute* EU:C:2011:503 [60].

50 Case C-269/90 *Technische Universität München* EU:C:1991:438 [14].

51 See n 44 in this chapter.

52 Opinion of Advocate General Léger in Case C-40/03 P *Rica Foods* (n 48) [49].

53 Case C-62/14 *Gauweiler* (n 44) [75]; Case C-493/17 *Weiss* (n 44) [91].

54 Case T-79/13 *Accorinti and Others v ECB* EU:T:2015:756 [68].

55 This circularity as the defining feature of ECB's constitutive powers has been highlighted by Mendes as the feature that constitutes a 'breakdown between law creation and law application'. Mendes (n 42).

monetary policy decisions that are of a controversial nature: one can only know what a necessary monetary policy decision is if one has specific expert knowledge about this field.[56] The two discretions therefore reinforce each other to fortify the untouchable character of ECB action. It is difficult to argue against this background that ECB's independence and accountability carry equal weight. It is rather that legal accountability appears as the secondary, residual category: it is engaged so long as independence is not interfered with.

This construct may not be as problematic in a legal (constitutional) system where other forms of accountability would be in store for the ECB. Yet, given its Treaty-protected independence and the self-defined nature of its mandate, there appears to be no other political or administrative forum that is equipped with accountability tools with as direct consequences for ECB decisions as that in the arsenal of EU courts.[57] National courts, with the bombshell exception of the Bundesverfassungsgericht in respect of the PSPP Programme,[58] have not made a mark in the overall accountability of the ECB. This is all the more visible in the area of banking supervision, where EU courts explicitly deprived[59] national courts from reviewing national preparatory acts that serve as the basis for the ECB's supervisory decisions.[60] This significantly changed the interlocutors of legal accountability: in the SSM, no longer are national courts the ones engaging with the Court of Justice through the preliminary reference procedure. Instead, given the shift to direct actions, judicial interactions now remain in house, where the appellate power of the Court of Justice over the General Court places it at the centre of the legal accountability discourse.

56 Summed up by the Court of Justice in *Gauweiler*: '(. . .) given that questions of monetary policy are usually of a controversial nature and in view of the ESCB's broad discretion, nothing more can be required of the ESCB apart from that it use its economic expertise and the necessary technical means at its disposal to carry out that analysis with all care and accuracy'. Case C-62/14 *Gauweiler* (n 44) [75].

57 See also L Dragomir, 'The ECB's Accountability: Adjusting Accountability Arrangements to the ECB's Evolving Roles' (2019) 26(1) *Maastricht Journal of European and Comparative Law* 35, 44–46; A Bobić and M Dawson, 'How Can Law Contribute to Accountability in EU Monetary Policy?' in D Adamski, F Amtenbrink and J de Haan (eds), *The Cambridge Handbook on European Monetary, Economic and Financial Market Integration* (Cambridge University Press 2023).

58 Cases 2 BvR 859/15, 2 BvR 980/16, 2 BvR 2006/15, 2 BvR 1651/15 *Weiss* Judgment of 5 May 2020. For an extensive analysis of that decision, see A Bobić and M Dawson, 'Making Sense of the "Incomprehensible": The PSPP Judgment of the German Federal Constitutional Court' (2020) 57(6) *Common Market Law Review* 1953. For a further analysis of national judicial review in the area of monetary policy, see Chapter 4.

59 Case C-219/17 *Berlusconi* EU:C:2018:1023 [44].

60 See Chapter 5 for a detailed presentation of this case law.

The high level of independence granted to the ECB translates thus into a wide margin of discretion for it to implement its policies,[61] with a low level of interference by courts. That EU courts apply procedural review in conditions of high discretion[62] is common in other areas of EU law.[63] Still, the effects of monetary policy decisions carry redistributive impacts for the entire monetary union and cannot be ascribed merely to expertise, which is only the starting point for the ECB's decision-making process.[64] In other words, no matter the expertise behind its monetary policy decisions, this process inevitably involves also the weighing of different interests of actors across the eurozone. For example, a bond-buying programme will have asymmetric effects on different parts of financial markets that needs to be acknowledged as a crucial part of the ECB's decision-making process.[65] To sum up, the results of discretionary decisions of the ECB have effects beyond achieving price stability (the primary objective of ECB action).[66] Treating this discretion as being outside the courts' control thus leaves a large number of affected individuals without recourse to legal accountability. To ensure that the effects of the ECB's mandate are taken into account and balanced against each other with impunity, a more intense judicial review than that currently witnessed is imperative.

61 Mendes describes the mandate of the ECB as granting it constitutive powers. She defines such powers as arising in the following scenario: 'legal norms define the mandates of executive and administrative bodies, but the meaning of those norms is determined through the action of those bodies'. Mendes (n 42) 7.

62 As regards the duty to state reasons, the Court of Justice stated: '[...] it should be recalled that, in situations such as that at issue in the present case, in which an EU institution enjoys broad discretion, a review of compliance with certain procedural safeguards – including the obligation for the ESCB to examine carefully and impartially all the relevant elements of the situation in question and to give an adequate statement of the reasons for its decisions – is of fundamental importance [...].' When it comes to the proportionality analysis, the Court further stated that: 'As regards judicial review of compliance with those conditions, since the ESCB is required, when it prepares and implements an open market operations programme of the kind provided for in Decision 2015/774, to make choices of a technical nature and to undertake complex forecasts and assessments, it must be allowed, in that context, a broad discretion [...].' Case C-493/17 *Weiss* (n 44) [30], [73].

63 See, for example, in the field of State aid, Case C-148/19 P *BTB Holding Investments and Duferco Participations Holding v Commission* EU:C:2020:354 [56] and the case-law cited.

64 For a critique of the Court's often artificial distinction between technical expertise and value judgments, see Mendes (n 15).

65 This was an argument raised by the Bundesverfassungsgericht, albeit focusing merely on the effects within Germany. *Weiss* (n 58) [139].

66 For an in-depth analysis of distributive effects of ECB action in the monetary field and constitutional consequences of demanding the ECB to take these into account, see D Argyroulis and N Vagdoutis, 'Tackling Economic Inequality: Reorienting ECB's Role?' Manuscript on file with author, cited with the authors' permission.

2.2.3 *Soft Law Instruments*

Finally, the rules in economic governance resulted in the Commission taking up a prominent position,[67] making use of its discretionary powers to enact a sea of secondary acts of general application, as well as additionally issuing an accompanying set of recommendations, guidelines, and the like on how it intends to interpret and apply them.[68] For example, in the context of the multilateral surveillance procedure under Article 121 TFEU, the Council formulates broad economic policy guidelines. These concern macroeconomic and structural policies in an attempt to coordinate Member States' economic policies for achieving common goals. The multilateral surveillance mechanism is then used to ensure that Member States comply with the guidelines, but these are not formally binding.[69] Another example is the Commission's communication outlining its views on the flexibility regime under the Stability and Growth Pact.[70] Again while not legally binding, the communication is of 'structural importance'[71] for the Commission's approach to the application of fiscal policy rules.

The Commission also participated in the Troika, outside the constitutional framework of EU law proper. While for different reasons than the ECB, the Commission is also in a position where it is difficult to subject it to judicial control. The essence of the issue with judicial review of Commission action in economic governance[72] is its predominantly soft law character.[73] Arguments against judicial review would in this context lead us to conclude

67 P Dermine, *The New Economic Governance of the Eurozone: A Rule of Law Analysis* (Cambridge University Press 2022) 119–121; M W Bauer and S Becker, 'The Unexpected Winner of the Crisis: The European Commission's Strengthened Role in Economic Governance' (2014) 36(3) *Journal of European Integration* 213.

68 For a presentation of the complex legal framework applicable in the EMU, see Dermine (n 67) chapter 1.

69 ibid 35.

70 Communication from the Commission to the European Parliament, the Council, the European Central Bank, the Economic and Social Committee, the Committee of Regions and the European Investment Bank, 'Making the Best Use of the Flexibility within the Existing Rules of the Stability and Growth Pact' COM (2015) 12 final.

71 Dermine (n 67) 45.

72 For an analysis of soft law instruments in EU fiscal surveillance, see P Dermine, 'The Instruments of Eurozone Fiscal Surveillance through the Lens of the Soft Law/Hard Law Dichotomy – Looking for a New Approach' (2021) 23(7) *Journal of Banking Regulation* 18.

73 The literature on the emergence of soft law instruments in EU law is vast. For comprehensive accounts, see M Dawson, *New Governance and the Transformation of European Law: Coordinating EU Social Law and Policy* (Cambridge University Press 2011); M Eliantonio and O Stefan (eds), Special section 'Soft Law in the EU Legal Order: Reflections and Contemporary Trends' (2018) 37 *Yearbook of European Law*; M Eliantonio, E Korkea-aho and

that once a body has been given the power to enact soft law instruments by delegation from the legislator, courts should refrain from reviewing those powers.[74] Specifically, because soft law instruments do not have binding force, there is no need for judicial review. Soft law is, in addition, seen as part of the policymaking process that will ultimately result in enacting binding decisions. At this stage, policymakers should be able to change their position without being held responsible.

Yet, the multilevel nature of economic governance makes it more complicated to determine accountability channels at the EU and national level. The Commission cannot lift the entire economic governance weight on its own – it needs national authorities to implement and abide by requirements concerning prudent budgetary management, comply with instructions concerning fiscal surveillance, implement targets, and meet benchmarks (to name a few). These latter authorities arguably have a narrower public that can hold them to account, but it is equally difficult to achieve legal accountability given that the Commission's legal toolbox produces different obligations for national authorities, adding complexity to the relevant standard for review. This means that national authorities often act based on formally non-binding documents, but those may still create rights and obligations for individuals at the national level.[75] How are national courts to deal with disputes resulting therefrom? In addition, is there any space for EU courts to have a say in the matter? The case law of the Court of Justice, as the following paragraphs will show, provides limited guidance on the matter.

Let us begin with what the Treaties say. Under Article 288(5) TFEU, recommendations and opinions are listed as acts having no binding force. In line with this, they are under Article 263(1) TFEU excluded from acts that are reviewable through an action for annulment. Conversely, Article 267(1)(b) TFEU does not make any such differentiation and instead refers to 'acts of the institutions, bodies, offices or agencies of the Union'. Finally, Article 277 TFEU provides that, regardless of the deadline in Article 263 TFEU,

O Stefan (eds), *EU Soft Law in the Member States: Theoretical Findings and Empirical Evidence* (Hart 2021).

74 Traditionally under the *Meroni* doctrine, executive powers delegated to agencies could not involve the use of discretion. Case 9/56 *Meroni* EU:C:1958:7 at 152. On the Court of Justice changing its 'no discretion through delegation' approach, see M Scholten and M van Rijsbergen, 'The *ESMA-Short Selling* Case: Erecting a New Delegation Doctrine in the EU upon the *Meroni-Romano* Remnants' (2014) 41(4) *Legal Issues of Economic Integration* 389.

75 G Gentile, 'Ensuring Effective Judicial Review of EU Soft Law via the Action for Annulment before the EU Courts: A Plea for a Liberal-Constitutional Approach' (2020) 16(3) *European Constitutional Law Review* 466, 488 and the literature cited.

'any party may, in proceedings in which an act of general application adopted by an institution, body, office or agency of the Union is at issue, plead the grounds specified in Article 263, second paragraph, in order to invoke before the Court of Justice of the European Union the inapplicability of that act'. On its face, then, Article 263 TFEU is the odd one out in terms of what is a reviewable act.

Against this background, let us take a look at what the Court of Justice said on the matter. It is well-known by now that soft law is sourced in a variety of acts beyond recommendations and opinions (e.g. guidelines, communications, notices, recommendations, information notes, letters, or press releases).[76] While without legally binding force, they 'nevertheless may have practical effects'.[77] The Court of Justice stated in *Grimaldi* that (in the concrete case) a recommendation cannot 'be regarded as having no legal effect'.[78] Rather, national courts are under an obligation to take soft law instruments 'into consideration'.[79] In *Belgium v Commission*, the Court explained that soft law instruments have the 'power to exhort and to persuade',[80] but without creating binding legal effects. The Court grounded this in the joint reading of Articles 263 and 288 TFEU.[81] The inconsistency among these findings is difficult to miss: we are either within or outside the letter of the Treaties, but the Court attempts to achieve both at the same time.[82] If recommendations and opinions are non-binding and non-reviewable acts, where does the duty of national courts to take them into consideration come from?[83] In the same vein, where does the authority for soft

[76] For a useful theorisation and typology, see F Terpan, 'Soft Law in the European Union – The Changing Nature of EU Law' (2015) 21(1) *European Law Journal* 68, and in particular 77–86; most recently see also B Cappellina, A Ausfelder, A Eick, R Mespoulet, M Hartlapp, S Saurugger and F Terpan, 'Ever More Soft Law? A Dataset to Compare Binding and Non-binding EU Law across Policy Areas and over Time (2004–2019)' (2022) 23(4) *European Union Politics* 741.

[77] F Snyder, 'The Effectiveness of Community Law: Institutions, Processes, Tools and Techniques' (1993) 56 *Modern Law Review* 19, 32.

[78] Case C-322/88 *Grimaldi* EU:C:1989:646 [18].

[79] 'The national courts are bound to take recommendations into consideration in order to decide disputes submitted to them, in particular where they cast light on the interpretation of national measures adopted in order to implement them or where they are designed to supplement binding Community provisions.' ibid.

[80] Case C-16/16 P *Belgium v Commission* (n 20) [26].

[81] ibid [30].

[82] A Arnull, 'EU Recommendations and Judicial Review' (2018) 14 *European Constitutional Law Review* 609, 620.

[83] ibid 617, referring also to Opinion of Advocate General Bobek in Case C-16/16 P *Belgium v Commission* EU:C:2017:959 [168].

law instruments 'to exhort and to persuade' come from? Certainly not from the text of the Treaties.

In the context of direct actions, the Court of Justice defined a challengeable act as one which has 'binding legal effects'. How does one reach that conclusion? Back in the famous *ERTA* judgment, the Court introduced a 'substance over form' approach: 'an action for annulment must therefore be available in the case of all measures adopted by the institutions, whatever their nature or form, which are intended to have legal effects'.[84] As a consequence, an EU act cannot be shielded from judicial review simply because its author misnamed it. It is relevant to look into the 'wording and context',[85] the 'substance'[86] of the act in question, and the intention of its author[87] as to the nature of its legal effects. Over time, the requirement of 'legal effects' has turned into 'binding legal effects'.[88] The Court in *Belgium v Commission* arguably departed, or at least distorted, its substance over form approach,[89] by focusing on recommendations not being expressly included in Article 263(1) TFEU. According to Arnull, this has consequences for the institutional balance in the EU, because the Commission will have an easier job in circumventing the otherwise required participation of the Council and/or Parliament by resorting to the use of recommendations and opinions.[90]

However, the story does not end here. EU soft law instruments will be treated differently before the Court of Justice if a question of its interpretation is raised in a preliminary reference procedure. This is the result of the Court's abovementioned findings in *Grimaldi* and has recently been expanded to situations where the national court is questioning the validity of a soft law

84 Case 22/70 *Commission v Council* EU:C:1971:32 [42].

85 Case C-57/95 *France v Commission* EU:C:1997:164 [18]; Case C-301/03 *Italy v Commission* EU:C:2005:727 [21]–[23].

86 Case C-147/96 *Netherlands v Commission* EU:C:2000:335 [27] and case-law cited; Case C-366/88 *France v Commission* EU:C:1990:348 [23]; Case C-303/90 *France v Commission* EU:C:1991:424 [18]–[24]; Case C-325/91 *France v Commission* EU:C:1993:245 [20]–[23].

87 Case C-362/08 P *Internationaler Hilfsfonds v Commission* EU:C:2010:40 [52]; Case C-521/06 P *Athinaïki Techniki v Commission* EU:C:2008:422 [42].

88 Case 151/88 *Italy v Commission* EU:C:1989:201 [21]. The Court here refers to Case 60/81 *IBM v Commission* EU:C:1981:264 [9]: 'According to the consistent case-law of the Court any measure the *legal effects of which are binding on, and capable of affecting the interests of*, the applicant by bringing about a distinct change in his legal position is an act or decision which may be the subject of an action under Article 173 for a declaration that it is void' (emphasis added). Advocate General Bobek has found this change as narrowing the admissibility threshold for direct actions. Opinion of Advocate General Bobek in Case C-16/16 P *Belgium v Commission* (n 83) [72]–[73].

89 Gentile (n 75) 482–483; Arnull (n 82) 620.

90 Arnull (n 82) 618.

act (in *Kotnik*,[91] *Balgarska Narodna Banka*,[92] and *Fédération Bancaire Française*).[93] There is more. It is within the national procedural autonomy to determine *who* can initiate a challenge of validity before national courts.[94] That is so because Article 267 TFEU does not impose any autonomous requirements of standing, unlike Article 263 TFEU. Thus, a trade association was able to initiate a challenge of validity against non-binding EBA guidelines regardless of any individual and direct concern so long as the national procedural rules respected the principles of effectiveness and equivalence.[95]

Hence, an asymmetry. In direct actions, soft law instruments are not a reviewable act, but in the preliminary reference procedure, anything goes. We may well contrast this to the above asymmetry in effects: Member States may refuse to comply with a soft law instrument (and it remains open for the Commission to attempt to enforce it by way of an infringement procedure).[96] Conversely, under *Grimaldi*, national courts must[97] take into consideration soft law instruments and it is therefore not entirely illogical that they are able to submit preliminary references concerning their interpretation or validity.[98] In a framework of legal accountability that focuses on the individuals rather than on Member States, the openness of the Court of Justice towards preliminary references concerning any and all soft law instruments is not

91 Case C-526/14 *Kotnik* EU:C:2016:570 (concerning a Commission Communication).

92 Case C-501/18 *Balgarska Narodna Banka* EU:C:2021:249 (concerning a recommendation of the European Banking Authority (EBA)).

93 Case C-911/19 *Fédération bancaire française* EU:C:2021:599 (concerning EBA guidelines).

94 ibid [62]–[65].

95 National rules 'must not be less favourable than those concerning similar claims based on provisions of national law or arranged in such a way as to make the exercise of rights conferred by the EU legal order practically impossible'. See, for example, Case C-397/21 *HUMDA* EU:C:2022:790 [33].

96 See Case C-575/18 P *Czech Republic v Commission* EU:C:2020:530 [80]. The Court here specified that, because of the Commission's discretion in using Article 258 TFEU, there is no corresponding right of the Member States to initiate a direct action on the matter.

97 For an analysis of an intervening judgment where the Court seemingly forgot about *Grimaldi* and stated that national courts 'may' take into account soft law instruments, see E Korkea-aho, 'National Courts and European Soft Law: Is *Grimaldi* Still Good Law?' (2018) 37(1) *Yearbook of European Law* 470, 487–491. Nevertheless, given that the Court returned to *Grimaldi* in subsequent cases analysed above, it may be concluded that *Grimaldi* still is good law.

98 For a critique concerning the inability of Member States to challenge soft law measures as opposed to individuals before national courts, see H Marjosola, M van Rijsbergen and M Scholten, 'How to Exhort and to Persuade with(out Legal) Force: Challenging Soft Law after *Fédération bancaire française*. Case C-911/19, *Fédération bancaire française (FBF) v Autorité de contrôle prudential et de resolution (ACPR)*, Judgment of the Court (Grand Chamber) of 15 July 2021, EU:C:2021:559' (2022) 59 *Common Market Law Review* 1523, 1535–1537.

problematic. Nevertheless, this construct may lead to asymmetries with negative effects in the SSM, which is dominated by direct actions.

There is a caveat, however: national procedural rules govern access to remedies. So long as they do not go below the standards provided for remedies concerning rights stemming from national law, the Court of Justice will find no issue with effective judicial protection. Along the same lines, access to review of EU soft law will vary across Member States, without the fall-back ability of Member States to safeguard their citizens' rights by challenging the act in question by way of a direct action. Necessarily then, national courts should share with EU courts the burden of ensuring the political equality of citizens.[99] In what comes next, I will propose the role that judicial review should play in economic governance to overcome the deficiencies described throughout this section.

2.3 JUDICIAL REVIEW AS A TOOL FOR ACHIEVING THE POLITICAL EQUALITY OF CITIZENS IN THE EMU

I should like to make clear my position in respect of the debate on the legitimacy of judicial review: I consider judicial review a normatively desirable and necessary activity in a democratic society. Its main role is to protect those fundamental rights of citizens put into jeopardy by decisions delivered through a majoritarian democratic process. In addition, in a context where the democratic process creates wide and extensively used discretion, robust judicial review is all the more important. In this section, I will present why this is the case by recalling some of the central works that have promoted this position more generally (specifically those by Dworkin and Ely). Qualifying this against the background of an ever-expanding executive discretion in economic governance presented in the previous section, I will then offer my view on the role and operation of judicial review. This will lead me finally to argue that judicial review is capable of substantially contributing to the political equality of citizens in the EU by delivering legal accountability of decision-makers in EU's economic governance.

2.3.1 *Theoretical Inspiration*

I will ground my normative position towards judicial review in the work of Dworkin and Ely, as there is, in my opinion, no need to reinvent the

[99] An issue I will address in Section 2.3.4.

extraordinary wheel they created. In his book *Taking Rights Seriously*,[100] Dworkin puts forward what he calls 'the rights thesis': 'men have moral rights against the state (...) therefore a court that undertakes the burden of applying these clauses fully as law must be an activist court, in the sense that it must be prepared to frame and answer questions of political morality'.[101] According to this argument, 'judicial decisions enforce existing political rights'[102] that are 'creatures of both history and morality'.[103] They are (or should) never be a result of policy but instead always a result of principle.[104] As such, judicial decisions are of a political nature inasmuch as they need to respect individual or group rights. Dworkin argues that constitutional theory does not rest on simple majoritarian decision-making, but rather protects 'individual citizens and groups against certain decisions that a majority of citizens might want to make'.[105] While recognising the difficulty of defining which rights exactly are to be taken seriously, Dworkin argues that regardless, the logic behind their protection must rest on two important ideas: human dignity[106] and political equality.[107] On this view, courts serve as a counter-majoritarian force equipped with principles of ensuring human dignity and political equality of all citizens – and it is this idea that I subscribe to in devising my arguments for judicial review as an important accountability tool to ensure the political equality of citizens in the EU. If a majoritarian decision interferes to the extent that political equality is at risk, it is right that a judicial decision should protect an individual right pertaining to every member of a political community.[108]

[100] R Dworkin, *Taking Rights Seriously* (Harvard University Press 1977; Bloomsbury Revelations reprint 2022).
[101] ibid 181.
[102] ibid 111.
[103] ibid 112. It should also be added that Dworkin's thesis relies heavily on the idea of justice as fairness developed by Rawls. See J Rawls, *A Theory of Justice* (Harvard University Press 1971).
[104] Dworkin (n 100) 107–111.
[105] ibid 165.
[106] 'The idea (...) supposes that there are ways of treating a man that are inconsistent with recognizing him as a full member of the human community, and holds that such treatment is profoundly unjust.' ibid 239.
[107] 'This supposes that the weaker members of a political community are entitled to the same concern and respect of their government as the more powerful members have secured for themselves, so that if some men have freedom of decision whatever the effect on the general good, then all men must have the same freedom.' ibid 240.
[108] Dworkin's work (published as separate papers that were put together in *Taking Rights Seriously*) has of course been subject to critique, in particular as regards his conviction that every case has one right answer that a judge equipped with principles of morality can reach. See for example, Michigan Law Review, 'Dworkin's "Rights Thesis"' (1976) 74(6) *Michigan Law Review* 1167.

What is Ely doing in Dworkin's company? That is a fair question, given that in his work he rejects the Dworkin's view that there are moral principles that ought to guide judicial activity.[109] Indeed when reading Ely's *Democracy and Distrust*, it is difficult to shake off the impression that the two have little to nothing in common, as they take entirely different routes to arrive at the point of advocating for judicial review. My intention here is not to reconcile their approaches. Instead, I am adding the work of Ely to this section because he too is an advocate of political equality as the underlying rationale[110] for justifying judicial review.[111] Before focusing on what interests me in Ely's work (the role of structural inequalities), I also want to distance myself from his strict separation between substance and process,[112] which seems to have inspired numerous proposals in the EU legal scholarship to the effect that the Court of Justice should conduct a process-oriented review.[113] When Ely argues that the protection of minorities is the necessary constraint on governmental action, his focus is on procedural requirements pertaining to the demand of equality. This, to ensure that judges do not substitute the government's legitimate policy choice with their own substantive view on a certain value.[114] However, it has been convincingly showed by others that if Ely himself can present any right as procedural, so can any judge.[115] That means that it is possible to disagree with Ely on his over-characterisation of what is procedural. This is precisely a drawback of the EU law literature that applies his process–

[109] 'There simply does not exist *a* method of moral philosophy. Ronald Dworkin also succumbs to this error.' Ely (n 4) 58.

[110] Although he would likely have disagreed with my characterisation that some ultimate moral principle guided his arguments. But there are traces of such a position. For example: 'There *are* ethical positions so hopelessly at odds with assumptions most of us hold that we would be justified in labelling them (if not with absolute precision) "irrational".' ibid 52.

[111] 'Naturally that cannot mean that groups that constitute minorities of the population can never be treated less favourably than the rest, but it does preclude a refusal to *represent* them, the denial to minorities of what Professor Dworkin has called "equal concern and respect in the design and administration of the political institutions that govern them".' ibid 82.

[112] ibid 88–101. Ely attempts here to show that the American Constitution, as well as the large part of the Bill of Rights, is in fact ridden with values that are procedural rather than substantive. For a critique of this point, see, for example, G E Lynch, 'Democracy and Distrust: A Theory of Judicial Review' (1980) 80 *Columbia Law Review* 857, 860; M Tushnet, 'Darkness at the Edge of Town: The Contributions of John Hart Ely to Constitutional Theory' (1980) 89 *Yale Law Journal* 1037; P Brest, 'The Puzzling Persistence of Process-Based Constitutional Theories' (1980) 89 *Yale Law Journal* 1063, 1065.

[113] For a broader critique of this phenomenon, see A Woodhouse, 'Process Review as Panacea: A Critique of Process Review Advocacy in the European Union' (2020) 45(3) *European Law Review* 373.

[114] Ely (n 4) 104.

[115] For a presentation of this critique, see Woodhouse (n 113) 376–379.

substance distinction in claiming that even proportionality review can be merely procedural.[116]

But it is also possible to agree with him that judicial review is necessary *precisely because* minority rights require protection, not because their protection is nothing more than ensuring due process.[117] What makes his argument pertinent is that he drives home the point of structural inequalities as unavoidably present in majoritarian decision-making, thus rendering counter-majoritarian judicial control indispensable. Differently from Dworkin, who focuses on the protection of rights, Ely recognises the inherently precarious position of those 'whose interests differ from the interests of most of the rest of us'.[118] While we could certainly engage in a logical exercise to reach the conclusion that each injustice to a member of a minority would fall under Dworkin's rights thesis, what interests me here is the recognition of the *structural* nature of such injustices in a majoritarian system. Ely stresses that these cannot be remedied through political accountability. Transposed to the context of the EU's economic governance and particularly the deficiencies described in the previous section, it is right to recognise that it is by (its current) design permeated with structural inequalities between citizens across the EU both in terms of their ability to influence decision-making and in respect of the (redistributive) outcomes such decisions bring about.[119] To sum up, I subscribe to Dworkin's value-based approach to judicial review that underscores the centrality of political equality of individuals, whereby the courts have an obligation to safeguard these moral principles against the

[116] For example, the acceptance by the Court of Justice of an impact assessment and its findings represented for Lenaerts a proof that proportionality review is entirely procedural. Yet, this is not what Ely's argument is about: ensuring that democratic representation is complied with is a thicker obligation, one that looks at structural relationships among citizens impacted by a rule or an individual decision. Without exploring those choices made, it is not possible for the courts to properly discharge their function. See K Lenaerts, 'The European Court of Justice and Process-Oriented Review' (2012) 31(1) *Yearbook of European Law* 3, 8.

[117] A critique to my approach may be that his argument on minority protection would not be possible without the process–substance distinction and that he would simply not support a substance-oriented view of judicial review because this would mean providing judges with the ability to make policy based on their personal values. But Ely is himself guilty of trying to have his cake and eat it: try as he might, he is unable to avoid the conclusion that the development or sustaining of inequalities in a purely majoritarian (procedural, if you will) system are issues deeply connected to values. For such a reading of his approach to democracy and political equality, see J S Schacter, 'Ely and the Idea of Democracy' (2004) 57 *Stanford Law Review* 737, 741–742. See also J Habermas, *Between Facts and Norms: Contributions to a Discourse Theory of Law and Democracy* (MIT Press 1996) 266. I am grateful to Wayne V Walton for challenging me on this point.

[118] Ely (n 4) 78.

[119] These correspond broadly to Ely's two levels of representation. ibid 89.

government. In addition, a proper understanding of the role of judicial review is impossible to grasp without accepting the inherent structural inequalities of the constitutional system we are analysing – in this book, the EU's economic and monetary union.

2.3.2 *On Discretion*

In appreciating both these levels, I consider it necessary to address another point that will shape our conclusions on judicial review as a remedy against structural inequalities specific to the EMU: the role of executive discretion. In the previous section, I have described the main contours of the deficiencies that executive discretion brought about in financial assistance, and due to the role of the ECB and the Commission in other areas of economic governance. Of course, both Dworkin and Ely developed their arguments in the context of the US constitutional system, and I use them in an abstract manner. Yet, delegation of authority from the legislator to the executive and the resulting discretion is an unavoidable trend in national systems as well as the EU,[120] noticed even before it appeared in its version on steroids after the financial crisis. This is not a place to explore the (now) old literature of how the regulatory state (in the words of Majone) came about. But the discussions on discretion still yield some common misconceptions in EU law that it is useful to bring to light.

The first of those concerns defining discretion in the first place. Opinions vary: each of the following definitions, keep in mind, has a different relationship to understanding the limits of discretion. Let us begin again with Dworkin. Unlike Ely,[121] he devoted some attention to the role of discretion and its relationship to judicial review. Famously, he began his analysis with: 'Discretion, like the hole in a doughnut, does not exist except as an area left open by a surrounding belt of restriction.'[122] In his view, discretion is only there because a norm has granted it, and by doing so, it necessarily determined its scope and limits. Depending on how far a particular action is from the centre of the doughnut, we may speak of weak or strong discretion, but

[120] D J Galligan, 'Arbitrariness and Formal Justice in Discretionary Decisions' in D J Galligan (ed), *Essays in Legal Theory: A Collaborative Work* (Melbourne University Press 1984) 145; G Majone, 'The Rise of the Regulatory State in Europe' (1994) 17(3) *West European Politics* 77.

[121] The closest connection to the discussion on the relationship between the administration and courts in *Democracy and Distrust* is one where Ely discusses the motivation of legislation that he considers applicable also to the administration. See Ely (n 4) 136–145.

[122] Dworkin (n 100) 48.

Dworkin acknowledges that even the strongest discretion (at the centre of the doughnut) does not amount to licence, as we are ultimately, in all our actions, bound by such principles as rationality, fairness, and effectiveness.[123]

Similarly to this was discretion defined by Lord Diplock of the UK's House of Lords: 'The very concept of administrative discretion involves a right to choose between more than one possible course of action upon which there is room for reasonable people to hold differing opinions as to which is to be preferred.'[124] For both Dworkin and Lord Diplock, control is inevitable, no matter the extent of discretion granted, as there is always at least a rationality requirement underlying any use of discretion. Constraints have been similarly set out by Galligan: 'the fundamental duties governing the exercise of discretion are threefold: a duty to decide according to rational considerations; a duty to advance the purposes and objects for which power has been granted; and a duty to comply with a variety of moral and political principles, such as fairness in various of its senses.'[125] Note that both these definitions share Dworkin's approach of higher principles guiding and limiting the exercise of discretion without distinguishing the reasons and extents of the discretion granted.

Consider, in opposition to these, the following two definitions coming from the EU law literature. First, Ritleng: '(…) discretion can be defined as the freedom of action which the holder of public authority enjoys in its decision-making or rule-making activity. It is the part of its activity that falls outside the ambit of judicial review'.[126] Second, Fritzsche: 'discretion can be defined as the power and competence of a decision-maker to decide, with highest authority, about the application of the law to a specific fact pattern or certain elements thereof. This power derives from the absence of a statutory predetermination and subsequent *de novo* decision by the controlling court'.[127] Here, discretion is seen in purely negative terms, as the nucleus of public authority not subject to judicial control.[128] It would result from this approach that once discretion is acknowledged, the body in question has free rein over the specific

[123] R Dworkin, 'The Model of Rules' (1967) 35 *University of Chicago Law Review* 14, 33–34.

[124] *Secretary of State for Education and Science v Tameside MBC* [1976] UKHL 6, 17. Mendes calls for a similar approach: 'discretion should be conceived as the authority attributed to decision-makers to choose between different alternatives when concretising legal norms with a view to achieving the ends that those norms identify'. Mendes (n 15) 462. See also Opinion of Advocate General Emiliou in Case C-389/21 P *ECB v Crédit Lyonnais* (n 12) [44].

[125] Galligan (n 120) 147.

[126] Ritleng (n 13) 184.

[127] A Fritzsche, 'Discretion, Scope of Judicial Review and Institutional Balance in European Law' (2010) 47 *Common Market Law Review* 361, 364.

[128] For a critique of this approach, see Mendes (n 15) 461.

matter within its competence. It is particularly important also to note that Fritzsche's definition stems from the case law of EU courts.

The second misconception concerns the extent to which courts review discretionary decisions. This discussion is necessarily contingent on the first, of course. 'Positive' definitions of discretion focus on its content but maintain that control of its rational use is necessary. 'Negative' definitions of discretion instead require that courts display in respect of the administrative body a degree of deference. Here reasons for granting discretion become relevant and condition the extent of judicial control. Kavanagh accordingly distinguishes between minimal and substantive deference: the first is justified by arguments pertaining to the separation of powers, the second by the specific expertise of the body in question, its institutional features, and the procedures under which it operates.[129] In the EU context, the separation of powers, referred to as institutional balance, is often highlighted as the main reason for a light standard of review of discretion.[130]

Yet, it already became visible in Section 2.2 that the traditional arguments on the position of discretion and judicial review do not bite in the post-crisis context in several respects. The persistence in maintaining the same justifications as those imported from the context of the nation-state with different chains of accountability is inadequate. The pattern visible in decision-making post-crisis is a counter-intuitive one: while in the nation-state context deliberative processes create discretionary powers, for the post-crisis economic and monetary governance, the opposite is true. Specifically, decisions with high redistributive impacts, such as the ECB's bond-buying programmes and decisions on financial assistance to debtor Member States, lacked any deliberative process at their origins.[131]

My proposal on the proper treatment of discretion by courts takes inspiration from the criticism by Mendes, according to which the Court of Justice artificially separates discretion in making complex findings based on technical expertise (cognition), on the one hand, and discretion that involves a value judgment based on the balancing of interests (volition), on the other.[132]

[129] A Kavanagh, 'Deference or Defiance? The Limits of the Judicial Role in Constitutional Adjudication' in G Huscroft (ed), *Expounding the Constitution: Essays in Constitutional Theory* (Cambridge University Press 2008) 184.

[130] See Opinion of Advocate General Emiliou in Case C-389/21 P *ECB v Crédit Lyonnais* (n 12) [33].

[131] See above, in particular, Section 2.2.1.

[132] Mendes (n 15) 449. See also H P Nehl, 'Judicial Review of Complex Socio-Economic, Technical, and Scientific Assessments in the European Union' in J Mendes (ed), *EU Executive Discretion and the Limits of Law* (Oxford University Press 2019) 176.

Mendes is certainly right in claiming that the two activities of an administrative body necessarily overlap and it is not always possible to clearly distinguish them so as to then determine the relevant standard of judicial review – in particular after the financial crisis, which exacerbated the need for executive discretionary decision-making.[133] We should accordingly abandon distinctions that focus on predetermined categories of discretion, obscuring its effects. Courts should, as I will show in the following section, regard discretion as a unitary concept by focusing instead on their effects on the common interest and how these were balanced in the exercise of discretion by the decision-making body in question.

2.3.3 *What Type of Judicial Review?*

Informed by these important contributions from the theory of judicial review, I propose approaching the issue with a starting position of a rebuttable presumption of full review. An important consideration behind this approach is the high redistributive effects of decisions in the EMU.[134] Yet, opportunities for input from the individuals were few and far between, at best along national lines. No legitimacy routes were created for the individuals to connect along socioeconomic lines, where wealth redistribution takes shape. The Troika, as we will see in Chapter 3, only considered the financial effects of conditionality measures, instead of including a reflection on their socioeconomic effects. Likewise, we will see in Chapter 4, for example, that the ECB became the largest creditor of eurozone Member States through its quantitative easing programme, with significant effects in the prices of assets. Such a decision was not subject to any sort of *ex ante* scrutiny of the different socioeconomic interests that are inevitably affected. In this context, measures that carry political and socioeconomic outcomes for individuals must be pursued in the common interest and judicial review is there to ensure that is the case. But how exactly?

In every case that comes before a court and involves discretion, the presumption should be that it is to perform a high standard of review. This includes an intensive examination of all the factual, legal, as well as political considerations that went into reaching the decision under review. The legitimacy structure behind the granting of discretion to the decision-making body

[133] Mendes (n 15) 448.

[134] Most recently, see 'ECB Confronts a Cold Reality: Companies Are Cashing in on Inflation', *Reuters* (2 March 2023). Available at <www.reuters.com/markets/europe/ecb-confronts-cold-reality-companies-are-cashing-inflation-2023-03-02/>.

is also relevant: what limitations and conditions are attached to the granting of discretion and what are the accountability duties in other spheres (e.g., political, administrative) that the decision-maker was or will be subject to.[135] The burden then shifts to the parties to demonstrate not only who should win the case, but also, preliminarily, what should be the appropriate standard of review and all the necessary evidence to allow a court to reach conclusions on that point. In this way, the duty to state reasons becomes a central feature of legal accountability.

The parties thus carry the full burden of substantiating at least five elements determinative of the ultimate standard of review to be applied. First, that the power of the body in question involves (or does not) an area that is either complex, uncertain, highly politicised, carries redistributive effects, or any combination of these elements. The second element concerns the need that the decision-maker in question had (or did not have) a high duty of care in collecting all the relevant evidence for reaching a decision. Third, that an obligation was (or not) met to explain carefully and in a detailed manner what information was (or not) considered and why. Fourth, what values and/or societal interests have been at play in this intellectual process and how they were (or should have been) balanced. Fifth and finally, what would have been the alternative outcomes had a different path been opted for and why these would (or would not) have achieved the aim as mandated by the norm granting discretion.

It is, of course, a matter of fact that to a certain extent, these evidentiary activities are already present in the submissions of parties before EU and national courts. For example, the ECB argued in *Gauweiler* that the information that was taken into account in creating the Outright Monetary Transaction mechanism was sufficient and necessary in light of the ECB's assessment of the functioning of the monetary policy transmission mechanism.[136] However, my proposal goes further in that it places the burden on the parties also to justify the nature of the discretion and how it was used in all its facets (cognition and volition, and the extent to which either is present). To take the monetary policy field as an example again, I have already mentioned that the exercise of the price stability mandate of the ECB necessarily entails value choices that materialise in the redistribution field. In this scenario, I see nothing controversial in demanding the ECB to justify and

[135] This approach is echoed by the Bundesverfassungsgericht where it argued that the lack of political accountability of the ECB (i.e., its special status under the Treaties) should be the reason for a more stringent judicial review. *Weiss* (n 58) [143].

[136] Case C-62/14 *Gauweiler* (n 44) [73].

explain the choices it made, the reasons and data behind those choices, what alternatives were possible, and why they were not pursued. The opposing party then has the parallel task of demonstrating the inconsistencies or deficiencies in the ECB's submissions.

These elements go against the traditional wisdom whereby the more politicised the mandate of an institution, the less intense judicial scrutiny should be, lest the court does not replace the decision of that institution with its own. My approach is the reverse: the more politicised the mandate and the resulting decision under review, the higher the burden on the institution in question publicly to demonstrate the different interests and values it took into account in its decision-making process.[137] Here is where the institution's duty to state reasons plays a central role: should it become obvious that the institution in question needs to explain its conduct additionally, the likelier it is that it lacked in its obligation sufficiently to state reasons in the decision under review. This point is also crucial as a bridge between procedural and substantive judicial control, because it is the institution itself who ultimately needs to demonstrate the substantive qualities of its decision. The court merely rubber-stamps the outcome that becomes clear in public judicial proceedings.

Presented with this rich evidentiary basis, the task of courts is then to assess and weigh it to reach the conclusion on the normative basis of the discretion in question, the context in which it was exercised, and the credibility and persuasiveness in showing that the proper duty of care was employed.[138] This is where the activity of the Court of Justice can surpass its modest procedural approach to reviewing decisions in the economic and monetary field.[139]

[137] This point broadly follows the logic introduced by Dawson and Maricut-Akbik concerning the accountability good of publicness. They explain publicness as follows: 'The final good is publicness or the idea that official action should be oriented towards the common good – and therefore justified by public or universal reasons. This involves demonstrating both that officials were not personally enriched and that their decisions are fairly balanced, taking into account different societal interests and perspectives. Once again, accountability can ensure the publicness of official action in this sense – when parliamentarians scrutinise government agencies, or courts conduct judicial review, a key demand is that actors show how their activities forwarded the national or collective interest. Accountability is thus a device to advance the normative good of public policy grounded in the public interest.' M Dawson and A Maricut-Akbik, 'Procedural vs Substantive Accountability in EMU Governance: Between Payoffs and Trade-offs' (2021) 28(11) *Journal of European Public Policy* 1707, 1714 (references omitted).

[138] This is no novel obligation. In the context of Article 41 of the Charter, guaranteeing the right to good administration, the Court stated: 'the right to good administration encompasses the obligation of the administration to give reasons for its decisions (see, to that effect, judgment of 8 May 2019, *PI*, C-230/18, EU:C:2019:383, paragraph 57 and the case-law cited)'. Joined Cases C-225/19 and C-226/19 *R.N.N.S. & K.A.* EU:C:2020:951 [34].

[139] Dawson, Maricut-Akbik and Bobić (n 40).

By demanding of the parties a full evidentiary analysis of the decision under review, courts will have before them a complete picture of the procedural as well as substantive considerations and outcomes and will be able to scrutinise both aspects of the decision. The legitimacy of this activity will be sourced in the normative obligation of the parties, and at the very least of the body in question, to justify itself in respect of the procedure followed and the aims it pursued. The public interests or values that were disregarded or sacrificed in this process will also be on full display for the public.[140]

This exercise for the decision-making body and the opposing party is in addition crucial for understanding the way in which that body safeguarded the common interest embedded in the norm granting it discretion in the first place.[141] This is central to the normative framework I use in this book and propose should guide decision-making in the EMU for the purposes of achieving political equality. It will be achieved when citizens are provided with a forum that protects their legitimate demands to seek recognition in shaping the common interest and its enforcement. Contestation is in this context the necessary condition of political equality, given that all citizens have entrusted the institutions to pursue and achieve goals in the common interest. Parties who challenge decisions before courts engage in contestation and do so in pursuit of the common interest. Their access to legal accountability is thus one mode of using the rights accorded to all EU citizens.

To achieve this aim, I have argued in Chapter 1 that the principles of solidarity and equality of Member States should be given a different interpretation to move away from a state-centred, conditionality-oriented focus. The common interest, in turn, is contingent upon Member States and the EU acting in respect of the principle of solidarity. We have learned from Ely that judicial review is a tool able effectively to remedy heterogeneous conditions in a political community. An analogous asymmetry pervades the EMU, both in the starting positions and in the outcomes of decisions on the different groups of society. The normative objectives embedded in the granting of discretionary powers with distributive effects, characteristic for the EMU, are translated into commitments of decision-makers towards all EU citizens in the achievement of the common interest. In Chapter 1, I have presented further arguments on

[140] This approach is also consistent with the role of courts as spaces for deliberation as argued by Habermas (n 117) 274–276.

[141] See also J Mendes, 'The Foundations of the Duty to Give Reasons and a Normative Reconstruction' in E Fisher, J King and A Young (eds), *The Foundations and Future of Public Law: Essays in Honour of Paul Craig* (Oxford University Press 2020) 304.

what considerations normatively pertain to the pursuit of the common interest in the EMU even when the enabling norm is indeterminate.[142]

Finally, this arrangement of judicial review allows for a proportionality-based balancing exercise to take place. The balancing here will not lead the Court to engage in a *de novo* decision-making and substitution of the original decision with its own. Instead, it will be for the body whose decision is under review thoroughly to demonstrate how far it has gone to reconcile the competing interests its decision influenced. To return to the example of distributive effects, the question would be how the ECB has ensured, while working on achieving price stability, to prevent income inequality or similar redistributive outcomes. This echoes the approach taken by Scott and Sturm in touting courts as catalysts, whereby they are able to require that decision-makers 'justify their particular conception of a norm both in relation to the processes they use to produce that norm and in relation to more general normative commitments that must be articulated in context in order to assume meaning'.[143] In some ways, my proposal is that courts outsource the activity of balancing to the parties, and, in the exercise of their authority to say what the law is, endorse the outcome faithful to the enabling norm and the objectives underpinning it.

The court hearing the case is also able to invite independent experts to aid its assessment of the comprehensiveness and veracity of the facts submitted by the decision-maker and the opposing party. A good example of such a practice is the litigation that took place before the Bundesverfassungsgericht concerning the Own Resources Decision. There, a number of experts participated at the hearing and provided their views on the likelihood that the Next Generation EU measures carry a risk to the budgets of Member States.[144] These opinions at times provided contradicting prognoses, enabling the court to form an idea of what sort of fact-finding process should guide the decision-maker in assessing the risks and economic effects of a certain decision. This has an additional benefit of legitimising judicial review in scientific areas with high uncertainty, as the court hearing the case can decide it based on comprehensive information from the relevant expert community.

Comparing and assessing the credibility and persuasiveness of the different pieces of evidence presented to it is at the heart of the intellectual activity

[142] See Sections 2.3 and 2.4 in particular.

[143] J Scott and S Sturm, 'Courts as Catalysts: Rethinking the Judicial Role in New Governance' (2007) 13 *Columbia Journal of European Law* 565, 571.

[144] Cases 2 BvR 547/21 and 2 BvR 798/21 *Own Resources Decision* Judgment of 6 December 2022 [96], [179], [181], [201], [208], [221], [225]. For a further analysis of this decision, see section "Judicial Review at the National Level" in the Epilogue.

inherent to judicial activity that takes place across virtually all areas of human life.[145] In the same way that the Court of Justice is able to assess the proper use of discretion in highly scientific or uncertain areas,[146] so it is in the economic and monetary field.[147] This constellation allows the Court to dodge the most difficult bullet directed to its review of decisions in the EMU: that it does not have sufficient expertise in this area and should not interfere.[148] Instead, the Court's role is to have those with the necessary expertise justify themselves both in terms of the procedure followed and the substantive outcome reached in relation to the normative values that every decision-maker in the EMU should achieve. The party opposing the decision-maker represents, through its action before the Court, the interests of those affected by the decision under review. It is, of course, possible that the interests of that specific party are not representative of the common interest.[149] Procedurally, it should be said that in direct actions and appeals, EU courts examine the legal interest in bringing the case of their own motion.[150] This is contingent also upon the interpretation of the common interest, where the courts are not prevented, but are

[145] Nehl (n 132) 180. See also Opinion of Advocate General Ćapeta in Case C-268/21 *Norra Stockholm* EU:C:2022:755 [66]–[83].

[146] For example, the Court of Justice instructed national courts how to treat scientific evidence in the application of the Medicinal Products Directive and defined what might be considered 'beneficial effects on health' for the purposes of its application, in Case C-616/20 *M2Beauté Cosmetics GmbH* EU:C:2022:781 [38], [51]. We can all agree that the Court does not have the necessary expertise to make those conclusions, but it does have the intellectual tools available to assess different options and evidence presented to it. For a critique on the Court's overly intrusive review of scientific methodology, see G C Leonelli, 'The Fine Line between Procedural and Substantive Review in Cases Involving Complex Technical-Scientific Evaluations: *Bilbaína*' (2018) 55(4) *Common Market Law Review* 1217.

[147] Case C-12/03 P *Tetra Laval* EU:C:2005:87 [39]: 'Whilst the Court recognises that the Commission has a margin of discretion with regard to economic matters, that does not mean that the Community Courts must refrain from reviewing the Commission's interpretation of information of an economic nature. Not only must the Community Courts, inter alia, establish whether the evidence relied on is factually accurate, reliable and consistent but also whether that evidence contains all the information which must be taken into account in order to assess a complex situation and whether it is capable of substantiating the conclusions drawn from it. Such a review is all the more necessary in the case of a prospective analysis required when examining a planned merger with conglomerate effect.'

[148] Most clearly expressed by M Goldmann, 'Adjudicating Economics? Central Bank Independence and the Appropriate Standard of Judicial Review' (2014) 15(2) *German Law Journal* 265.

[149] On this risk and the normative proposal to remedy it, see M Morvillo and M Weimer, 'Who Shapes the CJEU Regulatory Jurisprudence? On the Epistemic Power of Economic Actors and Ways to Counter It' (2022) 1(3) *European Law Open* 510.

[150] See Opinion of Advocate General Mengozzi in Case C-401/09 P *Evropaïki Dynamiki v ECB* EU:C:2011:31 [60] and in particular footnote 21.

rather obliged, to adjudicate in line with the constitutional principles underlying the common interest.

2.3.4 *On the Division of Judicial Labour*

In this last section, I want briefly to turn to the question of who should do what in the multilevel judicial structure of the EU. That question will be answered by determining the relevant interlocutors in the European judicial space and the way to ensure the quality of their work.

First, to interlocutors: why is it relevant that courts should 'talk to' and challenge each other? Without entering the well-travelled universe of the judicial dialogue literature, suffice it to say here that the EU's judicial set-up, with the preliminary reference procedure in the centre, depends on national and EU courts mutually contesting each other's decisions and thereby keeping each other in check.[151] Their interactions are of equal importance in the EMU. Thus, the starting position should be as elsewhere in EU law: EU courts deal with issues pertaining to EU law; national courts deal with issues pertaining to national law. When these two legal orders interact, so do the courts. This may take place through the preliminary reference procedure or through parallel decisions on the same subject matter. So far so good.

EMU law is, however, slightly different from other areas of EU law in that it is often made up of composite structures including the national and EU level. For example, monetary policy is exercised by the European System of Central Banks, which is composed of the ECB and national central banks of the euro area. Furthermore, the SSM equally operates in composition of the ECB and the relevant national authorities. There is more. In the operation of the SSM, the ECB operates on the basis of both EU and national law, therefore blurring the division of powers and applicable law. As will be described in Chapter 5 dealing with the SSM, EU courts have reserved for themselves the exclusive power to adjudicate matters in which the ECB has exclusive powers, even when it applies national law.[152] This exclusion removes one point of control in the legal accountability structure and is in my view deeply problematic. It also provides EU courts with the power to interpret national law, which goes beyond the powers granted to them under

[151] In my work, I have been a strong supporter of constructive constitutional conflict between the Court of Justice and national constitutional courts, arguing it is a vehicle of mutual checks and balances. See Bobić (n 17).

[152] Case C-219/17 *Berlusconi* (n 59).

Article 19(1) TEU and may lead to problematic outcomes should that interpretation be erroneous without any subsequent control.

From the perspective of access, knowledge, and democratic legitimacy, my view is that the traditional division of work in EU law should remain in place also in the EMU. This can at present be achieved by national courts accepting jurisdiction in contravention of the *Berlusconi* decision of the Court of Justice, and maintain, where necessary, the use of the preliminary reference procedure. This will also reduce the dominance of direct actions in the Banking Union more generally. Important improvements would arise in terms of access to justice as well, given the already mentioned high threshold for standing when it comes to non-privileged applicants, a problem less pronounced at the national level.

2.4 CONCLUSION

Judicial review is a contested concept in constitutional theory, for reasons concerning the democratic legitimacy of judges and the democratic consequences of their decisions. These concerns become more complex when courts get involved in reviewing the decisions of the administration and the executive who have been granted discretionary powers, where courts should arguably exercise deference not to replace the original decision with their own. Regardless of which side in this debate one takes, I have shown that arguments against judicial review are not compelling in respect of decision-making patterns in the EMU, an area where decisions inherently carry high redistributive outcomes. These latter are characterised by novel arenas of non-deliberative decision-making, a high degree of executive discretion, and a widespread use of soft law instruments.

Against this background, I have then presented my own vision of the role of judicial review in the EMU, grounded in the work of Dworkin and Ely. I used their work as normative support for judicial review, which is an efficient tool to safeguard political equality under conditions of structural inequalities. I have also relied on Mendes's work in arguing that we should employ a unitary understanding of discretion when approaching judicial control. With this in mind, I have proposed that the burden should be placed on the parties in the litigation to present a rich evidentiary basis that is to serve as ammunition aimed at endorsing or rebutting the presumption of full judicial review. This judicial activity should be shared between national and EU courts, as it is done in other areas of EU law. This is particularly important given the changes that took place in the division of tasks between national and EU courts in the SSM, where national courts lost the ability to review measures where the ECB applies national law, and has the final say on supervisory decisions. With these lessons and proposals in mind, I now turn to explore in detail three areas of EMU governance: financial assistance mechanisms, monetary policy of the ECB, and the SSM. My aim will be to present EU and national judicial review of decisions in these areas and test them against the normative framework of accountability from Chapter 1, and how this should be done according to my proposal in this chapter.

3

Financial Assistance Mechanisms

3.1 INTRODUCTION

After the Annual Meeting of the European Stability Mechanism (ESM) Board of Governors on 13 June 2019, the ESM Managing Director Klaus Regling stated in a press conference:

> For this Annual Report, we recalculated the annual savings that Greece derives from our assistance. The number is €13 billion in savings for the Greek budget in 2018. That represents 7% of Greek GDP. And this will happen again every year. It is the largest support and *largest solidarity ever given to any country in the world.*[1] (emphasis added)

From the creditor's point of view, the principle of solidarity appears to be the cornerstone of all financial assistance: money is given out of solidarity the creditors felt towards a Member State in trouble. This statement represents the mainstream view on solidarity in the EU, as direct help given to a Member State in need. But for such solidarity not to be mistaken for a transfer union, measures of financial assistance have been designed to ensure the principle of equality of Member States as articulated in Article 4(2) of the Treaty of the European Union (TEU). The principle of equality prevents the development of a transfer union, for example, by prohibiting monetary financing of national budgets (Article 123 of the Treaty on the Functioning of the European Union (TFEU)). In addition, the no-bailout clause (Article 125 TFEU) presumes that a Member State cannot be held liable for the debt of another, as all Member States are to be treated equally.

1 See <www.esm.europa.eu/press-releases/klaus-regling-press-conference-after-annual-meeting-esm-board-governors>.

A common denominator found in these measures is that they grant decision-making powers to national governments and ultimately reduce the influence of individuals in economic governance to national elections only. This looks like equality only on the surface: debtor governments and parliaments have had little power to negotiate the terms of financial assistance, unlike the power that was reserved for the creditor Member States. This is furthermore true given that the post-crisis economic governance is increasingly regulated through ad hoc and non-typical instruments, which results in both a decreased ability to use contestation fora at the EU level, as well as differentiation in terms of the variety of contestation routes and mechanisms at the national level.[2]

In this context, judicial review carried out by national courts and the Court of Justice in EU economic governance is problematic as it departs from focusing on individual rights, instead focusing on national budgetary sovereignty and the resulting conditionality embedded in measures of financial assistance. This is due to the legal nature of austerity obligations, which are outside the realm of EU law proper, remaining in the sphere of public international law.[3] Judicial review of measures of financial assistance at the EU level was initially light,[4] stemming primarily from the fact that each of those measures had a peculiar legal status, meaning that the Court of Justice was not able to apply the Charter of Fundamental Rights.[5] The Court of Justice appears to be changing its approach, by imposing an obligation on the Commission, when acting outside its Treaty-based functions, to ensure the Charter is respected.[6] The same obligation is now placed on the European Central Bank (ECB),[7] while national measures implementing austerity

2 See, for example, Opinion of Advocate General Pitruzzella in Joined Cases C-597/18 P, C-598/18 P, C-603/18 P and C-604/18 P *Chrysostomides* EU:C:2020:390 [48], [54].

3 See, on this point, R Repasi, 'Judicial Protection against Austerity Measures in the Euro Area: Ledra and Mallis' (2017) 54 *Common Market Law Review* 1123, 1140.

4 Case C-370/12 *Pringle* EU:C:2012:756. Initially, the review of financial assistance measures based on Memoranda of Understanding was rejected as inadmissible. See A Hinarejos, 'The Role of Courts in the Wake of the Eurozone Crisis' in M Dawson, H Enderlein and C Joerges (eds), *Beyond the Crisis: The Governance of Europe's Economic, Political, and Legal Transformation* (Oxford University Press 2019) 119.

5 Case C-370/12 *Pringle* (n 4) [180].

6 Joined Cases C-8/15 P to C-10/15 P *Ledra Advertising and Others v Commission* EU:C:2016:701.

7 Case T-107/17 *Steinhoff* EU:T:2019:353. The Court of Justice found the appeal against this decision is manifestly inadmissible and in part manifestly non-founded. See Case C-571/19 P *EMB Consulting SE v ECB* EU:C:2020:208.

requirements have been reviewed in limited circumstances.[8] Still, when it comes to the central institutions actually deciding on the conditions of financial assistance, legal accountability at the EU level remains weak. For example, the decision-making processes of the Euro Group are not amenable to judicial review by EU courts, as it is considered an informal discussion forum,[9] not affecting rights of individuals given that their decisions do not produce binding legal effects.[10] Individuals are required to take a number of indirect routes[11] that have as yet not resulted in successful judicial redress.[12]

Turning to the national level, not all national courts have the same position and powers in their constitutional set-up to review measures resulting from financial assistance. For example, the German Bundesverfassungsgericht (the German Federal Constitutional Court) is seen as the dominant national constitutional court in the EU, being one of the most cited courts EU-wide, and the most prominent in questioning the decisions of the Court of Justice.[13] However, the Bundesverfassungsgericht is also seen as pushing the ordoliberal agenda in the EU's economic policy,[14] therefore depriving citizens of other Member States of having any say in the economic rationale behind governance mechanisms. This ultimately means that the extent of contestation before national courts depends on their behaviour and position in national

[8] When reviewing a cut in judges' salaries, an austerity measure introduced to meet the requirements of the bailout, the Court of Justice did not mention the ESM or any other financial assistance mechanism in the legal context of the judgment, but focused solely on the interpretation of the principle of judicial independence from Article 19(1) TEU, which it concluded was not impaired by the measure in question. Case C-64/16 *Associação dos Juízes Portugueses* EU:C:2018:117. See also Chapter 2, Section 2.2.1.

[9] Joined Cases C-597/18 P, C-598/18 P, C-603/18 P and C-604/18 P *Chrysostomides* EU:C:2020:1028 [88].

[10] Opinion of Advocate General Wathelet in Joined Cases C-105/15 P to C-109/15 P *Mallis* EU:C:2016:294 [66]. On the concept of binding legal effects, see Chapter 2, Section 2.2.3.

[11] Opinion of Advocate General Pitruzzella in Joined Cases C-597/18 P, C-598/18 P, C-603/18 P and C-604/18 P *Chrysostomides* (n 2) [32].

[12] See also P Craig, 'The Eurogroup, Power and Accountability' (2017) 23 *European Law Journal* 234, 248.

[13] G Anagnostaras, 'Activation of the *ultra vires* Review: The *Slovak Pensions* Judgment of the Czech Constitutional Court' (2013) 14(7) *German Law Journal* 959, 959; R D Kelemen, 'On the Unsustainability of Constitutional Pluralism: European Supremacy and the Survival of the Eurozone' (2016) 23 *Maastricht Journal of European and Comparative Law* 136, 136; F Mayer, 'Rashomon in Karlsruhe: A Reflection on Democracy and Identity in the European Union: The German Constitutional Court's Lisbon Decision and the Changing Landscape of European Constitutionalism' (2011) 9(3) *International Journal of Constitutional Law* 757.

[14] C Joerges, '"Brother, Can You Paradigm?"' (2014) 12(3) *International Journal of Constitutional Law* 772, 780.

legal systems.[15] Fragmented judicial review of austerity measures therefore prevents a more homogeneous approach towards the social conflicts taking place across and within Member States.[16]

In essence, thus, this chapter looks at the intersection between the substance of the EU economic governance and the procedure by which EU citizens can and should be able to contest it. In so doing, the aim is to determine the position of individuals and their ability to make use of existing routes of judicial contestation in the current set-up of EU economic governance, characterised by its normative focus on the equality of Member States. It explores the role accorded to the principle of equality of Member States in the case law of the Court of Justice and national courts reviewing measures of financial assistance, while at the same time investigating the extent to which the common interest, as the expression of the principle of solidarity,[17] features as a consideration before those courts. In that sense, I will argue that courts are able to contribute to the overall state of accountability in the EMU by reinterpreting the normative preferences of the constitutional system and ensuring political equality of citizens. Methods for doing so include a teleological interpretation of rules on access and the scope of remedies, and a substantive interpretation of the common interest.

In what follows, Section 3.2 will offer a brief description of financial assistance measures to gain a sense of how their versatile nature influenced judicial review. Section 3.3 will look at the judicial review of the European Stability Mechanism[18] and the resulting Memoranda of Understanding at the national level. Section 3.4 will conduct the analogous exercise in respect of EU courts. Section 3.5 will finally reflect upon judicial interactions taking place between the EU and the Member States to connect the findings from the previous sections and comment on the overall status of legal accountability in financial assistance.

3.2 THE LEGAL FRAMEWORK OF FINANCIAL ASSISTANCE

The number, complexity, and variety of financial assistance mechanisms employed during the Euro crisis is well documented in the

[15] See also Transparency International, 'From Crisis to Stability: How to Make the European Stability Mechanism Transparent and Accountable' (2017), <https://transparency.eu/wp-content/uploads/2017/03/ESM_Report_DIGITAL-version.pdf> 36.

[16] See A Farahat and X Arzoz (eds), *Contesting Austerity: A Socio-Legal Inquiry* (Bloomsbury 2021).

[17] See Chapter 1 for a more detailed elaboration of this connection.

[18] Treaty Establishing the European Stability Mechanism (ESM Treaty) T/ESM 2012-LT/en 1.

literature.[19] What binds all these instruments together is their non-typical, hybrid,[20] legal nature, placed partially within and partially outside EU law, essentially transforming the Treaty-based EU method of action.[21] The sources considered here as instruments of financial assistance are the earlier European Financial Stabilisation Mechanism (EFSM)[22] and the European Financial Stability Facility (EFSF),[23] which was later replaced by the European Stability Mechanism (ESM).[24] Both have been accompanied by loans provided by the International Monetary Fund (IMF) as well as bilateral loans. However, to add to the complexity, the so-called Six-Pack[25] of EU law instruments, later

[19] E Chiti and P G Teixeira, 'The Constitutional Implications of the European Responses to the Financial and Public Debt Crisis' (2013) 50 *Common Market Law Review* 683, 686; C Kilpatrick, 'Are the Bailouts Immune to EU Social Challenge Because They Are Not EU Law?' (2014) 10 *European Constitutional Law Review* 393, 394; C Kilpatrick, 'On the Rule of Law and Economic Emergency: The Degradation of Basic Legal Values in Europe's Bailouts' (2015) 35(2) *Oxford Journal of Legal Studies* 325, 333; A Poulou, 'Financial Assistance Conditionality and Human Rights Protection: What Is the Role of the EU Charter of Fundamental Rights?' (2017) 54 *Common Market Law Review* 991, 995.

[20] Poulou (n 19) 995.

[21] The political reasons behind these choices are also presented in detail in Chiti and Teixeira (n 19) 685 ff, and will not be covered here.

[22] Council Regulation (EU) No 407/2010 of 11 May 2010 establishing a European financial stabilisation mechanism (OJ 2010 L 118) p. 1.

[23] The EFSF is a company governed by private law incorporated in Luxembourg. Full text available at <www.esm.europa.eu/system/files/document/20111019_efsf_framework_agreement_en.pdf>. See also U Forsthoff and J Aerts, 'Financial Assistance to Euro Area Members (EFSF and ESM)' in F Amtenbrink and C Herrmann (eds), *The EU Law of Economic and Monetary Union* (Oxford University Press 2020).

[24] It should be added that the ESM Treaty has been reformed and was ratified by all its members except Italy. This reform will thus be excluded from analysis but will be reflected upon in the Conclusion. For more information, see <www.esm.europa.eu/about-esm/esm-reform>.

[25] Council Directive 2011/85/EU of the Council of 8 November 2011 on the requirements for budgetary frameworks of the Member States (OJ 2011 L306) p. 41; Regulation (EU) 1173/2011 of the European Parliament and of the Council of 16 November 2011 on the effective enforcement of budgetary surveillance in the euro area (OJ 2011 L306) p. 1; Regulation (EU) 1174/2011 of the European Parliament and of the Council of 16 November 2011 on enforcement measures to correct excessive macroeconomic imbalances in the euro area (OJ 2011 L306) p. 8; Regulation (EU) 1175/2011 of the European Parliament and of the Council of 16 November 2011 amending Council Regulation (EC) No 1466/97 on the strengthening of the surveillance of budgetary positions and the surveillance and coordination of economic policies (OJ 2011 L306) p. 12; Regulation (EU) 1176/2011 of the European Parliament and of the Council of 16 November 2011 on the prevention and correction of macroeconomic imbalances (OJ 2011 L306) p. 25; Council Regulation (EU) 1177/2011 of 8 November 2011 amending Regulation (EC) No 1467/97 on speeding up and clarifying the implementation of the excessive deficit procedure (OJ 2011 L306) p. 33. The Six-Pack is available in OJ 2011 L301/1, p. 1.

replaced by the 'Two-Pack',[26] was attached to the ESM to ensure consistency between the conditionality attached to financial assistance and economic and budgetary surveillance of euro zone countries.[27] Surveillance mechanisms are, however, pure EU law instruments, invoking different legal consequences than an international treaty such as the ESM. What is important to note is that each of the individual instances of financial assistance has been granted as a combination of one or more of these facilities.[28]

The actual financial assistance to be disbursed and the conditions attached to it are negotiated between the Troika (representatives of the Commission, the ECB, and the IMF) and the Member State in need of assistance. The ultimate conditions of the assistance are then agreed in a Memorandum of Understanding, another instrument without a clear answer concerning its legal nature.[29] The same conditions are then also confirmed by a Council Decision, which, however, does not contain the same amount of detail as the Memoranda of Understanding.[30] In sum, then, even this brief summary demonstrates the complex network of instruments in place. How judicial review before national and EU courts dealt with this complexity is presented in the following sections.

3.3 JUDICIAL REVIEW AT THE NATIONAL LEVEL

A feature shared by all national decisions on the ratification of the ESM Treaty is a focus on sovereignty and more specifically on parliamentary budgetary prerogatives as its most direct expression.[31] While the ESM Treaty regulates parliamentary involvement in decisions concerning the

[26] Regulation (EU) 472/2013 of the European Parliament and of the Council of 21 May 2013 on the strengthening of economic and budgetary surveillance of Member States in the euro area experiencing or threatened with serious difficulties with respect to their financial stability (OJ 2013 L140) p. 1; Regulation (EU) 473/2013 of the European Parliament and of the Council of 21 May 2013 on common provisions for monitoring and assessing draft budgetary plans and ensuring the correction of excessive deficit of the Member States in the euro area (OJ 2013 L140) p. 11.

[27] Poulou (n 19) 995.

[28] Kilpatrick, 'On the Rule of Law and Economic Emergency' (n 19) 336.

[29] For an analysis and presentation of differing views in the literature, see M Markakis and P Dermine, 'Bailouts, the Legal Status of Memoranda of Understanding, and the Scope of Application of the EU Charter: *Florescu*' (2017) 55(2) *Common Market Law Review* 643, 654.

[30] Poulou (n 19) 1002.

[31] S Bardutzky and E Fahey, 'Who Got to Adjudicate the EU's Financial Crisis and Why? Judicial Review of the Legal Instruments of the Eurozone' in M Adams, F Fabbrini, and P Larouche (eds), *The Constitutionalization of European Budgetary Constraints* (Hart 2014) 347.

disbursement of aid at length, the case law makes hardly any mention of the Treaty's solutions concerning judicial review. This is not surprising, though: Article 37 of the ESM Treaty is the only provision concerning judicial review, providing that the Court of Justice is to decide on appeals against decisions made by the Board of Governors on the interpretation or dispute between ESM Members. At the national level, the ESM Treaty was challenged before the highest courts[32] in Austria, Estonia, France, Germany, Ireland, the Netherlands, and Poland. Only the Irish case resulted in a preliminary reference to the Court of Justice concerning the compliance of the ESM Treaty with EU law, in the now famous *Pringle* reference.[33] The following subsections seek to shed light on the impact of the ESM Treaty and other legal instruments developed to manage the eurozone crisis on judicial review and the role of courts at the national level. In that respect, I will first look at the procedural aspects of judicial review, more specifically the scope of access to courts by individuals and the remedies available to them. Second, I will analyse how national courts interpreted the principle of equality grounded in national budgetary sovereignty and the resulting conditionality of financial assistance, and whether the common interest of the EU has been taken into account.

3.3.1 *Access and Remedies*

The practice of national courts in respect of access to judicial review by individuals and available remedies will be the focus of this section. Certainly, the expectation of this exercise is not to establish that the diversity of access rules and remedies at the national level immediately results in political inequality of EU citizens. This would disregard decades of Court of Justice's case law on national judicial autonomy[34] and would reduce the argument to a need for full harmonisation in this area. The purpose is rather to provide an illustration of different rules in order better to understand the diverse thresholds in place for individuals to contest decision-making in economic governance before national courts.

Individuals challenged the ratification legislation in Germany and the Netherlands. The German ratification of the ESM Treaty was subject to

[32] Depending on the national judicial systems of constitutional review, these included both supreme and constitutional courts.

[33] The lack of a wider engagement in the preliminary reference procedure was heavily criticised by Bardutzky and Fahey (n 31) 354.

[34] M Dougan, *National Remedies before the Court of Justice Issues of Harmonisation and Differentiation* (Hart 2004).

several constitutional complaints, one of them by a group of private citizens seeking to protect their fundamental right to vote and parliamentary budgetary responsibility. The standard applied by the Bundesverfassungsgericht in order to admit a constitutional complaint is the 'injury to the permanent budgetary autonomy of the German Bundestag'.[35] After analysing the academic criticism concerning the wide access granted to individuals in challenging measures resulting from European integration,[36] the German court stated that it will not change its approach, as citizens must be able to challenge the transfer of competences as a way of defending the set-up of the Basic Law.[37] The complaint must substantiate the alleged erosion of the right to vote.[38] In the specific case of the ESM, this meant showing when guarantee authorisations might result in 'massive adverse effects'[39] for the Bundestag's budgetary autonomy. In that respect, while the access granted to individuals is wide, it is confined solely to the preservation of German-specific budgetary interests. In other words, a German citizen would not be able to challenge a measure that might have adverse effects on the stability of the eurozone as a whole, which may ultimately have consequences for the budgetary autonomy of the Bundestag. Yet, a measure applicable to a debtor Member State can produce effects on the remainder of the eurozone members, as evidenced by the Greek sovereign debt crisis.

In the Netherlands, the ratification bill of the ESM Treaty was challenged by members of parliament acting in their capacity as private citizens before the Hague Civil Court.[40] Importantly, one of the arguments put forward by the applicants concerns the silence of the ESM Treaty as regards judicial review and accountability.[41] This is particularly relevant in the context of the Dutch Constitution, which prohibits judicial review against the Constitution, resting upon a strong tradition of judicial self-restraint.[42] Accordingly, the court emphasised this point by stating that it is not the appropriate forum for

[35] Case 2 BvR 987/10 *ESM Treaty* Judgment of the Second Senate of 07 September 2011 [93].
[36] Connected to access in the Maastricht and Lisbon decisions (ibid [101]).
[37] ibid.
[38] ibid [102].
[39] ibid [103].
[40] *Wilders and Others v the Dutch State*, case no 419556 / KG ZA 12-523 Judgment in summary proceedings of 1 June 2012 [2.2], [3.1].
[41] ibid [3.3].
[42] Article 120 of the Dutch Constitution prohibits judicial constitutional review. See G van der Schyff, 'Constitutional Review by the Judiciary in the Netherlands: A Bridge Too Far?' (2010) 11 *German Law Journal* 175, 177; G Yein Ng, 'Judicialisation and the End of Parliamentary Supremacy: Shifting Paradigms in the Protection of the Rule of Law and Human Rights in the UK, France and the Netherlands' (2014) 3 *Global Journal of Comparative Law* 50.

assessing the ESM ratification bill as this is the role of the legislative branch.[43] The Dutch court did not put forward any legal standard for access but summarily addressed the main substantive points raised by the applicants.

In all other cases dealing with the ESM Treaty, the action was initiated by members of parliament (the remainder of German decisions and Ireland), the provincial government (Austria), the president (France), and the public prosecutor (Estonia and Poland). Thus, when it comes to challenging the ratification of the ESM Treaty at the national level, a clear dominance of privileged applicants is visible. It should be said that this does not immediately deteriorate the position of the individual, as her political representatives in the legislative branch are challenging the treaty in advance of its ratification to regulate any and all future measures of financial assistance.

Remedies that can be awarded as a result of judicial review of individual measures enacted as a requirement of financial assistance demonstrates a similar pattern. In Portugal, for example, the number of cases initiated by private individuals is not known, but the outcome of an individual case would not result in the invalidation of the national measure under review, as the decisions are binding only *inter partes*,[44] thereby excluding more general accountability effects for decision-makers.[45] When it comes to abstract constitutional review, all national measures challenged before the Constitutional Tribunal were initiated by privileged applicants, such as the president, members of the legislature, or regions.[46] While these decisions have *erga omnes* effects, such an outcome is only possible through indirect dependence of individuals on the constitutional organs of their Member State. In Greece, after the initial deadline for contestation before the Council of State expires, implementing administrative acts can be challenged as regards their constitutionality, but only for the purposes of the main proceedings, thereby also

43 *Wilders and Others* (n 40) [3.3].

44 According to Almeida Ribeiro, this legal solution is arcane and departs from traditional set-ups of constitutional review in Europe. G Almeida Ribeiro, 'Judicial Review of Legislation in Portugal: A Brief Genealogy' in F Biagi, J O Frosini and J Mazzone (eds), *Constitutional History: Comparative Perspectives* (Brill 2020) 4.

45 M Canotilho, T Violante and R Lanceiro, 'Austerity Measures under Judicial Scrutiny: The Portuguese Constitutional Case-Law' (2015) 11 *European Constitutional Law Review* 155, 158.

46 R De Brito Gião Hanek and D Gallo, *Constitutional Change through Euro Crisis Law: Report of Portugal* (2015) <https://eurocrisislaw.eui.eu/wp-content/uploads/sites/44/2019/05/Portugal.pdf>, Annex I. The reports were made as part of a research project carried out by the European University Institute.

limiting the effects to *inter partes*.[47] Even if the Council of State does find an administrative act unconstitutional, the precedent is not legally binding.[48]

Rules on access and remedies can be, and to some extent were, interpreted in a teleological manner. Legal innovation, or at least a novel interpretation of access and remedies, was in fact visible at the national level. For Germany, a broad interpretation of access was introduced in the Maastricht and Lisbon decisions.[49] In Portugal, the Constitutional Tribunal temporarily suspended the effects of its decision when it found the budget based on new austerity measures unconstitutional, also a novelty in its remedies.[50] Therefore, it is not inconceivable that the courts deciding a case can take into account specific interests that will possibly be affected by decisions stemming from financial assistance. In this respect, while the approach of the German court allows individuals to trigger constitutional review of legislation, it does so only in relation to possible deteriorations of budgetary powers of the Bundestag. In that sense, it would not be possible to initiate a constitutional complaint when interests of the eurozone, or a significant portion thereof, are jeopardised due to measures of economic governance.

The opposite would require a dynamic approach to judicial interpretation, demanding the decision-makers to justify their decisions based on EU-wide considerations. For example, in its recent decision concerning monetary policy in *Weiss*,[51] the Bundesverfassungsgericht argued that the European Central Bank did not sufficiently take into account the effects that its bond purchase programme would have on different societal groups, albeit its focus was regrettably on such groups only in Germany.[52] Yet, it is impossible to carry out such an analysis without looking deeper into the redistributive effects across Member States, thereby reducing the importance of the principle of equality of Member States. This aligns with the understanding of the common interest as presented in Chapter 1. It would also require courts conducting judicial review to demand more of the parties in terms of justifying their

47 A I Marketou and M Dekastros, *Constitutional Change through Euro Crisis Law: Report of Greece* (2017) <https://eurocrisislaw.eui.eu/wp-content/uploads/sites/55/2019/05/Greece.pdf> section X.8.

48 ibid.

49 A Bobić, *The Jurisprudence of Constitutional Conflict in the European Union* (Oxford University Press 2022) 95–106.

50 De Brito Gião Hanek and Gallo (n 46) Annex I, 10.

51 Cases 2 BvR 859/15, 2 BvR 980/16, 2 BvR 2006/15, 2 BvR 1651/15 *Weiss* Judgment of 5 May 2020.

52 M Dawson and A Bobić, 'Quantitative Easing at the Court of Justice – Doing Whatever It Takes to Save the Euro: *Weiss and Others*' (2019) 56(4) *Common Market Law Review* 1005.

decisions, using expert knowledge to corroborate or oppose the claims of decision-makers, all against the standards of the common interest.

3.3.2 *Solidarity and Equality*

In what follows, the case law concerning the crisis measures will be analysed by looking at how national courts interpreted the principle of equality of Member States and whether EU-wide considerations were of any relevance. It should be added that courts have not referred explicitly to the principle of equality of Member States. Rather, as explained in the Introduction, the logic of the principle of equality permeates the rules on conditionality as well as in treaty prohibition of monetary financing and the no-bailout clause. All these aim at protecting national budgetary sovereignty, and it is this jurisprudence that is of interest here. Thus, the following analysis will look at, on the one hand, the ways in which national courts have treated conditionality and national budgetary sovereignty, and, on the other hand, the stability of the entire eurozone as the expression of the common interest. In order to determine the latter, special attention will be paid to whether, and if yes, how, the principle of solidarity played a role in this interpretative process.

The near-universal commonality of the decisions under analysis is that sovereignty is preserved so long as the constitutionally granted powers of the national legislature remain intact. The individual is only ever mentioned in this context, most prominently in the German decisions, because the right to vote and the ensuing parliamentary budgetary sovereignty were considered a fundamental right, warranting direct interest necessary for the submission of a constitutional complaint.[53] This means that the variety of societal interests end up being conflated to one: that of participating in national elections. This, as was explained in Chapter 1, prevents the connection between EU citizens along lines different from the national ones. There is no possibility for the creation of an interest group along transnational socioeconomic lines and accordingly no platform exists for the expression of their regulatory preferences.

Another consequence of the focus on parliamentary budgetary responsibility is that the debate concerning the ESM focused more on the competence clashes between the EU and Member States concerning fiscal policy, to the detriment of transnational benefits that a stability mechanism may possibly carry. This very question then directed attention to the issue of conditionality

[53] Case 2 BVerfG 1390/12 *ESM Treaty II* Judgment of the Second Senate of 12 September 2012 [92].

in order to ensure that no debtor state abuses the aid given to it in times of need or departs from following a sound budgetary policy. The dangers of such an approach are now dominating the Italian debate on the reformed ESM Treaty and may be one of the reasons why there is no political support to ratify it.[54]

The principle of solidarity did not feature prominently in the case law of either creditor or debtor states. The German analysis in relation to the first aid package to Greece, later reiterated in the ESM review, mentions solidarity only in the following context: 'The Bundestag must specifically approve every large-scale measure of aid of the Federal Government taken in a spirit of solidarity and involving public expenditure on the international or European Union level.'[55] Consequently, aid is considered an act of solidarity and the decision does not dwell upon the importance of the aid for the stability of the eurozone as a whole. The consequences of conditionality, such as the inequality of representation and participation, remain unaddressed. Rather, the insular view of each Member State concerning budgetary sovereignty prevents austerity conflicts among different societal interests to be resolved transnationally by taking into account the interdependence of the euro area.

The need to regard the eurozone as a common project with shared risks was presented as a justification in the Greek decision of the Council of State concerning the first Memorandum of Understanding.[56] More specifically, when carrying out the proportionality test concerning the cuts in salaries, benefits, and pensions of public sector employees, the Council of State found these necessary for achieving the aim of consolidating public finances, an aim in the common interest of eurozone states.[57] Similarly, the Estonian Supreme Court's decision comes closer to viewing the eurozone as a risk-sharing area and the ESM as a tool necessary for preserving its stability to the benefit of all its members: 'Estonia is a euro area Member State and therefore a threat to the economic and financial sustainability of the euro area is also a threat to the economic and financial sustainability of Estonia.'[58] While solidarity is not mentioned, the approach taken is one where financial aid is not simply a handout but an investment in the prosperity of the euro area and all its members. Among creditor states, in the Dutch decision mentioned above,

54 G Galli, 'The Reform of the ESM and Why It Is So Controversial in Italy' (2020) 15(3) *Capital Markets Law Journal* 262.

55 Case 2 BvR 987/10 *ESM Treaty* Judgment of 7 September 2011 [128].

56 Decision 668/2012, 20 February 2012.

57 Marketou and Dekastros (n 47) section X.8.

58 Estonian Supreme Court, *Constitutional Judgment* 3-4-1-6-12 *(ESM Treaty)*, 12 July 2012 [165].

an important consideration accepted by the Hague Civil Court was put forward by the State Secretary for Foreign Affairs, who stated that:

> The interconnectedness of the Member States, and in particular of the Member States whose currency is the euro, means that economic and budgetary policies in one Member State can have disproportionate consequences for the other Member States. The consequences of not supporting the Member State can have consequences for the other Member States that are greater than the consequences for that Member State alone.[59]

In the Portuguese line of cases before the Constitutional Tribunal, solidarity among the Portuguese people and between different regions of the country was used as a justification for limiting regional autonomy that were interfered with due to austerity measures.[60] In the same vein, an 'extraordinary solidarity contribution' imposed on pension contributions was considered constitutional in line with the principle of national solidarity.[61]

3.4 JUDICIAL REVIEW AT THE EU LEVEL

The individual has throughout the decades of European integration and the development of the Court's case law been a central figure, an important difference from other international organisations where relevant subjects are states. In that vein, the Court of Justice has early on[62] established the Union's system of judicial review:[63] privileged applicants[64] are entitled to initiate a direct action, whereas natural and legal persons can do so when an act is of a direct and individual concern to them.[65] In addition, the preliminary

[59] *Wilders and Others* (n 40) [1.9], [3.6].

[60] De Brito Gião Hanek and Gallo (n 46) Annex I, 6, 38, 57.

[61] ibid Annex I, 17, 20.

[62] Case 294/83 *Les Verts* EU:C:1986:166 [23]; Case 314/85 *Foto-Frost* EU:C:1987:452 [16].

[63] See also K Lenaerts, 'The Rule of Law and the Coherence of the Judicial System of the European Union' (2007) 44 *Common Market Law Review* 1625, 1626.

[64] According to Article 263(2) TFEU, these are Member States, the European Parliament, the Council, and the Commission. Article 263(3) TFEU accords to the Court of Auditors, the European Central Bank, and the Committee of the Regions the right to initiate a direct action for the purpose of protecting their prerogatives.

[65] The Treaty of Lisbon was revised in relation to individual concern when it comes to a direct action against regulatory acts that do not entail implementing measures (Article 263(4) TFEU). This sparked further problems into what exactly regulatory acts are, and the General Court defined them as 'all acts of general application apart from legislative acts' in Case T-18/10 *Inuit* EU:T:2011:419 [56]. On appeal, the Court of Justice confirmed this interpretation in Case C-583/11 P *Inuit Tapiriit Kanatami* EU:C:2013:625 [61]. For an overview, see M Kucko, 'The Status of Natural or Legal Persons According to the Annulment Procedure Post-Lisbon' (2017) 2 *LSE Law Review* 101.

reference procedure provides another avenue for natural and legal persons to question the validity of a Union act, when such a doubt arises before national courts.[66] In anti-crisis judicial review, both the preliminary reference procedure and direct actions were used in order to challenge measures of financial assistance. They will be analysed with regard to the interpretation of access and remedies and the developments concerning the review of the merits in relation to the common interest.

3.4.1 *Access and Remedies*

Compliance of the ESM Treaty with EU law and the validity of the Council Decision amending Article 136 TFEU was, as mentioned, tested through the preliminary reference submitted by the Irish Supreme Court. When discussing admissibility of preliminary references, the Court of Justice's case law established that it has jurisdiction when a connection to EU law exists in relation to the case at hand, whereas the questions must not be hypothetical in relation to the facts of the case.[67] A presumption of relevance is, in addition, attached to preliminary references.[68] In addition, a case must be referred to the Court when a national court considers that an EU act is invalid, as it has the exclusive jurisdiction to conclude on its invalidity.[69]

The Court's decision in *Pringle*[70] is relevant as regards two points. First, the Court's jurisdiction was widely questioned,[71] claiming that assessing the validity of the Council Decision amending Article 136 TFEU would breach Article 267 TFEU, which does not accord it the power to review primary law. The Court found that because the amendment was carried out through a simplified revision procedure, it is necessary to verify whether such a procedure was used for a proper purpose and under the prescribed conditions. Given

66 The special role of the preliminary reference procedure in the system of judicial review of Union acts was confirmed explicitly in, for example, Case C-50/00 P *UPA* EU:C:2002:462 [40]; Case C-491/01 *BAT and Imperial Tobacco* EU:C:2002:741 [39].

67 Case 244/80 *Foglia v Novello* EU:C:1981:302 [21]; Case C-343/90 *Dias* EU:C:1992:327 [18]–[19].

68 For example in Case C-35/19 *Belgian State (Indemnité pour personnes handicapées)* EU:C:2019:894 [29].

69 Case 314/85 *Foto-Frost* (n 62) [16].

70 Case C-370/12 *Pringle* (n 4). For a comment on the implications of the decision on the crisis resolution itself, rather than issues of accountability presented here, see B de Witte and T Beukers, 'The Court of Justice Approves the Creation of the European Stability Mechanism outside the EU Legal Order: *Pringle*' (2013) 50 *Common Market Law Review* 805.

71 By Austria, Belgium, Cyprus, France, Germany, Ireland, Italy, the Netherlands, Slovakia, Spain, as well as the European Council and the Commission.

that Article 19 TEU grants it jurisdiction for ensuring 'that the law is observed', the Court concluded it has jurisdiction in this case.[72]

Second, the admissibility of the reference was questioned by Ireland, claiming that questions of validity should have been submitted by way of a direct action within the prescribed time limit, or within a reasonable time limit before a national court.[73] Conversely, the Court found the case admissible, by underlining that a time limit would be relevant only in the case when it is beyond doubt that the applicant would have standing under Article 263 TFEU.[74] As mentioned above, the threshold for direct action for natural persons is high, and the Court could not have established beyond doubt that Mr Pringle would have met its conditions.[75] Such a reading of standing for the purposes of admitting the preliminary reference procedure should be regarded positively from the perspective of the protection of the individual and her ability to challenge decision-makers at EU level, given the difficulties of accessing the Court directly. It also serves to include national courts in a participatory process of ensuring legal accountability through submitting preliminary references.

Turning to judicial review of the Memoranda of Understanding signed after agreeing on the conditions of financial assistance, questions of access and remedies available have not followed a steady course. As explained in the introduction to this chapter, measures of financial assistance were outside traditional EU acts, and when financial assistance was granted, its conditions were set out in the Memoranda concluded between the Member State receiving the assistance and the creditors. What needs to be pointed out is that Memoranda have been concluded in all areas of financial assistance, including balance of payment assistance and bailouts issued within the ESM Treaty framework, where the latter were placed within the EU legal order by way of a Council Decision. Different Memoranda have therefore followed various routes when it comes to their reviewability before EU courts.

When it comes to Memoranda of Understanding stemming from balance of payments assistance, the Court of Justice has initially rejected the admissibility of preliminary references questioning their validity, arguing that Portugal and Romania, the relevant Member States, were not implementing EU law.[76]

[72] Case C-370/12 *Pringle* (n 4) [33]–[37].

[73] ibid [38].

[74] ibid [41]. On this, see Case C-188/92 *TWD Textilwerke Deggendorf GmbH* EU:C:1994:90 [18].

[75] ibid [42].

[76] Case C-434/11 *Corpul National al Politistilor v MAI* EU:C:2011:830; Case C-462/11 *Cozman v Teatrul Municipal Targoviste* EU:C:2011:831; Case C-134/12 *MAI et al. v Corpul National*

A change took place with the Court's decision in *Florescu*,[77] where it found the case admissible, determining that the Memorandum of Understanding based on balance of payments assistance is an act of an EU institution.[78] This welcome development therefore extended judicial review to matters of interpretation and validity of Memoranda of Understanding, which have previously only been dealt with by the Court in cases of an indirect connection to EU law (such as an implementing Council Decision) or an action for damages against an EU institution.[79]

Another development concerns the question of whether a Memorandum of Understanding grounded in the EFSM is subject to the same treatment. The Court decided it is in *Juízes Portugueses*.[80] This unlikely champion of legal accountability in economic governance owes its importance to the current salience of judicial independence in the EU.[81] Namely, the association of judges in Portugal challenged a temporary reduction in their salaries, arguing it interfered with their independence guaranteed by Articles 2 and 19 TEU. The Court of Justice, arguably in need of establishing a legal precedent for its jurisdiction concerning the rule of law challenges taking place in Poland and Hungary,[82] found that Article 19(1) TEU, which states that 'Member States shall provide remedies sufficient to ensure effective legal protection in the fields covered by Union law', is engaged and the preliminary reference is admissible. Rule of law issues aside, the decision of the Court nevertheless further extended access and remedies for Memoranda of Understanding grounded in the EFSM. Consequently, taking the analysed case law into account, Memoranda are susceptible to judicial review before the Court of Justice as regards their validity and interpretation and can also be subject to a possible action for damages resulting from actions of EU institutions in this context.

al Politistilor EU:C:2012:288; Case C-369/12 *Corpul National al Politistilor v MAI* EU:C:2012:725; Case C-128/12 *Sindicato dos Bancarios do Norte et al. v BPN* EU:C:2013:149; Case C-264/12 *Sindicato Nacional dos Profissionais de Seguros e Afins v Fidelitate Mundial* EU:C:2014:2036; Case C-665/13 *Sindicato Nacional dos Profissionais de Seguros e Afins v Via Directa* EU:C:2014:2327.

77 Case C-258/14 *Florescu* EU:C:2017:448.

78 ibid [36].

79 Markakis and Dermine (n 29) 651.

80 Case C-64/16 *Juízes Portugueses* (n 8) [19]–[26].

81 M Bonelli and M Claes, 'Judicial Serendipity: How Portuguese Judges Came to the Rescue of the Polish Judiciary ECJ 27 February 2018, Case C-64/16, *Associação Sindical dos Juízes Portugueses*' (2018) 14 *European Constitutional Law Review* 622.

82 ibid 623.

The question of access and remedies for Memoranda of Understanding agreed under the ESM, a legal facility unequivocally outside the EU law framework, was addressed in *Ledra*[83] and *Mallis*.[84] Revolving around the haircut of deposits in order to secure emergency liquidity assistance to the banking sector in Cyprus, a number of deposit holders sought to annul the Euro Group statement that was the basis for the assistance and conditioned upon the haircut. In *Mallis*, the applicants addressed the action for annulment against the Commission and the ECB, arguing they are the real creators of the conditionality statement, given that the Euro Group is not formally recognised as an institution in the Treaties. In *Ledra*, the applicants sought to establish non-contractual liability of the Commission for the damage incurred as the result of the haircuts of deposits. They argued that the Commission and the ECB, based on *Pringle*, had an obligation to ensure the consistency of the Memoranda of Understanding with EU law.

In *Mallis*, the Advocate General dismissed the ability of individuals to seek judicial redress against the Euro Group, underlining that it is an informal forum for discussion.[85] In *Ledra*, another Advocate General equally dismissed the argument that the Commission has a strict obligation to ensure consistency with EU law in the negotiation of the Memorandum of Understanding.[86] The only redress available to individuals, according to the former Advocate General, would be attacking the Council Decision, which transposes the Memoranda of Understanding to EU law, however, through national judicial proceedings, as the applicants would never be able to meet the standard of direct concern required for direct actions under Article 263 TFEU.[87]

Following the Advocate General, the Court of Justice concluded in *Ledra*[88] that no act stemming from the ESM can be considered an act of an EU institution. However, the decision is important as it nevertheless obliges the EU institutions acting within the ESM (the Commission and the ECB) to act in compliance with EU law. This opened the door for individuals to seek

83 Joined Cases C-8/15 P to C-10/15 P *Ledra* (n 6).

84 Joined Cases C-105/15 P to C-109/15 P *Mallis* EU:C:2016:702.

85 Opinion of Advocate General Wathelet in Joined Cases C-105/15 P to C-109/15 P *Mallis* (n 9) [66].

86 Opinion of Advocate General Wahl in Joined Cases C-8/15 P to C-10/15 P *Ledra* EU:C:2016:290 [71], [72], [74].

87 Opinion of Advocate General Wathelet in Joined Cases C-105/15 P to C-109/15 P *Mallis* (n 9) [91], [98].

88 Joined Cases C-8/15 P to C-10/15 P *Ledra* (n 6) [52]–[54]. For a more general comment on the decision, see Repasi (n 3) 1123.

damages under Articles 268 and 340 TFEU when the Commission acts contrary to EU law while operating within the ESM.[89] Similarly to *Ledra*, the Court of Justice found in *Mallis* that a statement of the Euro Group within the ESM framework is not susceptible to judicial review despite the fact that the ECB and the Commission take part in it.[90]

A somewhat unexpected and revolutionary change in relation to the accountability of the Euro Group almost took place after the 2018 judgment of the General Court in *Chrysostomides*.[91] This litigation is based on the same financial assistance measures to the Cypriot banking system as in the *Ledra* and *Mallis* procedures. Dealing once more with the legal status of the Euro Group in relation to ESM conditionality, the General Court decided that, while it cannot be considered an institution in the sense of Article 263 TFEU, Article 340 TFEU does allow for such an interpretation:

> Article 137 TFEU and Protocol No 14 [...] annexed to the TFEU, make provision, inter alia, for the existence, the composition, the procedural rules and the functions of the Euro Group. [...] Those questions concern, under Article 119(2) TFEU, the activities of the European Union for the purposes of the objectives set out in Article 3 TEU, which include the establishment of an economic and monetary union whose currency is the Euro. It follows that the Euro Group is a body of the Union formally established by the Treaties and intended to contribute to achieving the objectives of the Union. The acts and conduct of the Euro Group in the exercise of its powers under EU law are therefore attributable to the European Union.
>
> Any contrary solution would clash with the principle of the Union based on the rule of law, in so far as it would allow the establishment, within the legal system of the European Union itself, of entities whose acts and conduct could not result in the European Union incurring liability.[92]

In this remarkable move, the General Court, while not allowing a direct action against the Euro Group under Article 263 TFEU, considered nevertheless that the latter can be subject to non-contractual liability. As a result, individuals would be able to seek damages resulting from the harm attributable to the European Union. The General Court nevertheless decided that neither of the institutions under review (the Euro Group, the Commission, or the ECB) had breached EU law by way of a manifest error of assessment.[93]

89 Joined Cases C-8/15 P to C-10/15 P *Ledra* (n 6) [55].
90 Joined Cases C-105/15 P to C-109/15 P *Mallis* (n 84) [57].
91 Case T-680/13 *Chrysostomides* EU:T:2018:486.
92 ibid [113]–[114].
93 ibid [295].

The Council appealed this decision and in December 2020 the Court of Justice overturned the finding of the General Court.[94] The Advocate General's Opinion is of relevance as it focuses on the informal nature of the Euro Group, thus finding that it has no power in making legally binding decisions.[95] The Advocate General argued that this outcome does not undermine effective judicial protection, as individuals are able to contest the decisions of the Commission, the Council, and the ECB instead.[96] The Advocate General also emphasised that these institutions remain bound by the Charter in carrying out their tasks, whether within or outside the framework of EU law.[97]

The Court of Justice followed the Advocate General[98] and overturned the finding of the General Court that the Euro Group can be considered an EU body for the purposes of establishing non-contractual liability of the Union under Article 340 TFEU.[99] Addressing the status of effective judicial protection resulting from this finding, the Court of Justice merely referred to the ability of individuals to seek damages against the Council, the ECB, and the Commission, in respect of their participation in the ESM, the agreement and implementation of assistance, and conditionality requirements.[100] The Court therefore re-emphasised the indirect route for individuals to access judicial review as the centre of legal accountability in the ESM, as the acts of the institutions in question can only bind the ESM.[101] This formalistic view of the Euro Group disregards the evolution of its role and influence from its creation throughout the financial crisis and up to today.[102]

3.4.2 *Solidarity and Equality*

When it comes to the substance of the decisions analysed above, and the way in which the Court of Justice approached the question of achieving the common interest (including the principle of solidarity), *Pringle* is again the starting point of analysis. An important issue considered in its decision was the applicability of the Charter, specifically its Article 47 providing for the right to

94 Joined Cases C-597/18 P, C-598/18 P, C-603/18 P and C-604/18 P *Chrysostomides* (n 9).
95 Opinion of Advocate General Pitruzzella in *Chrysostomides* (n 2) [89], [96].
96 ibid [111], [113], [114].
97 ibid [124].
98 Joined Cases C-597/18 P, C-598/18 P, C-603/18 P and C-604/18 P *Chrysostomides* (n 9) [88].
99 ibid [90].
100 ibid [93]–[97].
101 ibid [131].
102 Craig (n 12) 248–249.

an effective remedy. While the ESM Treaty itself does not set forth any mechanisms of judicial control, the Court found that the Charter is not applicable to it as an instrument outside of EU law.[103]

However, the Court of Justice has incrementally opened up space for the Charter's applicability, namely in response to challenges concerning Memoranda of Understanding. The already mentioned decisions in *Florescu*, *Ledra*, and *Juízes Portugueses* are relevant in this regard. The first one considered the interpretation of the Memorandum of Understanding concluded based on balance of payments assistance to Romania and placed it within the scope of EU law. Consequently, it also found the Charter applicable and assessed whether the right to property protected by its Article 17 was breached.[104] In *Ledra*, while the Court found that Memoranda of Understanding under the ESM are not part of EU law, EU institutions participating in its decision-making are still bound by EU law,[105] and equally as in *Florescu* engaged in the analysis of a possible breach of Article 17 of the Charter. Finally, given the wide interpretation of judicial independence, the Court in *Juízes Portugueses* also found the Charter applicable, namely its Article 47.[106]

Nevertheless, when assessing the proportionality of the measures in question as a restriction to the right to property, the Court found in *Ledra* that 'ensuring the stability of the banking system of the euro area as a whole' is an objective pursued in the general interest and thus legitimate for curtailing the right to property.[107] In that respect, the common interest relating to the stability of the entire euro zone was acknowledged by the Court. In analysing the treatment of the common interest at the EU level, the decision of the Court of Justice in *Dowling*[108] is relevant. The Irish High Court submitted a preliminary reference seeking to ascertain whether its compliance with the conditions of financial assistance within the EFSM

[103] Case C-370/12 *Pringle* (n 4) [178]–[182].

[104] Case C-258/14 *Florescu* (n 77) [43]–[48].

[105] Joined Cases C-8/15 P to C-10/15 P *Ledra* (n 6) [67].

[106] Case C-64/16 *Juízes Portugueses* (n 8) [29], [35].

[107] Joined Cases C-8/15 P to C-10/15 P *Ledra* (n 6) [71]. In *Florescu*, given that it concerned Romania, a Member State not part of the eurozone, the context of the global financial crisis was used to justify the restriction to the right to property. Case C-258/14 *Florescu* (n 77) [56]. Similarly, the Court found Portugal's compliance with financial assistance conditions as a legitimate aim for interfering with salaries of judges. Case C-64/16 *Juízes Portugueses* (n 8) [49].

[108] Case C-41/15 *Dowling* EU:C:2016:836.

is a justifiable breach of Directive 77/91/EEC.[109] The Court of Justice stated that:

> The provisions of the Second Directive do not therefore preclude an exceptional measure affecting the share capital of a public limited liability company, such as the Direction Order, taken by the national authorities where there is a serious disturbance of the economy and financial system of a Member State, without the approval of the general meeting of that company, *with the objective of preventing a systemic risk and ensuring the financial stability of the European Union*.[110] (emphasis added)

Furthermore, and in the same vein as in *Dowling*, the stability of the Cypriot financial system and that of the euro area as a whole was accepted as a legitimate aim by the Court of Justice in *Chrysostomides*.[111] The applicants in that case argued that the General Court erred in assessing the principle of proportionality and the existence of a less restrictive measure. The General Court engaged in a substantive analysis of possible outcomes of alternative measures based on the acts and conduct of the Council as well as the Cypriot Republic. The General Court not only made an assessment of these measures and their effects on the banking system of Cyprus, but also how this would affect the entire euro zone, which was ultimately accepted by the Court of Justice as a proper proportionality analysis.[112] Two conclusions can be drawn from this analysis. First, the Court of Justice confirmed the analysis of the substance of the measures by the General Court and the alternatives proposed by the applicants in the first instance.[113] The General Court assessed this in relation to the specificities of the Cypriot situation and the characteristics of its financial sector. In this type of substantive review, courts should be tracing the fact-finding process of the decision-making institutions in detail and can demand that they take into account the relevant interests of a wide variety of social groups and interests.[114] While the courts may not possess the expertise relevant to make final conclusions on the feasibility of the measures

[109] Second Council Directive 77/91/EEC of 13 December 1976 on coordination of safeguards which, for the protection of the interests of members and others, are required by Member States of companies within the meaning of the second paragraph of Article 58 of the Treaty, in respect of the formation of public limited liability companies and the maintenance and alteration of their capital, with a view to making such safeguards equivalent (OJ 1977 L 26) p. 1.

[110] Case C-41/15 *Dowling* (n 108) [51].

[111] Joined Cases C-597/18 P, C-598/18 P, C-603/18 P and C-604/18 P *Chrysostomides* (n 9) [161].

[112] ibid [163]–[164].

[113] Case T-680/13 *Chrysostomides* (n 91) [311]–[312].

[114] Dawson and Bobić (n 52) 1023–1024.

themselves, they are able to exercise peer-review by taking into account a variety of sources in the proportionality assessment, beyond the reasons stated by the decision-makers.[115]

Second, both courts took into account the common interest of the euro zone in conducting the proportionality analysis and the possible contagion effects in the absence of the measures under review, or in the context of alternative measures. This reasoning, while not altering the essential characteristic of aid disbursement to Cyprus being rooted in strict conditionality, opens the doors to common interest becoming a more prominent aim, rather than a merely transactional view of debtors and creditors. This may result in judicial review more generally placing emphasis on decision-makers to justify the assistance not in relation to ensuring that the aid granted be orderly returned, but rather that such measures generally benefit the whole euro zone. Taking into account the redistributive effects that conditions to aid have had in the debtor states, an approach which arguably surpasses a formal reading of equality of Member States can contribute to the interests of all citizens being taken into account in the creation of financial assistance mechanisms.

As regards the principle of solidarity more specifically, it has not been explicitly mentioned in any of the preliminary references or direct actions before the Court of Justice in the area of financial assistance.[116] It has only been mentioned by Advocate General Kokott in *Pringle*[117] as necessarily justifying the establishment of the ESM and its compliance with the no-bailout clause enshrined in Article 125 TFEU. According to Maduro's interpretation of the Court's decision in *Pringle*, solidarity cannot, in and of itself, justify financial assistance if the interests of the entire eurozone are not at stake.[118] This would be somewhat closer to the definition of solidarity proposed in Chapter 1. However, the Court of Justice insisted on conditionality as central to financial assistance in order to ensure sound budgetary policy being pursued by the Member State in question.[119] Given that the Court of Justice makes no mention of the principle of solidarity, but focuses strongly on conditionality, Maduro's interpretation of solidarity appears too generous.

[115] See Chapter 2, Section 2.3.3.

[116] On this point explicitly, see also the Opinion of Advocate General Campos Sanchez-Bordona in Case C-848/19 P *Germany v Poland* EU:C:2021:218 [67].

[117] View of Advocate General Kokott in Case C-370/12 *Pringle* EU:C:2012:675 [142]–[143].

[118] M P Maduro, 'EU Law and Sovereign Debt Relief' in K Lenaerts, J-C Bonichot, H Kanninen, C Naômé and P Pohjankoski (eds), *An Ever-Changing Union? Perspectives on the Future of EU Law in Honour of Allan Rosas* (Hart 2019) 77.

[119] Case C-370/12 *Pringle* (n 4) [135]–[137].

3.5 ON JUDICIAL INTERACTIONS

The intensity of judicial interactions in the area of financial assistance progressed alongside the developments of the mechanisms under review themselves. What this means is that national constitutional review of an international treaty such as the ESM expectedly did not give rise to any significant number of preliminary references (save for *Pringle*). National courts were reviewing the ESM Treaty (and the revision of Article 136 TFEU) as they traditionally would for the ratification of an international agreement under their respective constitutional requirements.[120] However, as Memoranda of Understanding and the resulting Council Decisions proliferated, so did interactions in the form of preliminary references.

These developments are not surprising and they do not depart from regular judicial interactions in the EU, where Treaty revisions by domestic courts are not submitted as a preliminary reference to the Court of Justice. The legal status of a Treaty amendment naturally strengthens the position of national courts vis-à-vis the Court of Justice. First, it needs to be ratified by all Member States according to their respective constitutional procedures,[121] which allows national courts to determine constitutional limits as regards a particular Treaty amendment.[122] Second, they have the ability to reject the ratification of the amendment if it is contrary to national constitutional requirements. In addition, because Treaty amendments are acts awaiting national ratification, they are not (yet) in the system of binding EU law and therefore fall outside the exclusive jurisdiction of the Court of Justice.[123]

When it comes to the revision of Article 136 TFEU, a new dynamic can be observed. The Court of Justice has been put in a position to decide on conditionality requirements which increasingly concern areas of social

[120] For an overview, see 'Article 136 TFEU, ESM, Fiscal Stability Treaty Ratification Requirements and Present Situation in the Member States' European Parliament's Committee on Constitutional Affairs, June 2013, <www.europarl.europa.eu/meetdocs/2009_2014/documents/afco/dv/2013-06-12_pe462455-v16_/2013-06-12_pe462455-v16_en.pdf> 4–5.

[121] While the process of negotiation of the amendments varied for each Treaty amendment, the final process of ratification is done according to the respective rules of Member States on the ratification of international treaties. On the development of the former, see J Pollak and P Slominski, 'The Representative Quality of EU Treaty Reform: A Comparison between the IGC and the Convention' (2004) 26(3) *Journal of European Integration* 201.

[122] M Claes and J-H Reestman, 'The Protection of National Constitutional Identity and the Limits of European Integration at the Occasion of the Gauweiler Case' (2015) 16(4) *German Law Journal* 917, 943.

[123] Case 314/85 *Foto-Frost* (n 62) [15].

security, labour rights, and protection of vulnerable societal groups[124] – areas only marginally within the scope of EU competence. Invariably this only takes place in relation to debtor states. This most certainly appears problematic from the perspective of equality of Member States, whereby the Court of Justice is intruding in the way debtor Member States exercise their competences, without doing the same in relation to creditor Member States.

The principle of solidarity, however, may justify differentiation[125] when it comes to intrusion into domestic policymaking, if conducted in the common interest. If we take into account the different access requirements and degrees of judicial engagement with the substance of anti-crisis measures at the national level, the use of the preliminary reference procedure appears as a helpful instrument setting common pointers and limits to the dynamic and teleological interpretation to be employed at the national level. At the same time, as was shown in the section concerning the EU level, preliminary references resulted in the Court of Justice expanding the applicability of the Charter and extending admissibility conditions to measures stemming from the Memoranda of Understanding. Another problem relates to the fact that while the Council Decisions confirming the Memoranda conditions are within the scope of EU law and thus subject to well-established routes of legal accountability, they do not always faithfully transpose the amount of detail contained in the Memoranda. Thus, in order for EU citizens impacted by conditionality requirements to be able effectively to hold the institutions participating in the Troika to account, the preliminary reference procedure appears as the necessary outlet, as opposed the exclusively institutional access that Member States have as part of their negotiations with the Troika. Using judicial review and the preliminary reference procedure to relocate the individual in EMU (a policy field otherwise dominated by states and EU institutions) could yet constitute a major contribution of judicial review to the wider system of accountability in the EMU.

Furthermore, judicial interactions between the EU and the national level may lead to improvements of review on the EU level in three ways. First, national courts are able to propose their own interpretation in light of the existing jurisprudence and relevant legal sources, providing the Court of Justice with a wide perspective on the issue at hand, while also ensuring the

124 S Garben, 'The Constitutional (Im)balance between "the Market" and "the Social" in the European Union' (2017) 13(1) *European Constitutional Law Review* 23.

125 For a proposal to formalise differentiation in the ESM through enhanced cooperation, see M Schwarz, 'A Memorandum of Misunderstanding – The Doomed Road of the European Stability Mechanism and a Possible Way Out: Enhanced Cooperation' (2014) 51 *Common Market Law Review* 389.

coherence of such review. By holding the Court of Justice to its standards, national courts are able to create long-term legitimate expectations, and ultimately, contribute to the uniformity and coherence of EU law.[126] Second, national courts can use their questions to direct the Court of Justice towards specific heads of review through their questions, thus ensuring that the common interest is served and a broad variety of societal interests taken into account. Finally, national courts can provide additional reasoning, interpretation, and (expert) evidence. The use of the preliminary reference procedure and the view of the referring national court may shed light on the differences in economic philosophies of Member States, which might find their place in the review stage, not least through the application of the national identity clause set out in Article 4(2) TEU.

However, any proposal placing reliance on the preliminary reference procedure as the locus of legal accountability is to be taken with a grain of salt. Can the Court of Justice be trusted to ensure that political equality of EU citizens is preserved simply due to the mere dynamic of centralisation of judicial review? As set out in Chapter 1, political equality of EU citizens at times requires differentiation, in particular between citizens of creditor and debtor Member States. In addition, varying traditions of social protection across Member States also lead to demands for context-specific interpretation of the common interest. For this purpose, issues of extreme salience in constitutional orders of individual Member States will benefit from judicial activity at the national level, which is arguably more assertive in protecting their constitutional traditions (as was the case in Portugal). This will in turn require the Court of Justice, when acting on the same issues, to apply deference to national constitutional courts, as applied in other areas of EU law.[127]

126 A Bobić and M Dawson, 'Making Sense of the "Incomprehensible": The *PSPP* Judgment of the German Federal Constitutional Court' (2020) 57 *Common Market Law Review* 1953, 1985–1986.

127 A Bobić, 'Constitutional Pluralism Is Not Dead: An Analysis of Interactions between the European Court of Justice and Constitutional Courts of Member States' (2017) 18(6) *German Law Journal* 1395, 1425–1426.

4

The Monetary Policy of the European Central Bank

4.1 INTRODUCTION

> 'When *I* use a word,' Humpty Dumpty said in rather a scornful tone, 'it means just what I choose it to mean – neither more nor less.'[1]

In the story about monetary policy, the European Central Bank (ECB) is our Humpty Dumpty: when it uses the words 'monetary policy', they mean just what it chooses them to mean. This ability of the ECB comes from Article 119(2) TFEU, which states that the competence includes 'the *definition* and conduct of a single monetary policy' (emphasis added).[2] This undoubtedly makes the ECB extremely powerful. The Treaties have also endowed the ECB with a high level of independence:[3] one that has developed into an almost impervious screen shielding it from legal accountability demands.[4] The ability to define its own mandate, coupled with a high level of independence, created an ECB that wields enormous power, influencing the lives and livelihoods of EU citizens. The nature of the ECB's mandate has important consequences for its accountability, which was highlighted by the Court of Justice,[5] the Bundesverfassungsgericht,[6] as well as in

1 L Carroll, *Through the Looking Glass* (Oxford World's Classics 2022) 68.

2 See also Article 127(2) TFEU and Article 3.1 of the Statute of the European System of Central Banks and the European Central Bank (ESCB Statute).

3 Article 130 TFEU.

4 F Amtenbrink, 'The European Central Bank's Intricate Independence versus Accountability Conundrum in the Post-crisis Governance Framework' (2019) 26(1) *Maastricht Journal of European and Comparative Law* 165, 167.

5 Case C-11/00 *Commission v ECB* EU:C:2003:395 [134], [137].

6 Case 2 BvR 2728/13 *Gauweiler* Order of 14 January 2014 [187].

the literature.[7] In a nutshell, ECB's independence and accountability act as counterforces where independence most commonly prevails. How so?

Following a joint reading of Articles 127(1) TFEU and 282(2) TFEU, the primary objective of the Union's monetary policy is to maintain price stability. In addition, Article 127(1) TFEU tells us that without prejudice to this primary objective, the European System of Central Banks (ESCB, headed by the ECB) shall also 'support the general economic policies in the Union', with the aim of contributing to the achievement of the objectives enshrined in Article 3 TEU.[8] The 'without prejudice' phrasing in this provision is of enormous consequence for the common interest: it tells us that Treaty objectives that should guide all Union action hold but a secondary importance for the ECB's price stability mandate.[9] The ECB's high level of independence at the same time makes any contestation in that regard nearly impossible. Yet, there seems to be no unified stance among central bankers regarding the beneficial or detrimental nature of the relationship between the price stability mandate and the ECB's possible role in more general policies aimed at economic growth.[10] Such an environment creates significant leeway for the ECB to make its own assessments in a virtually unfettered manner.

Fears about the precarious status of ECB's accountability on paper materialised in practice. The overlap between monetary and economic policy effects became most vivid with the ECB's use of quantitative easing (the Public Sector Purchase Programme (PSPP)), which made the ECB the largest creditor of eurozone Member States.[11] This creditor role of the ECB makes it more difficult to achieve accountability via routes that theoretically may be open to Member States under the Treaties. It also places governments in a subordinate position to the ECB, with a decreased ability

7 T Violante, 'Bring Back the Politics: The PSPP Ruling in Its Institutional Context' (2020) 21 *German Law Journal* 1045, 1053–1056; M Dawson, A Maricut-Akbik and A Bobić, 'Reconciling Independence and Accountability at the European Central Bank: The False Promise of Proceduralism' (2019) 25(1) *European Law Journal* 75, 77–80.

8 These include balanced economic growth and price stability, a highly competitive social market economy, aiming at full employment and social progress. The same provision also refers to economic, social, and territorial cohesion, and solidarity between Member States.

9 S Egidy, 'Proportionality and Procedure of Monetary Policy-Making' (2021) 19(1) *International Journal of Constitutional Law* 285, 291.

10 D Adamski, *Redefining European Economic Integration* (Cambridge University Press 2018) 109; E Monnet, 'The Democratic Challenge of Central Bank Credit Policies' (2023) *Accounting, Economics, and Law: A Convivium* 1, 2.

11 K Tuori, 'The ECB's Quantitative Easing Programme as a Constitutional Game Changer' (2019) 26(1) *Maastricht Journal of European and Comparative Law* 94, 95.

to be responsive to their citizens. In some ways, this construct is similar to how the Troika-led creditors obstructed the chains of accountability of governments to their citizens in the area of financial assistance.

The ECB is also undoubtedly making value-based choices on how the PSPP is to be implemented, deciding on the desired consequences in the prices of assets, which arguably led to a significant income redistribution.[12] Another important consequence tied to the PSPP's rollout is that due to its sheer size and influence on the prices of assets, discontinuing the programme may result in significant uneven shocks across Member States, ultimately endangering financial stability.[13] As we will see below, the multifaceted consequences of ECB action caused a rift between the Court of Justice and the Bundesverfassungsgericht. The former took the view that so long as the ECB claims it is acting within its primary mandate (price stability), there is nothing problematic in its policies having other effects as well. In contrast to this, the latter argued that the ECB should do no more than act within its monetary policy mandate, which should be interpreted narrowly given its high level of independence under the Treaties.

The aim of this chapter is thus to highlight how these tensions influence the accountability of the ECB from the perspective of the individual and the achievement of the common interest as presented in Chapter 1. As a first step, I will present the legal framework of monetary policy within the system of the ESCB and explain in more detail the quantitative easing programmes of the ECB. Here, I will also provide a summary of the back-and-forth litigation on the scope of monetary policy between the Court of Justice and the Bundesverfassungsgericht in *Gauweiler* and *Weiss*. This background will allow for a further in-depth analysis of these decisions in the remainder of the chapter. To do so, I will then focus on the judicial review of monetary policy decisions by the Court of Justice (Section 4.3) and by national courts (Section 4.4). Both these sections will follow the same structure: I will focus, first, on access to courts and remedies, and second, on the ways in which the courts under analysis approached the principles of equality and solidarity for the purposes of achieving the common interest. The last section will focus on judicial interactions between the EU and national courts and the role they play in the legal accountability of the ECB.

[12] ibid 100.
[13] ibid 105.

4.2 MONETARY POLICY AND THE EUROPEAN SYSTEM OF CENTRAL BANKS

An exclusive competence of the EU, monetary policy and the EU's single currency may be one of the most visible symbols of EU integration after the establishment of the internal market. Its particular position within the EMU was a result of a decades-long debate between the so-called 'monetarists' and 'economists'. In a nutshell, the former argued that a common currency should precede the coordination of economic policies, whereas the latter focused on economic policy coordination as the necessary precondition for the introduction of the common currency.[14] While the monetarists prevailed, the creation of an asymmetrical EMU prevented the creation of a transfer union: every Member State continues to be competent for its economic and fiscal policy and remains solely responsible for its debt. This is ensured by the prohibition of monetary financing (Article 123(1) TFEU)[15] and the no-bailout clause (Article 125(1) TFEU).[16] In economic policy, fiscal surveillance at the EU level serves to ensure that Member States pursue a sound economic policy, thus minimising the likelihood of any possible shocks manifesting themselves across the eurozone.[17]

Within this legal scheme, the ECB is the governing institution of the European System of Central Banks, comprised also of central banks of eurozone Member States.[18] To achieve the objectives of monetary policy, national central banks and the ECB may operate in financial markets and conduct

[14] A Hinarejos, 'Economic and Monetary Union: Evolution and Conflict' in P Craig and G de Búrca (eds), *Evolution of EU Law* (Oxford University Press, 3rd ed 2021) 722 and the references cited.

[15] 'Overdraft facilities or any other type of credit facility with the European Central Bank or with the central banks of the Member States (hereinafter referred to as "national central banks") in favour of Union institutions, bodies, offices or agencies, central governments, regional, local or other public authorities, other bodies governed by public law, or public undertakings of Member States shall be prohibited, as shall the purchase directly from them by the European Central Bank or national central banks of debt instruments.'

[16] 'The Union shall not be liable for or assume the commitments of central governments, regional, local or other public authorities, other bodies governed by public law, or public undertakings of any Member State, without prejudice to mutual financial guarantees for the joint execution of a specific project. A Member State shall not be liable for or assume the commitments of central governments, regional, local or other public authorities, other bodies governed by public law, or public undertakings of another Member State, without prejudice to mutual financial guarantees for the joint execution of a specific project.'

[17] Fiscal surveillance is outside the scope of this book. For a detailed analysis of this area, see P Dermine, *The New Economic Governance of the Eurozone: A Rule of Law Analysis* (Cambridge University Press 2022).

[18] Articles 1 and 14.3 of the ESCB Statute.

credit operations with credit institutions and other market participants following the general principles established by the ECB.[19] They also conduct prudential supervision, and as will be detailed in Chapter 5, here the ECB also has a central role, whereas national supervisors act under its instructions and control.[20] The ECB is subject to judicial control at both the EU and national levels: under the general Treaty rules concerning the procedures before the Court of Justice and before national courts concerning disputes with creditors, debtors, or any other person.[21] The ESCB can be seen as a novel institutional system in which national central banks now wear two hats: they are national but are also EU authorities when acting under the ESCB.[22] In their latter function, the Governing Council of the ECB is entitled to decide that a central bank, while wearing its national hat, is acting in conflict with what is required of it while wearing its ESCB hat.[23]

The ECB's role changed significantly during and after the Euro crisis. It participated, alongside the Commission and the International Monetary Fund, in the Troika, negotiating financial assistance, the conditions under which it would be granted, and supervised national compliance.[24] Aside from its new role in banking supervision, it also added to its arsenal of powers the use of a non-conventional monetary policy mechanism: quantitative easing. This includes purchasing government bonds indirectly on the secondary market, thereby incentivising private purchases of bonds issued by troubled eurozone countries and providing the latter with a fresh supply of money.[25] While in the nation-state context the central bank usually buys government bonds directly,[26] the ECB had to work around the prohibition of monetary financing of Member States from Article 123 TFEU. The first quantitative easing programme to cause a legal ruffling of feathers[27] is the Outright

[19] Article 18 of the ESCB Statute.

[20] See Chapter 5, Section 5.2.

[21] Article 35.1 and 35.2 of the ESCB Statute.

[22] Case C-316/19 *Commission v Slovenia* EU:C:2020:1030 [83]; Case C-45/21 *Banka Slovenije* EU:C:2022:670 [52].

[23] Article 14.4 of the ESCB Statute.

[24] More generally on this role of the ECB, see T Beukers, 'The New ECB and Its Relationship with the Eurozone Member States: Between Central Bank Independence and Central Bank Intervention' (2013) 50 *Common Market Law Review* 1579.

[25] Hinarejos (n 14) 731.

[26] D Andolfato and L Li, 'Quantitative Easing in Japan: Past and Present' (2014) 1 *Economic Synopses* 1.

[27] The earlier Securities Market Programme (SMP) was focused on secondary market bond-buying from 2010 to 2012 of bonds from Italy, Spain, Greece, Portugal, and Ireland. However, the SMP provided for a preferential creditor status for the ECB. It was also not linked to conditionality requirements.

Monetary Transactions (OMT) programme – without ever even being implemented. The programme was announced in the form of a press release,[28] outlining that purchases would be done only for Member States undergoing a financial assistance programme and so long as they complied with the conditionality attached. Apart from this constraint, there were no other quantitative limits to purchases, while the bonds to be purchased would be those with a maturity between one and three years.

The quantitative easing programme that actually did get to see the light of day was the PSPP.[29] The PSPP formed part of the ECB's extended asset purchase programme (APP) alongside the asset-backed securities purchase programme (ABSSP), the bond purchase programme (CBPP3) (both introduced in September 2014), and the corporate sector purchase programme (introduced in March 2016).[30] Unlike the OMT, the PSPP contained no restrictions in terms of compliance with the conditionality requirements. Instead, purchases were to be done across the entire eurozone according to the capital key contributions of eurozone Member States. The PSPP did initially contain a limitation on the volume of purchases to €60 billion, but these were continually extended and are today at a level of €2.5 trillion.[31] Another change in comparison to the OMT is that eligible bonds were now those with a maturity of between one and thirty years. The PSPP ran from 9 March 2015 to 19 December 2018 and from 1 November 2019 until 30 June 2022.

Finally, the ECB also instituted the Pandemic Emergency Purchase Programme (PEPP)[32] 'to counter the serious risks to the monetary policy

[28] Technical features of Outright Monetary Transactions, 6 September 2012, <www.ecb.europa.eu/press/pr/date/2012/html/pr120906_1.en.html>.

[29] ECB Decision 2015/774 of 4 March 2015 on a secondary markets public sector asset purchase programme (OJ 2015 L121) 20, amended by Decision 2015/2101 of 5 November 2015 amending Decision (EU) 2015/774 on a secondary markets public sector asset purchase programme (OJ 2015 L303) 106, Decision 2015/2464 of 16 December 2015 amending Decision (EU) 2015/774 on a secondary markets public sector asset purchase programme (OJ 2015 L344) 1, Decision 2016/702 of 18 April 2016 amending Decision (EU) 2015/774 on a secondary markets public sector asset purchase programme (OJ 2016 L121) 24, and Decision (EU) 2017/100 of 11 January 2017 amending Decision (EU) 2015/774 on a secondary markets public sector asset purchase programme (OJ 2017 L16) 51. For a more detailed presentation of the programme, see S Grund and F Grle, 'The European Central Bank's Public Sector Purchase Programme (PSPP), the Prohibition of Monetary Financing and Sovereign Debt Restructuring Scenarios' (2016) 41 *European Law Review* 781.

[30] For more information on the programmes of the APP, see <www.ecb.europa.eu/mopo/implement/app/html/index.en.html#pspp>.

[31] ibid.

[32] Decision 2020/440 of the ECB of 24 March 2020 on a temporary pandemic emergency purchase programme (OJ 2020 L91) 1.

transmission mechanism and the outlook for the euro area posed by the coronavirus (COVID-19) outbreak'.[33] Initiated in March 2020 with an envelope of €750 billion, it was ultimately expanded to €1,850 billion. Purchases were discontinued in March 2022. In terms of its characteristics, it resembles the PSPP in that it does not restrict its applicability to Member States receiving financial assistance but includes all eurozone members according to the capital key. This, with the caveat that purchases will be carried out with flexibility that might entail fluctuations over time. Eligibility of the bonds in terms of their maturity is set to from 70 days up to a maximum of 30 years and 364 days.

In addition to this general legal framework and the non-conventional mechanisms used by the ECB, it is useful in this section to introduce the main outlines of the litigation concerning quantitative easing that took place between the Court of Justice and the Bundesverfassungsgericht through the preliminary reference procedure. The two courts have been discussing the appropriate level of control of the ECB as an idiosyncratically independent institution extensively,[34] beginning with the announcement of the OMT. The judgment of the German court in *Weiss* concerning the PSPP is at present the last instance of this back-and-forth. Three main threads run through and shape these interactions: the legality of ECB action, *ultra vires* review, and the role of constitutional identity, culminating in the German rejection of the interpretation provided by the Court of Justice.

In *Gauweiler*, the Bundesverfassungsgericht raised doubts concerning the compatibility of the OMT mechanism with primary EU law. More specifically, for the OMT to be *ultra vires*, it needed to exceed the monetary policy mandate of the ECB and the prohibition of monetary financing, resulting in an encroachment of Member States' economic policy.[35] The Court of Justice's response confirmed the legality of the OMT programme: it first analysed the powers of the ECB and concluded that the indirect effects of monetary policy on economic policy do not make them equivalent, leading to the conclusion that the ECB was acting within its mandate.[36] The Court of

33 ECB <www.ecb.europa.eu/mopo/implement/pepp/html/index.en.html>.

34 See also D Grimm, 'A Long Time Coming' (2020) 21 *German Law Journal* 944.

35 Case 2 BvR 2728/13 *Gauweiler* Order of 14 January 2014 [36], [39], [63] and [80]. It is important to note here that the clear distinction between the two areas of competence is grounded in the Treaty text. However, issues related to the ECB's competence and accountability arose precisely because this formal division does not correspond to economic reality.

36 Case C-62/14 *Gauweiler* EU:C:2015:400 [52], [56], relying also on its findings in Case C-370/12 *Pringle* EU:C:2012:756.

Justice further provided the conditions necessary for compliance with the Treaties,[37] albeit differently than what the Bundesverfassungsgericht proposed in its order for reference.[38] In respect of the relationship between the two courts, the Court of Justice omitted any analysis of the claims to constitutional identity and *ultra vires* review of the Bundesverfassungsgericht, stating only that the decisions under the preliminary reference procedure on the interpretation and validity of Union acts are binding on national courts.[39] The Bundesverfassungsgericht accepted the findings of the Court of Justice by setting out the relationship between the principle of primacy and the German Basic Law, addressing also the identity and *ultra vires* review it carries out in relation to EU acts. It concluded that any such review must be done cautiously, with restraint, and in a way that is open to European integration.[40]

This background shaped the second preliminary reference that was submitted by the Bundesverfassungsgericht concerning the PSPP.[41] This second reference revolved around three issues: the ECB's obligation to state reasons in devising the PSPP programme, the scope of the monetary policy mandate of the ECB, and the PSPP's compliance with the Treaty prohibition of monetary financing. The principle of proportionality was mentioned by the Bundesverfassungsgericht only in relation to the first two issues.

Regarding the duty to state reasons, the Court of Justice concurred with the Advocate General's broad assessment of which documents are relevant for making this finding,[42] such as the publication of press releases, statements of the President of the ECB, answers to the questions raised by the press, and by the ECB Governing Council's monetary policy meetings.[43] Therefore, the Court found that the ECB complied with its duty to state reasons. In determining next whether the PSPP falls within the sphere of monetary policy, the Court focused on the objectives and instruments of the measure in question.[44] It found that regardless of any possible indirect effects on

37 For a more detailed analysis of each of these conditions, see T Tridimas and N Xanthoulis, 'A Legal Analysis of the Gauweiler Case: Between Monetary Policy and Constitutional Conflict' (2016) 23(1) *Maastricht Journal of European and Comparative Law* 17, 23–30.

38 ibid 30–31.

39 Case C-62/14 *Gauweiler* (n 36) [16].

40 Case 2 BvR 2728/13 *Gauweiler* Judgment of 21 June 2016 [121], [154], [156].

41 Cases 2 BvR 859/15, 2 BvR 980/16, 2 BvR 2006/15, 2 BvR 1651/15 *Weiss* Order of 18 July 2017.

42 Opinion of Advocate General Wathelet in Case C-493/17 *Weiss* EU:C:2018:815 [133].

43 Case C-493/17 *Weiss* EU:C:2018:1000 [37].

44 ibid [53].

economic policy, the PSPP cannot be treated as an economic policy measure.[45] As to what constitutes an indirect effect, the Court rejected the Bundesverfassungsgericht's interpretation, relying instead on *Gauweiler* and *Pringle*: indirect effects are the foreseeable consequences of measures, which have therefore been knowingly accepted at that time.[46]

Finally, the Court analysed whether the PSPP is in line with the prohibition of monetary financing.[47] The preliminary reference specifically invited the Court to apply the safeguards necessary for preventing a circumvention of that prohibition from *Gauweiler*.[48] The Court recalled the *Gauweiler* principle that the intervention must not have an effect equivalent to the direct purchase of bonds and the programme must contain sufficient safeguards not to reduce the impetus for Member States to pursue a sound budgetary policy.[49] On the first point, the Court acknowledged that there is some foreseeability in the ESCB's intervention given the publication of some of the programme's features.[50] However, numerous safeguards reduce certainty among market operators and keep it in line with Article 123(1) TFEU.[51] The Court then turned its attention to whether the impetus for Member States to conduct a sound budgetary policy is reduced. It recognised that monetary policy will always have an impact on interest rates, with consequences for the refinancing conditions of public debt.[52] However, the programme 'may not create certainty regarding a future purchase of Member State bonds'.[53] In conclusion, the PSPP survived.

After receiving the response from the Court of Justice, the Bundesverfassungsgericht found that the proportionality test as applied by the Court of Justice deprives the said principle of its ability to protect Member State competence.[54] It declared the judgment of the Court of Justice[55] and the PSPP programme[56] *ultra vires*. Having rejected the findings

45 ibid [61].
46 ibid [63].
47 ibid [102].
48 Cases 2 BvR 859/15, 2 BvR 980/16, 2 BvR 2006/15, 2 BvR 1651/15 *Weiss* (Order) (n 41) [79].
49 Case C-493/17 *Weiss* (n 43) [104]–[107].
50 ibid [111]–[112].
51 ibid [113]–[126].
52 ibid [130], in reference to Case C-62/14 *Gauweiler* (n 36) [110].
53 ibid [132], in reference to Case C-62/14 *Gauweiler* (n 36) [113]–[114].
54 Cases 2 BvR 859/15, 2 BvR 980/16, 2 BvR 2006/15, 2 BvR 1651/15 *Weiss* Judgment of 5 May 2020 [123].
55 ibid [116], [163].
56 ibid [117], [178].

of the Court of Justice, the Bundesverfassungsgericht then took it upon itself to interpret the scope of the ECB's monetary policy mandate: the ECB failed to take into account the economic policy effects of the PSPP programme and, importantly, balance a number of competing interests against each other.[57]

In defining the relevant steps of the proportionality test, the Bundesverfassungsgericht stated that the fourth *stricto sensu* step has been omitted by the Court of Justice[58] as there was no review of the sufficiency of information provided by the ECB in balancing the relevant interests.[59] The ECB thus failed in its duty to state reasons concerning the proportionality of the PSPP.[60] In relation to the prohibition of monetary financing, the Bundesverfassungsgericht raised some doubts with regard to the scrutiny applied by the Court of Justice, again related to the duty to state reasons.[61] Ultimately, it decided that the programme is in line with the prohibition of monetary financing and does not breach the constitutional identity of Germany.[62]

In consequence, the Bundesverfassungsgericht gave the Bundesbank a three-month deadline during which it was obliged to work together with the ECB to ensure that the programme meets the principle of proportionality. Otherwise, the Bundesbank will no longer be allowed to participate in the PSPP programme.[63] Since then, the ECB has decided to comply with the request of the Bundesverfassungsgericht,[64] which the President of the Bundesbank deemed to be in compliance with the proportionality analysis to be carried out and published by the ECB.[65] The conclusion of this litigation culminated in an Order of the Bundesverfassungsgericht, confirming its judgment was complied with.[66]

[57] ibid [133], [138]–[145].

[58] Here the Bundesverfassungsgericht infamously stated that the decision of the Court of Justice is 'simply not comprehensible'. ibid [116].

[59] ibid [169], [176].

[60] ibid [177].

[61] ibid [190].

[62] ibid [228]–[229].

[63] ibid [235].

[64] See the letter by ECB President Christine Lagarde to MEP Sven Simon on 29 June 2020, available at <www.ecb.europa.eu/pub/pdf/other/ecb.mepletter200629_Simon~ece6ead766.en.pdf>; Speech by Yves Mersch, Member of the Executive Board of the ECB, 'In the spirit of European cooperation', 2 July 2020, available at <www.ecb.europa.eu/press/key/date/2020/html/ecb.sp200702~87ce377373.en.html>.

[65] Frankfurter Allgemeine Zeitung, 'Weidmann sieht Forderungen des Verfassungsgerichts als erfüllt an', 3 August 2020, available at <www.faz.net/aktuell/finanzen/jens-weidmann-verfassungsgerichtsurteil-zur-ezb-erfuellt-16887907.html?GEPC=s3>.

[66] Cases 2 BvR 1651/15 and 2 BvR 2006/15 Order of 29 April 2021.

4.3 JUDICIAL REVIEW AT THE EU LEVEL

4.3.1 *Access and Remedies*

There is no specific scheme of the judicial review of ECB action provided by the Treaties. The ECB is, according to Article 35.1 of the ESCB Statute, caught by the general scheme of review provided by Article 263 TFEU as well as other ways to trigger a procedure before the Court of Justice, such as the action for damages under Article 340 TFEU. The same headings of review apply. There was thus no attempt by Treaty drafters to create a specific form of review or exclude ECB action from judicial oversight altogether. In the ten cases where the Court of Justice dealt with the interpretation of monetary policy,[67] six were initiated through a preliminary reference and four via direct action. This tells us little about the patterns of litigation that are more pronounced in financial assistance (in favour of preliminary references) and in the Single Supervisory Mechanism (in favour of direct actions).

In that respect, there is hardly anything special about monetary policy when it comes to admissibility – save for the fact that the Court of Justice reviewed a Press Release of the ECB in announcing the OMT mechanism.[68] A press release merely set out the main features of the programme but did not constitute a binding measure adopted by the ECB. In that respect, some of the participants in the preliminary reference claimed the case is hypothetical and thus inadmissible.[69] Another line of attack was that the press release is a preparatory act that cannot be subject to questions of validity, as it does not produce legal effects.[70] The Court of Justice dismissed these arguments, claiming instead that since an action against a possible future act is possible under German law, the questions submitted through the preliminary reference procedure are necessary for the Bundesverfassungsgericht to resolve the case before it.[71]

As we will see below in respect of access and remedies at the national level,[72] the action before the Bundesverfassungsgericht was brought in the

67 Cases concerning the European budgets, fiscal surveillance, or where monetary policy was mentioned in passing, were excluded.

68 The admissibility of the preliminary reference was challenged in one way or another by the governments of Finland, France, Greece, Italy, the Netherlands, Portugal, and Spain, the European Parliament, the European Commission, and the ECB. Case C-62/14 *Gauweiler* (n 36) [18]–[31].

69 ibid [20]–[21].

70 ibid [23].

71 ibid [27].

72 Section 4.4.1.

context of an abstract review. This means that the national court is not in fact solving a dispute between the parties but conducting an abstract review – does that make the question of the national court hypothetical and thus inadmissible?[73] The Court of Justice dealt with preliminary references resulting from an abstract review at the national level, which although in their nature are hypothetical, nevertheless represent a genuine procedure at the national level. Here, then, the rules of national procedural law determine the relevance of the preliminary reference, and the Court of Justice will accept it as admissible.[74]

The Bundesverfassungsgericht did ask one question in *Weiss* that the Court of Justice found hypothetical and thus inadmissible. Taking into account the scenario of a default by a Member State, and the resulting possibility that other national central banks become jointly responsible for the resulting liabilities, the German court asked about the compatibility of such a risk-sharing scenario with the prohibition of monetary financing and the no-bailout clause. The Court of Justice found that there is no possibility envisaged in the PSPP for such risk-sharing to take place, and thus concluded its answer would be either advisory or purely hypothetical.[75] For its part, the Bundesverfassungsgericht understood this reply as meaning that the Treaties outright prohibit risk-sharing ever to be envisaged, and concluded, as we will see below, that this would also be precluded by Germany's constitutional identity.[76]

The question of remedies took an interesting turn, one from which it is possible to imagine further creativity by the Court of Justice. In *Rimšēvičs*,[77] the Court of Justice invalidated a national measure in the application of the ESCB Statute.[78] It should first be said that nobody, in fact, requested the Court to do so.[79] The Court anchored its decision in the independence of the ECB. The relevant provision of the ESCB Statute provides for a referral to the

[73] See, for example, Case C-399/11 *Melloni* EU:C:2013:107 [29]; Joined Cases C-78/08 to C-80/08 *Paint Graphos and Others* EU:C:2011:550 [30]; Joined Cases C-188/10 and C-189/10 *Melki and Abdeli* EU:C:2010:363 [27].

[74] Case C-415/93 *Bosman* EU:C:1995:463 [65]; Case C-62/14 *Gauweiler* (n 36) [28]. After *Gauweiler*, the Court continued with this approach in, for example, Case C-621/18 *Whigtman* EU:C:2018:999 [31].

[75] Case C-493/17 *Weiss* (n 43) [162]–[167].

[76] Cases 2 BvR 859/15, 2 BvR 980/16, 2 BvR 2006/15, 2 BvR 1651/15 *Weiss* (Judgment) (n 54) [224]–[228].

[77] Joined Cases C-202/18 and C-238/18 *Rimšēvičs* EU:C:2019:139.

[78] For a comment on the novelties of the case, see A Hinarejos, 'The Court of Justice Annuls a National Measure Directly to Protect ECB Independence: *Rimšēvičs*' (2019) 56 *Common Market Law Review* 1649.

[79] Opinion of Advocate General Kokott in Joined Cases C-202/18 and C-238/18 *Rimšēvičs* EU:C:2018:1030 [40].

Court of Justice but nowhere explicitly allows annulling a national measure. Advocate General Kokott argued strongly against the Court of Justice directly annulling a national measure, explaining that this would amount to a transgression into the national sphere of competence. This, she argued, may only be granted by an express treaty provision.[80]

It is important to note that different language versions of Article 14.2 of the ESCB Statute open up space for some procedural ambiguity on its relationship to the annulment procedure from Article 263 TFEU and whether it may be extended to national measures. My analysis compared Article 14.2 ESCB Statute in English, French, Italian, Croatian, Slovenian, Bulgarian, Czech, Polish, and Slovakian. The variety of procedural solutions include: a referral (EN), an appeal (FR, PL, CZ), or simply an initiation or a proposal of a procedure (IT, HR, SL, BG, SK) before the Court of Justice. Yet, it is through the interpretation of the purpose of this provision that the Court found the legal justification for its action.[81] That is quite a powerful weapon that the Court of Justice now has in ensuring the independence of the ECB and national central banks.[82] Still, interpretative acrobatics need not be employed only for that purpose. It was discussed above that the relationship between the ECB's primary objective of maintaining price stability appears to take precedence over any and all other Treaty aims. The Court of Justice's mandate, under the framework of legal accountability presented in Chapter 1, should instead be used to promote aims beyond price stability,[83] even against the ECB when its decisions impact different interests across the eurozone.

4.3.2 *Solidarity and Equality*

Neither solidarity nor equality feature explicitly at any point in the analysis of the Court of Justice in the review of monetary policy activities of the ECB. Neither is it possible to discern the Court's approach to the common interest through the achievement of the objectives in Article 3 TEU and Articles 8 and 9 TFEU. This means that when the Court of Justice interprets the powers of the ECB and their possible limits, the aims associated with the common interest of the EMU do not seem to play a role. Taking this into account, the interpretation of the common interest in monetary policy will thus be

80 ibid [60].

81 Joined Cases C-202/18 and C-238/18 *Rimšēvičs* (n 77) [45]–[48].

82 Opinion of Advocate General Kokott in Joined Cases C-202/18 and C-238/18 *Rimšēvičs* (n 79) [59].

83 Such as those from Article 3 TEU.

approached through the lens of the balancing of interests through the proportionality test. In other words, looking at how the ECB balances different interests when making its decisions will be taken as the indirect route through which it is possible to establish how that institution makes value choices that hinge upon the achievement of the common interest. It is also the route through which it is possible to establish the relationship between the ECB's primary objective of price stability and the general objectives pertaining to the common interest in the EMU (found in Article 3 TEU and Articles 8 and 9 TFEU).

The proportionality analysis is particularly important as it was one of the main points of contention between the Court of Justice and the Bundesverfassungsgericht in the review of the PSPP. In what follows, I will thus focus on what is proportionality for and how to use it in respect of the ECB when it balances different interests that influence the achievement of the common interest. One of the central criticisms directed at the decision of the Bundesverfassungsgericht in *Weiss* revolves around whether proportionality is the correct answer when the question is how competences are divided between the EU and the Member States.[84] On this view, the Bundesverfassungsgericht was wrong to use the principle of proportionality in delineating competences between the EU and the national level, which should instead be applied to the way in which existing competences are exercised. This criticism is grounded in the wording of the Treaty: Article 5(1) TEU clearly separates the existence of competence (which is guided by the principle of conferral) from its exercise (to which the principle of proportionality applies).

It is easy to say that the principle of conferral can be straightforwardly applied to whether something is, for example, an action in the area of competition law under Article 3(1)(b) TFEU, further specified in Articles 101 and 102 TFEU. The European Commission, tasked with implementing competition law, does not have the mandate to define that it is the agreements between undertakings that are prohibited by competition law, nor can it include or exclude the abuse of a dominant position from the scope of competition law. How it applies these concepts in the *exercise* of its competence is then subject to the principle of proportionality. However, this separation is not as straightforward when it comes to the monetary policy mandate

[84] F C Mayer, 'To Boldly Go Where No Court Has Gone Before: The German Federal Constitutional Court's *ultra vires* decision of May 5, 2020' (2020) 21 *German Law Journal* 1116, 1119; Editorial Comments, 'Not Mastering the Treaties: The German Federal Constitutional Court's PSPP Judgment' (2020) 57 *Common Market Law Review* 965, 969.

of the ECB and its separation from economic policy. In turn, this has important consequences for the accountability of the ECB.

Let us then take a closer look at how the Court of Justice separates the analysis of existence from the exercise of monetary policy for the purposes of applying the principle of proportionality. In both *Gauweiler* and *Weiss*, 'delimitation of monetary policy' and 'proportionality' are separate headings, keeping in line with the division of Article 5(1) TEU.[85] Upon closer inspection, nevertheless, the proportionality analysis runs through both headings. In other words, due to how Article 119(2) TFEU sets out the monetary policy competence, the very *existence* of monetary policy is impossible to separate from and already forms part of its *exercise*: in order to find out whether the ECB acted *within* its mandate, we need to find out *how* it defined its mandate.[86]

In the proportionality section in *Gauweiler*, the Court of Justice defined it as requiring that acts of EU institutions be appropriate for attaining the objectives pursued and not go beyond what is necessary for achieving those objectives.[87] Back to the section on delimiting monetary policy, the Court of Justice analysed whether the OMT mechanism *contributes to* achieving the objective of singleness of monetary policy and maintaining price stability.[88] Furthermore, the Court went on to assess whether the *means* to achieve the objectives of the OMT are in line with the objectives of monetary policy,[89] methods that we would intuitively expect in the review of how a certain institution exercised its competence. The language of whether a measure contributes to an objective and is the means chosen to achieve it is used regularly in the proportionality analysis of the Court.[90] Precisely because a measure may have both monetary policy and economic policy effects[91] and these are difficult to separate,[92] the Court is inevitably engaging in an

85 The literature does not seem to dispute this formalist division in the analysis. See, for example, M Wendel, 'Paradoxes of Ultra-Vires Review: A Critical Review of the PSPP Decision and Its Initial Reception' (2020) 21 *German Law Journal* 979, 985.

86 See also N de Boer and J van 't Klooster, 'The ECB, the Courts and the Issue of Democratic Legitimacy after *Weiss*' (2020) 57(6) *Common Market Law Review* 1689. They argue that the crisis has changed the operation of the ECB in such a way that judicial review has shifted from assessing the limits of its mandate, to reviewing measures with significant choices even within its mandate that might still lack democratic legitimacy.

87 Case C-62/14 *Gauweiler* (n 36) [67].

88 ibid [48], [49].

89 ibid [53].

90 See, for example, Case C-817/19 *Ligue des droits humains* EU:C:2022:491 [121]–[124].

91 Case C-62/14 *Gauweiler* (n 36) [51], [52].

92 ibid [110]. See also Case C-493/17 *Weiss* (n 43) [60], [64].

assessment of whether the decision-maker (the ECB) by enacting its measures (the OMT, the PSPP) went *beyond what is necessary* to define and exercise its mandate (monetary policy).[93] The inability of separating existence from exercise is even more apparent in *Weiss*:

> It does not appear that the specification of the objective of maintaining price stability as the maintenance of inflation rates at levels below, but close to, 2% over the medium term, which the ESCB chose to adopt in 2003, is *vitiated by a manifest error of assessment and goes beyond* the framework established by the FEU Treaty.[94] (emphasis added)

A manifest error of assessment is a well-established standard for assessing the proportionality of exercise of competence of EU institutions.[95] Going beyond what is necessary is the explicitly stated third step of the proportionality test.[96] This approach is, in fact, not different from the way in which the Bundesverfassungsgericht phrased its standard of review in its order for reference: 'a manifest and structurally significant exceeding of competences'.[97] The argument here is not that the two tests are identical, but that both carry a logic of proportionality in assessing the ECB's compliance with its monetary policy mandate. From the perspective of ensuring ECB accountability in a set-up where it is empowered to define its own mandate, it thus seems inherently impossible to separate the existence and exercise stages of competence control. The ESCB, when defining the inflation target (which arguably should act as the outer limit of monetary policy), is in fact already also *exercising* it. Otherwise, would it at all be possible that the Court of Justice says such a determination is in compliance with the TFEU unless a manifest error of assessment is made?[98]

A positive consequence of applying the principle of proportionality to determine the limits of monetary policy is an increased standard of judicial review, an aim that has arguably been the root cause of both German preliminary references. Once applied to the PSPP programme, proportionality does have the potential of increasing the accountability of the ECB through a more stringent obligation of giving account, even in the stage of defining the

93 On balancing as central to the structural approach of the Court of Justice in applying the principle of proportionality when reviewing EU measures, see T-I Harbo, 'The Function of the Proportionality Principle in EU Law' (2010) 16(2) *European Law Journal* 158, 177–180; P Craig, *EU Administrative Law* (Oxford University Press 2012) 656.

94 Case C-493/17 *Weiss* (n 43) [56].

95 Harbo (n 93) 177.

96 Craig (n 93) 656–657.

97 Cases 2 BvR 859/15, 2 BvR 980/16, 2 BvR 2006/15, 2 BvR 1651/15 *Weiss* (Order) (n 41) [64].

98 Case C-493/17 *Weiss* (n 43) [56].

inflation target. For whom is a target of 2 per cent good and what consequences will it have on aims such as income equality, full employment, or social progress? As shown in Chapter 2,[99] the ECB should carry the burden of showing the different interests that are possibly affected by its decision, the redistributive consequences of the approaches it was able to take, and why it chose a particular solution among those available.

In contrast to this high standard, the Court of Justice has been subject to ample critique due to its light touch proportionality review in both *Gauweiler*[100] and *Weiss*,[101] reducing its review to the duty to state reasons and accepting any and all reasons provided by the ESCB as sufficient. The proportionality analysis in *Gauweiler* did not properly engage in the assessment of less burdensome alternatives and was reduced to the Court of Justice analysing and ultimately accepting solely the information provided by the ESCB, thus concluding:

> [. . .] the ESCB weighed up the various interests in play so as to actually prevent disadvantages from arising, when the programme in question is implemented, which are manifestly disproportionate to the programme's objectives.[102]

In light of the standard of review proposed in Chapter 2, the approach of the Court of Justice, whereby it accepts whatever the ECB says without any challenge from other parties and other possible expert views, is light years away from what might be termed proper scrutiny of a decision with wide-ranging consequences for the entire euro area. In *Weiss*, the Court of Justice was equally one-sided in the choice of information that it found relevant for assessing the proportionality of the PSPP, again accepting the information provided by the ESCB as the only relevant one.[103] In essence, the Court of Justice did not allow for a thorough peer-review of the duty to state reasons on the part of the ESCB.[104] This criticism has been picked up directly by the Bundesverfassungsgericht,[105] demanding that less burdensome alternatives

99 Section 2.3.3.

100 Tridimas and Xanthoulis (n 37) 31; A Steinbach, 'All's Well That Ends Well? Crisis Policy after the German Constitutional Court's Ruling in *Gauweiler*' (2017) 24(1) *Maastricht Journal of European and Comparative Law* 140, 145.

101 M Dawson and A Bobić, 'Quantitative Easing at the Court of Justice – Doing Whatever It Takes to Save the Euro: *Weiss and Others*' (2019) 56(4) *Common Market Law Review* 1005, 1022–1028.

102 Case C-62/14 *Gauweiler* (n 36) [91].

103 Case C-493/17 *Weiss* (n 92) [81].

104 Dawson and Bobić (n 101) 1023.

105 Cases 2 BvR 859/15, 2 BvR 980/16, 2 BvR 2006/15, 2 BvR 1651/15 *Weiss* (Judgment) (n 54) [184], [190].

be considered and a wide array of interests included in such considerations. The lesson learned from *Gauweiler* and *Weiss* may well be that the organisation of Article 5 TEU does not operate as well in the context of self-defined mandates, which would result in judicial review remaining confined to accepting any and all reasons provided by the institution in question.[106] Instead, the great power of the ECB to say what monetary policy is should be followed by great responsibility.

A possible consequence of this litigation is that other national courts follow the German example and begin imposing their own standards and demands for justification on the part of the ECB, leading to a proliferation of diverging national standards and resulting in the creation of an unrealistic burden for the ECB. However, I do not find it controversial that national courts demand more of the ECB when it comes to predicting, assessing, and selecting the specific redistributive effects of large-scale purchase programmes such as the PSPP. In some ways, it would create a race to the top: the ECB, by needing to comply with different levels of justification across Member States, will naturally provide information required by the highest standard for justification, thus automatically meeting the demands of lower standards. Does this harm the ECB's independence? I think not: the ECB has full independence in the implementation of its policies; it simply has a high burden of explaining them. In fact, the ECB, despite Article 130 TFEU explicitly prohibiting it from taking instructions from Member States, complied with the request of the Bundesverfassungsgericht[107] better to explain the proportionality of the PSPP. The ECB has, 'in line with the principle of sincere cooperation [...] decided to accommodate this request'.[108]

4.4 JUDICIAL REVIEW AT THE NATIONAL LEVEL

4.4.1 *Access and Remedies*

Standing before national courts is a matter of national law. If it results in a preliminary reference, it is of no importance whether the case concerns questions of interpretation or validity of Union law.[109] An exception to this rule is a possible abuse of the national procedure, in the event that the

[106] Arguably this seems to be the case in Case C-62/14 *Gauweiler* (n 36) [60] and Case C-493/17 *Weiss* (n 43) [56].

[107] Cases 2 BvR 859/15, 2 BvR 980/16, 2 BvR 2006/15, 2 BvR 1651/15 *Weiss* (Judgment) (n 54) [235].

[108] See n 64.

[109] Case C-911/19 *Fédération bancaire française* EU:C:2021:599 [61]–[62].

applicant failed to submit an action for annulment at the EU level within the prescribed time period.[110] The litigation on quantitative easing offers a vivid demonstration of how powerful national procedural autonomy may be in allowing a wide range of individuals to challenge EU measures, something that would be virtually impossible to do at the EU level due to high standing requirements. Questions of EU integration have since the *Maastricht* judgment of the Bundesverfassungsgericht been opened to a constitutional complaint by individuals, whenever there is a danger that German constitutional identity might be jeopardised by excessive integration.[111]

When Mario Draghi announced the OMT programme, indeed German citizens did not shy away from challenging it before the Bundesverfassungsgericht: a whopping 11,693 of them challenged the Press Release.[112] While not all challenges were found admissible by the German court, the following was:

> From the submissions of the complainants in proceedings I., II., and III. it appears possible that the European Central Bank exceeded its competences in a sufficiently qualified manner by adopting the policy decision of 6 September 2012 regarding the OMT Programme and its possible implementation, thus giving rise to duties to react on the part of the Federal Government, which can be invoked in court by the complainants.[113]

In respect of the PSPP, it was challenged by 1,734 German citizens, and the Bundesverfassungsgericht was as generous:

> The challenge directed against the omission on the part of the Federal Government and the Bundestag is admissible in constitutional complaint proceedings. The complainants in proceedings I to III have standing to the extent that they assert, in a sufficiently substantiated manner, that with the PSPP the Eurosystem manifestly exceeded its competences in a structurally significant manner and violated Art. 123(1) TFEU; they also have standing as regards the assertion that possible changes to the risk-sharing regime could infringe the overall budgetary responsibility (haushaltspolitische Gesamtverantwortung) of the German Bundestag. Moreover, the

[110] Case C-188/92 *TWD Textilwerke Deggendorf GmbH* EU:C:1994:90 [18].

[111] P Huber, 'The Federal Constitutional Court and European Integration' (2015) 21(1) *European Public Law* 83, 97–98.

[112] K F Gärditz, 'Beyond Symbolism: Towards a Constitutional Actio Popularis in EU Affairs? A Commentary on the OMT Decision of the Federal Constitutional Court' (2014) 15(2) *German Law Journal* 183, 185 note 9.

[113] Case 2 BvR 2728/13 *Gauweiler* (Judgment) (n 40) [79].

complainants in proceedings I and III continue to have a recognised legal interest in bringing proceedings (Rechtsschutzinteresse).[114]

Maintaining broad standards of admissibility may be seen as a destabilising element, bringing about uncertainty concerning the interpretation and validity of EU acts. In another way, it can also be seen as a source of imbalance given the differing standing requirements across Member States. But so what? If it is enough that the preliminary reference procedure is not used to circumvent the two-month deadline for an action for annulment under Article 263 TFEU, why should Member States not otherwise provide for a higher standard of effective judicial protection? So long as EU acts are subject to the preliminary reference procedure, the Court of Justice remains involved, all in the operation of the complete system of legal remedies set by the Treaties.[115]

Next, to remedies. The Bundesverfassungsgericht generally focuses on the constitutional organs and their obligations under the integration obligation from the Basic Law.[116] This includes actions as well as omissions of the constitutional organs.[117] In other words, because constitutional organs under the Basic Law have a responsibility towards European integration (*Integrationsverantwortung*), individuals must be able to exercise their influence through their right to vote. In the event that constitutional organs detract from electoral legitimation and exceed their integration mandate, individuals have legal claims against them. In *Gauweiler*, the Bundesverfassungsgericht accepted the interpretation of the Court of Justice – there were thus no remedies to be ordered.

In *Weiss*, however, a peculiar novelty took place in respect of remedies. First, the Bundesverfassungsgericht repeated its jurisprudence on the constitutional review in relation to acts of EU law.[118] The Bundesverfassungsgericht therefore declared the complaints admissible only insofar as they are directed against the omission of the constitutional organs to take action.[119] Given that the PSPP was in the eyes of the German court an act outside the competences

[114] Cases 2 BvR 859/15, 2 BvR 980/16, 2 BvR 2006/15, 2 BvR 1651/15 *Weiss* (Judgment) (n 54) [86].

[115] Case 294/83 *Les Verts* EU:C:1986:166 [23].

[116] See, for example, Case 2 BvR 2/08 *Lisbon Treaty* Judgment of 30 June 2009 [240]. See also Case 2 BvR 2728/13 *Gauweiler* (Judgment) (n 40) [143]; Cases 2 BvR 859/15, 2 BvR 980/16, 2 BvR 2006/15, 2 BvR 1651/15 *Weiss* (Judgment) (n 54) [110].

[117] Cases 2 BvR 859/15, 2 BvR 980/16, 2 BvR 2006/15, 2 BvR 1651/15 *Weiss* (Judgment) (n 54) [86].

[118] ibid [89].

[119] ibid [85].

of the ECB, this required a remedy under the Basic Law. Yet, the ECB is outside the authority of the Bundesverfassungsgericht, as it should also be independent from any instruction coming from another EU institution or Member State, under Article 130 TFEU. An indirect route was therefore necessary:

> As the PSPP constitutes an ultra vires act, given the ECB's failure to substantiate that the programme is proportionate, their responsibility with regard to European integration (Integrationsverantwortung) requires the Federal Government and the Bundestag to take steps seeking to ensure that the ECB conducts a proportionality assessment in relation to the PSPP. This duty does not conflict with the independence afforded both the ECB and the Bundesbank (Art. 130, Art. 282 TFEU, Art. 88(2) GG), as was already decided by the Second Senate. The Federal Government and the Bundestag must clearly communicate their legal view to the ECB or take other steps to ensure that conformity with the Treaties is restored.
>
> This applies accordingly with regard to the reinvestments under the PSPP that began on 1 January 2019 and the restart of the programme as of 1 November 2019 (cf. Decision of the ECB Governing Council of 12 September 2019). In this respect, the competent constitutional organs also have a duty to continue monitoring the decisions of the Eurosystem on the purchases of government bonds under the PSPP and use the means at their disposal to ensure that the ESCB stays within its mandate.[120]

The Bundesverfassungsgericht is treating ECB independence in the same cavalier manner we witnessed when the Court of Justice dealt with the ECB's duty to state reasons. We are simply to take them for their word: here, Article 130 TFEU would not be breached simply because the Bundesverfassungsgericht said so. Should the German constitutional organs fail in their obligation to put the ECB in its place when it comes to proportionality of the PSPP within three months, the Bundesbank would be prohibited from participating in the PSPP. The German court was thus willing to kill two EU law obligations with one stone: the independence of the ECB and the participation of the Bundesbank in the ESCB. As we now know, this did not materialise, given that the ECB exceptionally decided to comply with the request of the Bundesverfassungsgericht. Whether that action of the ECB was a breach of Article 130 TFEU is a question we will never know the answer to. This is all the more the case taking into account that the Governing Council of the ECB is supposed to ensure that national law

[120] ibid [232]–[233].

requirements imposed on the central banks do not go against their functions under the ESCB. A score of unanswered questions persist. Given, however, the already significant status of central bank independence under EU law, perhaps it is better they remain unanswered.

4.4.2 *Solidarity and Equality*

As was the case with the Court of Justice, the Bundesverfassungsgericht also omitted any reference to the principles of solidarity or equality. This means we are to discern the approach to the common interest indirectly: from its approach to what the ECB is required to do when balancing different interests and from its findings on risk-sharing. These two assessments took place in the context of *ultra vires* review, and a brief introduction into its operation is thus due. To declare a measure outside of EU competence, the existing jurisprudence of the German court sets a significant number of hurdles, formulated in the *Honeywell* decision.[121] The logic of these conditions is to maintain competence control a task shared and coordinated with the Court of Justice. In so doing, first, no other court in Germany except the Bundesverfassungsgericht can perform *ultra vires* review; second, a preliminary reference must be submitted to the Court of Justice prior to making a final decision; and third, the Court of Justice enjoys a tolerance of error in its judgment. Only after these requirements are met, the Bundesverfassungsgericht applies the substantive criteria for competence control by testing whether an EU act represents a 'manifest transgression' in an area that is 'highly significant' in the division of competences between the EU and its Member States.[122] In so doing, the Bundesverfassungsgericht explicitly acknowledges the 'precedence of application' of EU law.[123]

As already pointed to in the discussion on proportionality at the EU level,[124] controlling a possible transgression of the principle of conferral boils down to, in essence, a necessity analysis. In other words, the question is whether the constitutional organs *went beyond* what was allowed under the principle of conferral.[125] In so doing, they therefore exceed the democratic legitimation

[121] Case 2 BvR 2661/06 *Honeywell* Order of 6 July 2010.

[122] ibid [56], [60]–[61].

[123] Case 2 BvR 2728/13 *Gauweiler* (Judgment) (n 40) [146].

[124] Section 4.3.2.

[125] This is, according to the Bundesverfassungsgericht, what distinguishes *ultra vires* from identity review: the latter does not ask about the degree of a certain transgression, but rather whether an area that is excluded from European integration altogether was in fact regulated at the EU level. Case 2 BvR 2728/13 *Gauweiler* (Judgment) (n 40) [153].

granted to them by the citizens. If we compare the weight given to citizens' interests by the German court and the framework of political equality in achieving the common interest, the former focuses on the imperative that citizens are 'not subjected to a political power that they cannot escape and that they cannot in principle freely and equally choose in respect of persons and subject-matter'.[126] Still, this obligation appears limited to its procedural aspect: that democratic legitimation be given through elections. There is no monitoring of the content of what might be termed as the common interest, what is relevant is participation in democratic processes.[127]

In reviewing whether the ECB complied with its mandate and the aims it is supposed to achieve under the Treaties, the Bundesverfassungsgericht criticised the Court of Justice not only for accepting at face value the ECB's claims concerning the OMT's aims,[128] but also for assessing them individually, instead of conducting an 'overall evaluation'.[129] Yet, it assumed that the Court of Justice will hold the ECB to strict scrutiny in terms of the requirements of limits to monetary policy. It is central that Member States do not acquire the certainty that their bonds would be purchased, that they continue to comply with macroeconomic adjustment programmes and conditionality, and that the bond buying programme remains temporary.[130] In this way, the potential of a default and the ultimate risk-sharing between Member States would be negligible, but in any event, constitutional organs in Germany are required to approve individually any measure that involves a liability for the budget.[131] These conditions became central for the *ultra vires* finding the Bundesverfassungsgericht later made concerning the PSPP.

In conducting the *ultra vires* review in respect of the PSPP, the Bundesverfassungsgericht focused on two main issues: first, whether by adopting it, the ECB had overstepped its mandate by breaching the principle of proportionality and, consequently, whether it had infringed on the principle of conferral.[132] Here, the balancing of interests will become relevant, and we will see that the common interest for the Bundesverfassungsgericht regrettably remains one limited to Germany. The second relevant issue is the analysis of possible risk-sharing between the central banks of the eurozone, creating the

[126] ibid [166].
[127] ibid [126].
[128] ibid [183]–[184].
[129] ibid [190].
[130] ibid [196], [199], [202], [204].
[131] ibid [213]–[214], [219].
[132] Cases 2 BvR 859/15, 2 BvR 980/16, 2 BvR 2006/15, 2 BvR 1651/15 *Weiss* (Judgment) (n 54) [117]–[178].

possibility of a transfer union and the liability of Member States for each other's debts.[133] Here, no red lines have been crossed by the ECB, but a warning remains in the form of constitutional identity: no risk-sharing is possible under the Treaties as they stand.

On the first point, for determining whether the ECB had overstepped its mandate in a qualified manner, the Bundesverfassungsgericht explicitly did not rely on the findings of the Court of Justice in *Weiss*. According to the German court, the judgment itself represents an *ultra vires* act and does not, as a consequence, bind it in its review.[134] The German court instead argued that the proportionality review as exercised by the Court of Justice neutralises the principle of proportionality's function to protect Member State competence.[135]

Specifically, the Bundesverfassungsgericht highlighted that the Court of Justice had limited its review to the statement that the ECB had not committed a manifest error of assessment due its economic expertise when designing the PSPP.[136] The main point of criticism concerns the failure of the Court of Justice to consider the economic policy effects of the PSPP.[137] The justification for this brings us closer to the common interest: if we analyse the economic policy effects of the PSPP, it would become possible to determine the competing interests that the ECB was supposed to balance against each other. Or to put it differently, had the ECB conducted merely monetary policy, such highly politicised questions would not even be put before the ECB. The failure to take economic policy effects into account and the relaxed approach to separating the economic and monetary policy by the Court of Justice led the Bundesverfassungsgericht to the conclusion that there was no meaningful competence review of the ECB's action at the EU level.[138] The imperative that this be done is in the eyes of the German court at the heart of proportionality review.[139] Instead, the approach of the Court of Justice allowed the ECB to choose any means it deemed adequate to reach its monetary policy goal, without having to balance the beneficial effects and collateral damage of the measure in question.[140] In the Bundesverfassungsgericht's view, this conflicts with the ECB's limited

133 ibid [222].
134 ibid [116].
135 ibid [123].
136 ibid [129]–[131].
137 ibid [138]–[145].
138 ibid [140]–[142].
139 ibid [133].
140 ibid [140].

democratic legitimation, which would require its mandate to be narrowly defined.[141]

Furthermore, the Bundesverfassungsgericht took issue with the lack of *stricto sensu* balancing in the analysis of the Court of Justice, thus warranting the application of its own proportionality test. Yet, it had not applied the *stricto sensu* stage itself either, instead stating that 'it would have been incumbent for the ECB' to do so.[142] Taking into account the emphasis of the German court on the ECB's limited mandate and insufficient democratic legitimation,[143] it appears counter-intuitive that the ECB should do so.[144] The Bundesverfassungsgericht devoted considerable attention to analysing the difference in the proportionality test developed by the Court of Justice and itself respectively, opting unsurprisingly to favour its own standard. The German court has in consequence been accused of parochialism,[145] and 'framing a European legal question largely in terms of German constitutional law'.[146] The German court engaged in an analysis of how the test is applied in other Member States,[147] then explained to the Court of Justice its own proportionality test,[148] and concluded it is deficient for the delimitation of competences between the EU and the national level.[149] A similar approach was subject to critique on the occasion of the Bundesverfassungsgericht's order in *Mr R*[150] when refusing to execute a European Arrest Warrant without submitting a preliminary reference to the Court of Justice.[151]

141 ibid [144].
142 ibid [176].
143 ibid [136].
144 Davies rightly points out that this would result in the ECB concluding that, despite its mandate to achieve price stability, it would sometimes need to abandon that aim as ultimately too costly in relation to its benefits. G Davies, 'The German Constitutional Court Decides Price Stability May Not Be Worth Its Price' 20 May 2020, European Law Blog. Available at <https://europeanlawblog.eu/2020/05/21/the-german-federal-supreme-court-decides-price-stability-may-not-be-worth-its-price/>.
145 T Marzal, 'Is the BVerfG PSPP Decision "Simply Not Comprehensible"?' 9 May 2020, Verfassungsblog. Available at <https://verfassungsblog.de/is-the-bverfg-pspp-decision-simply-not-comprehensible/>.
146 Wendel (n 85) 993.
147 Cases 2 BvR 859/15, 2 BvR 980/16, 2 BvR 2006/15, 2 BvR 1651/15 *Weiss* (Judgment) (n 54) [125].
148 ibid [126].
149 ibid [127], [133], [138].
150 Case 2 BvR 2735/14 *Mr R*. Order of 15 December 2015.
151 J Nowag, 'EU Law, Constitutional Identity, and Human Dignity: A Toxic Mix? Bundesverfassungsgericht: *Mr R* 2 BvR 2735/14, *Mr R v Order of the Oberlandesgericht Düsseldorf* Order of the Bundesverfassungsgericht (Second Senate) of 15 December 2015, DE:BVerfG:2015:rs20151215.2bvr273514' (2016) 53(5) *Common Market Law Review* 1441.

There is a further parochialism issue in the German decision, one far more detrimental to the common interest and the political equality of EU citizens. The Bundesverfassungsgericht saw it fit to perform its own proportionality review of the PSPP. For the Bundesverfassungsgericht, the decisions of the ECB lack the information it would need to fulfil this task, as they do not give evidence of whether the ECB has considered and balanced the effects of the PSPP.[152] According to the German court, the oral proceedings have shown, however, that there are several negative effects to the PSPP, which should have been taken into consideration by the ECB. For instance, it has been shown that there is a risk that Member States will be discouraged to implement consolidation measures,[153] and there is a risk of losses for private savings.[154] Furthermore, the fact that the volume of the programme increases overtime renders the balancing of these effects all the more necessary.[155] However, the Bundesverfassungsgericht focused only on the interests of German citizens. It entirely disregarded the possibility of contagion in the eurozone, or the eventuality that the consequences of one Member State defaulting may be felt across different Member States. It finally also completely neglected that the interests of, for example, savers or pensioners, need not be perfectly aligned *within* a single Member State. Endorsing the *Weiss* judgment approach would mean completely to deprive EU citizens of connection beyond their own Member State. In sum, the Bundesverfassungsgericht therefore concluded that the failure of the ECB to state reasons on the balancing of interests is in breach of the principle of proportionality. As a result, the PSPP decisions were not covered by the ECB's mandate and were *ultra vires*.[156]

Finally, the Bundesverfassungsgericht turned to whether the PSPP decisions infringe on the prohibition of monetary financing laid down in Article 123 TFEU. The Bundesverfassungsgericht accepted the safeguards established in *Gauweiler* to guarantee compliance with Article 123 TFEU.[157] Nevertheless, the German court criticised the way these safeguards were examined in *Weiss*, as the Court of Justice has neither scrutinised them closely nor explored whether there were circumstances capable of disproving their actual effectiveness. The Bundesverfassungsgericht, therefore, argued that this

[152] Cases 2 BvR 859/15, 2 BvR 980/16, 2 BvR 2006/15, 2 BvR 1651/15 *Weiss* (Judgment) (n 54) [169], [176].
[153] ibid [170].
[154] ibid [169]–[175].
[155] ibid [169].
[156] ibid [177].
[157] ibid [183].

approach prevented meaningful judicial review.[158] These worries led to the final announcement of a red line for what the Basic Law would allow in terms of economic integration:[159] if the scheme of allocation of risks would redistribute sovereign debts among Member States.[160] After stating that such a redistribution would represent an assumption of liability illegal under the Basic Law,[161] the German court found that the ECB's decisions cannot violate Germany's constitutional identity. As it is prohibited by primary law, such a redistribution cannot, in fact, currently take place.[162] This once again cements the position of the Bundesverfassungsgericht as an exclusively Germany-oriented court without the ability to see and understand the interconnections inherent in the EMU.

4.5 ON JUDICIAL INTERACTIONS

If any Member State could readily invoke the authority to decide, through its own courts, on the validity of EU acts, this could undermine the precedence of application accorded to EU law and jeopardise its uniform application. Yet if the Member States were to completely refrain from conducting any kind of *ultra vires* review, they would grant EU organs exclusive authority over the Treaties even in cases where the EU adopts a legal interpretation that would essentially amount to a treaty amendment or an expansion of its competences.[163]

Voilà, the well-known conundrum of the European Union's constitutional set-up digested in one paragraph: who has the final say on the limits of EU competence? Because the principle of conferral is a shared concept of EU and national constitutional law,[164] its application is likewise shared between EU and national courts, inevitably creating conditions for the possibility of a constitutional conflict. In the EMU, it is in monetary policy that competence control materialised itself in judicial interactions most prominently,[165] thus

[158] ibid [184].
[159] The Bundesverfassungsgericht examined that issue in the context of its fifth preliminary question to the Court of Justice, which the latter found hypothetical and thus inadmissible. See Case C-493/17 *Weiss* (n 43) [166].
[160] Cases 2 BvR 859/15, 2 BvR 980/16, 2 BvR 2006/15, 2 BvR 1651/15 *Weiss* (Judgment) (n 54) [222].
[161] ibid [227].
[162] ibid [228].
[163] ibid [111].
[164] Case 2 BVerfG 2/08 *Lisbon Treaty* (n 116) [234]; Cases 2 BvR 859/15, 2 BvR 980/16, 2 BvR 2006/15, 2 BvR 1651/15 *Weiss* (Judgment) (n 54) [158].
[165] In addition to this, the Bundesverfassungsgericht also reviewed the SSM, however, without submitting a preliminary reference to the Court of Justice. See Chapter 5, Section 5.4.

resulting in specific consequences for the legal accountability of the ECB. *Ultra vires* review was first introduced in the *Maastricht* judgment of the Bundesverfassungsgericht, widely considered the foremother of constitutional pluralism.[166] That court maintained the thesis that Member States are the 'Masters of the Treaties',[167] that are 'continuously breathing life into the Treaty'.[168] This meant that primacy of EU law only extends to acts within *vires*,[169] and it was the Bundesverfassungsgericht which retained the right to control the division between *intra* and *ultra vires*.

Weiss, where competence control resulted in the rejection of the Court of Justice's decision, is the second preliminary reference submitted by the Bundesverfassungsgericht. Constitutional courts across the EU are in general rarely submitting preliminary references, opting rather for indirect procedural routes to send their message across,[170] with the notable exception of the Belgian Constitutional Court.[171] One reason is that the very structure of the preliminary reference procedure leaves the constitutional court with only the most extreme option of disregarding the decision of the Court of Justice should it find it contrary to the national constitution. Understandably, the Court of Justice has consistently underlined the importance of judicial cooperation put into effect through the preliminary reference procedure.[172] Judicial interactions in the EU bring about important benefits and have through the history of European integration pushed the Court of Justice to increase its standards when reviewing EU action.[173] From a *de lege ferenda* perspective, visible from judicial interactions in monetary policy, national courts can provide the impetus for a substantive review of ECB action to be

[166] N MacCormick, 'The Maastricht-Urteil: Sovereignty Now' (1995) 1(3) *European Law Journal* 259.

[167] Cases 2 BvR 2134/92 and 2159/92 *Maastricht Treaty* Judgment of 12 October 1993 [II.a)].

[168] ibid [II.d).2.1].

[169] J Kokott, 'Report on Germany' in A-M Slaughter, A Stone Sweet and J H H Weiler (eds), *The European Court and National Courts, Doctrine and Jurisprudence: Legal Change in Its Social Context* (Hart 1998) 81.

[170] For an analysis, see A Bobić, 'Constitutional Pluralism Is Not Dead: An Analysis of Interactions between the European Court of Justice and Constitutional Courts of Member States' (2017) 18(6) *German Law Journal* 1395; G Martinico, 'Judging in the Multilevel Legal Order: Exploring the Techniques of "Hidden Dialogue"' (2010) 21 *King's College Law Journal* 257.

[171] Leading with forty-five preliminary references submitted. Court of Justice, 2021 Annual Report on Judicial Activity, available at <https://curia.europa.eu/jcms/upload/docs/application/pdf/2022-07/qd-ap-22-001-en-n.pdf> 254.

[172] For example, Case 283/81 *Cilfit* EU:C:1982:335 [7].

[173] The area of fundamental rights review is the obvious suspect for describing how the Bundesverfassungsgericht pressured the Court of Justice into applying a higher standard for fundamental rights review. See also A Bobić, *The Jurisprudence of Constitutional Conflict in the European Union* (Oxford University Press 2022) 177–187.

carried out by EU courts. Using judicial review and the preliminary reference procedure to relocate the individual in the EMU (a policy field otherwise dominated by states and EU institutions) could yet constitute a major contribution of judicial review.

Is the judicial review of monetary policy decisions an illustration of fruitful judicial interactions? Not quite. The German court, in my opinion, did not stick to its own rules on competence control, as it did not clarify the concept of 'a competence highly significant in the structure of the division of competences' While constitutional identity from Article 79(3) of the Basic Law is excluded from European integration altogether,[174] little to nothing is known about the concept of 'highly significant'. To demand of the Bundesverfassungsgericht more clearly to define this boundary would be a welcome development.

Furthermore, the Bundesverfassungsgericht gave no signal on how important the proportionality test was in its preliminary reference.[175] By omitting this fairly crucial information, it is difficult to talk about a genuinely open dialogue with the Court of Justice.[176] This runs counter to its statement in *Gauweiler* that there is an obligation to 'respect judicial development of the law by the Court of Justice even when the Court of Justice adopts a view against which weighty arguments could be made'.[177] The Bundesverfassungsgericht, in its Order for reference in *Weiss*,[178] placed a great deal of emphasis on the fact that the Court of Justice should remain consistent with the standards from *Gauweiler*.[179] And yet, the German court itself behaved inconsistently: the *stricto sensu* step of the proportionality test touted as central to the review of the PSPP was only introduced in the response to the decision of the Court of Justice, whereas no such expectation was hinted at in the order for preliminary reference itself, and even less so in the *Gauweiler* litigation. The point is not that this excuses the Court of Justice from carrying out a meaningful review of ECB's quantitative easing programmes. It is rather that judicial interactions, if they are to be fruitful, should be carried out in the spirit of mutual respect and sincere cooperation.

In the structure of constitutional pluralism, mutual respect and sincere cooperation play a central role in incrementally managing interpretative differences and ensuring the constructive nature of a possible constitutional

[174] Case 2 BVerfG 2/08 *Lisbon Treaty* (n 116) [240]–[241].
[175] Editorial Comments (n 84) 971.
[176] Wendel (n 85) 987.
[177] Case 2 BvR 2728/13 *Gauweiler* (Judgment) (n 35) [161].
[178] Cases 2 BvR 859/15, 2 BvR 980/16, 2 BvR 2006/15, 2 BvR 1651/15 *Weiss* (Order) (n 97) [79].
[179] ibid [180], [193], [205].

conflict ensuing.[180] The preliminary reference procedure enables national courts to act as peer-reviewers ensuring the coherence of judicial review at the EU level. By holding the Court of Justice to its standards, national courts are able to create long-term legitimate expectations, and ultimately, contribute to the uniformity and coherence of EU law (an important consideration for all those who rely on ECB action). The way in which proportionality was introduced in *Weiss* can hardly be referred to as a role model for this approach. Language and expressions used by constitutional courts and the Court of Justice are of importance for how constitutional conflict and its resolution are managed, and there is a coherence in this sense among different constitutional courts in the EU.[181] The allegation of the Bundesverfassungsgericht that the judgment of the Court of Justice is 'simply not comprehensible'[182] is in that sense not the sort of language that should be employed between courts that have for so long interacted in a constructive manner, enhancing the EU's constitutional sphere. It departs from mutual respect and sincere cooperation and unnecessarily distracts from the issues that can constructively be addressed through constitutional conflict.

In addition, the Court of Justice on its part provided very little input as regards a possible rejection of its decision by the Bundesverfassungsgericht, restating its well-established case law on the binding nature of preliminary rulings,[183] despite the possibility left open in the reference to disregard a decision contrary to German constitutional identity. From the perspective of avoiding conflict, this tactic from *Gauweiler* has proven useful, as any interference by the Court of Justice in sensitive national constitutional matters may ultimately breach the obligation of the EU to respect national identities of Member States under Article 4(2) TEU. Nevertheless, taking into consideration that the Bundesverfassungsgericht has now twice raised serious concerns, emphasising the importance of German constitutional identity relating to the budgetary powers of the Bundestag, the Court of Justice will at a certain point need to define the room for manoeuvre available to the ECB

[180] M Goldmann, 'Constitutional Pluralism as Mutually Assured Discretion: The Court of Justice, the German Federal Constitutional Court, and the ECB' (2016) 23(1) *Maastricht Journal of European and Comparative Law* 119, 128; L D Spieker, 'Framing and Managing Constitutional Identity Conflicts: How to Stabilize the Modus Vivendi between the Court of Justice and National Constitutional Courts' (2020) 57(2) *Common Market Law Review* 361, 381; Bobić (n 173).

[181] Bobić (n 170) 1414–1423.

[182] Cases 2 BvR 859/15, 2 BvR 980/16, 2 BvR 2006/15, 2 BvR 1651/15 *Weiss* (Judgment) (n 54) [116], [153].

[183] Case C-493/17 *Weiss* (n 43) [19].

when implementing large-scale programmes such as the PSPP at the expense of national budgetary powers.

Part of academic reactions to the German decision in *Weiss* characterise the German decision as breaching the rule of law.[184] This is, in my view, a mistake. Hitherto, there is nothing in the decision of the Bundesverfassungsgericht that questions the judicial independence of the Court of Justice, nor do we have reason to assume that the judges of the Bundesverfassungsgericht itself were biased or partial. In my view, shielding the Court of Justice from any sort of criticism by national courts would gravely disregard the structural properties of judicial cooperation in the EU, which moves forward through constructive conflict.[185] Further, it also neglects the constitutional set-up of the EU, which does not contain a federal supremacy clause, nor does it subsume national constitutional orders. It is, however, far-fetched to praise the Bundesverfassungsgericht for single-handedly increasing the accountability of the ECB, as its reasoning does not comply with its usual adherence to mutual respect towards and sincere cooperation with the Court of Justice.

[184] See, for example, Editorial Comments (n 84) 966.

[185] A Bobić, 'Constructive versus Destructive Conflict: Taking Stock of the Recent Constitutional Jurisprudence in the EU' (2020) 22 *Cambridge Yearbook of European Legal Studies* 60.

5

The Single Supervisory Mechanism

5.1 INTRODUCTION

This case study is somewhat specific in terms of the addressees of the Single Supervisory Mechanism (SSM), these being banks and other financial institutions under the supervision of the ECB and national competent authorities (NCAs). Critics might argue that because banks were at the source of the crisis,[1] any attempt at improving their position in the system of legal accountability can hardly be seen as supportive of political equality of citizens. Can one really conceive of a role for the principles of solidarity and equality in banking supervision? Further still, can increasing the responsiveness of decision-makers towards banks contribute to the political equality of citizens? I agree that taking the road to this conclusion may involve some detours. Necessarily, the analysis of the consequences for accountability and the individual striving for political equality will, to a certain extent, appear indirect. In other words, what happens to banks and their ability to challenge the decisions of the ECB and national competent authorities before EU and national courts appears not to have an immediate impact on the ability of individuals to hold decision-makers in the EMU to account.

Why, then, including the SSM? As I hope to make clear in this chapter, the SSM's lack of immediate application to individuals does not make its impact any less important. Its peculiar legal set-up, organisation, and operation, all of which arguably stem from the shock of the financial crisis,[2] illustrates the inherent flexibility of the Treaty framework to adjust to exogenous shocks and exceptional circumstances. Legal experimentalism is thus undoubtedly the

[1] See, for example, Opinion of Advocate General Hogan in Case C-450/17 P *Landeskreditbank Baden-Württemberg* EU:C:2018:982 [1].

[2] D Howarth and L Quaglia, 'Internationalised Banking, Alternative Banks and the Single Supervisory Mechanism' (2016) 39 *West European Politics* 438.

shared common denominator of the SSM and earlier case studies in this book. The three case studies further share economic salience and impact in the Eurozone.[3] Centrally for the purposes of this book, the SSM brought about significant accountability distortions. The way that courts review decisions in this area thus undoubtedly carries consequences for the individual.

The legal experimentalism in the SSM that created accountability distortions may be seen as less haphazard than the solutions in financial assistance mechanisms and unconventional monetary policy programmes of the ECB. Prudential supervision is, under the SSM Regulation, an exclusive task for the ECB.[4] However, due to a lack of unanimous support in the legislative procedure,[5] this exclusive competence is unrestrained only for significant entities. Prudential supervision of less significant entities[6] is a task for national competent authorities.[7] The resulting composite structure of prudential supervision muddled the accountability routes available thus far.[8] Complicating matters further, the ECB has the power to apply national law[9] and EU courts accordingly the power exclusively to review national decisions in certain situations.[10] Three major themes thus arise: first, when the ECB applies national law, does it do so in the common interest of the EU or in the interest of the Member State that enacted that national law? Second, when an ECB decision is reviewed before the EU courts, do they also become competent to

3 As Schammo reports, significant entities that the SSM Regulation brought under direct supervision of the ECB account for almost 82 per cent of banking assets in the Eurozone. P Schammo, 'Institutional Change in the Banking Union: The Case of the Single Supervisory Mechanism' (2021) 40(1) *Yearbook of European Law* 265, 288, 304.

4 Article 4(1) of Council Regulation (EU) No 1024/2013 of 15 October 2013 conferring specific tasks on the European Central Bank concerning policies relating to the prudential supervision of credit institutions (OJ 2013 L 287) 63 (SSM Regulation). This statement is, as will become obvious in the analysis below, simple and straightforward only at first glance.

5 Schammo (n 3) 282.

6 Article 6(4) of the SSM Regulation provides criteria for determining what is a less significant institution. The final say on the significant/less significant characterisation lies with the ECB.

7 Article 6 of the SSM Regulation. It should be mentioned that a reclassification of an entity moves in both directions: from a significant to a less significant one and vice versa. In both cases, the ECB makes the final decision. For more details, see Section 5.2.

8 A Karagianni and M Scholten, 'Accountability Gaps in the Single Supervisory Mechanism Framework' (2018) 34(2) *Utrecht Journal of International and European Law* 185. For a more optimistic view, see M Goldmann, 'The Case for Intra-Executive Accountability in the Banking Union' in M Dawson (ed), *Towards Substantive Accountability in EU Economic Governance* (Cambridge University Press, forthcoming 2023).

9 Article 4(3) of the SSM Regulation.

10 Case C-219/17 *Berlusconi* EU:C:2018:1023 [47]. These concern national preparatory acts within the meaning of Article 4(1)(c) and Article 15 of the SSM Regulation.

interpret and apply the national law that the ECB relied on? Finally, what is left for the national courts to review in the structure of the SSM?

In addition to its composite structure, the SSM Regulation is characterised by a different kind of legal experimentalism due to the changes, often novel and unconventional, of the scope and manner of judicial review. More obviously than in the previous two case studies, the enforcement of the SSM by the ECB and national competent authorities resulted in unconventional judicial solutions and novel relationships between EU and national courts. It may even be said that the SSM framework left open a number of interpretative questions that were left to the courts to deal with for lack of another actor.[11] Thus, this legal regime lends itself remarkably well for testing the accountability framework presented in Chapter 1: this chapter will tackle the wiggle room available to the courts under analysis for rethinking the relationship between the principles of equality and solidarity, in respect of access, remedies, and interpretation of the common interest.

This chapter is structured as follows. In the next section I will present the legal framework of the SSM and the solutions chosen for its organisation and operation. This exercise will both aid our reading of the case law to come and highlight a number of accountability distortions problematic for the political equality of citizens. In Section 5.3, I will focus on judicial review concerning the SSM at the EU level, which will include the jurisprudence of the General Court and the Court of Justice. Section 5.4 will repeat this exercise in respect of the national level. In both sections, I will follow the approach taken in the previous two case studies and look specifically at how courts dealt with questions of access, remedies, and any possible interpretation of the principles of equality and solidarity. The final section of this chapter will then reflect upon the role that judicial interactions play in delivering accountability within the SSM.

5.2 THE LEGAL FRAMEWORK OF THE SSM

The first pillar of the Banking Union,[12] banking supervision, was created by the SSM Regulation that entered into force in 2014. The SSM Regulation

[11] Schammo (n 3) 289, 291.

[12] The second pillar of the Banking Union is the Single Resolution Mechanism (SRM), a system for effective and efficient resolution of non-viable credit institutions. The third pillar of the Banking Union, the European Deposit Insurance Scheme (EDIS), is still in the making. For more information, see <www.consilium.europa.eu/en/policies/banking-union/>.

was based on the competence for harmonising[13] prudential supervision in Article 127(6) TFEU.[14] The principal aim of the SSM is

> ensuring the safety and soundness of credit institutions and the stability of the financial system of the Union as well as of individual participating Member States and the unity and integrity of the internal market, thereby ensuring also the protection of depositors and improving the functioning of the internal market, in accordance with the single rulebook for financial services in the Union.[15]

Further details on the operation of the SSM were set out in the ECB SSM Framework Regulation.[16] The basic organisational principle of the SSM Regulation can be summarised as follows: the ECB supervises significant entities, whereas the supervision of less significant entities is left to national competent authorities.[17] The final decision on the significant character of an entity lies with the ECB,[18] based on the criteria for distinction from Article 6 of the SSM Regulation.[19] Crucially, the ECB has the power to take on the supervision of an entity having hitherto been classified as less significant[20] and vice versa.[21] The SSM Regulation is not explicit on the nature of ECB's powers in the supervisory field: it is inconclusive as to whether the ECB is the exclusive power holder who simply delegates tasks to national competent

[13] The literature underlines that using this legal basis did not resolve the nature of such harmonisation, namely, whether it forms part of the exclusive Union competence in monetary policy (given that Article 127(6) TFEU is positioned in the monetary policy chapter of the TFEU). See B Wolfers and T Voland, 'Level the Playing Field: The New Supervision of Credit Institutions by the European Central Bank' (2014) 51(5) *Common Market Law Review* 1463; T Tridimas, 'The Constitutional Dimension of Banking Union' in S Grundmann and H-W Micklitz, *The European Banking Union and Constitution–Beacon for Advanced Integration or Death-Knell for Democracy* (Hart 2019) 36–38.

[14] 'The Council, acting by means of regulations in accordance with a special legislative procedure, may unanimously, and after consulting the European Parliament and the European Central Bank, confer specific tasks upon the European Central Bank concerning policies relating to the prudential supervision of credit institutions and other financial institutions with the exception of insurance undertakings.'

[15] Recital 30 of the SSM Regulation. See also Recitals 16, 17, 27, 65, 87, and Article 1(1) of the SSM Regulation.

[16] Regulation (EU) No 468/2014 of the European Central Bank of 16 April 2014 establishing the framework for cooperation within the Single Supervisory Mechanism between the European Central Bank and national competent authorities and with national designated authorities (ECB/2014/17) (OJ 2014 L 141) 1 (SSM Framework Regulation).

[17] Article 6(4) of the SSM Regulation.

[18] Recitals 39–41 of the SSM Regulation.

[19] Detailed further in Part IV of the SSM Framework Regulation.

[20] See Article 6(4), subparagraphs (3)–(7) of the SSM Regulation.

[21] Article 6(4), subparagraphs (1) and (2) of the SSM Regulation.

authorities, or they share tasks along the dividing line of significance. The Court of Justice confirmed the former in *Landeskreditbank*: supervisory powers of the ECB are exclusive and national competent authorities are assisting the ECB in respect of less significant credit institutions.[22]

Supervisory tasks conferred upon the ECB are detailed in Article 4 of the SSM Regulation. These are shared with national competent authorities according to the significant/less significant division, save for the ECB's exclusive powers concerning the authorisation of credit institutions and its withdrawal[23] and the assessment of notifications of the acquisition and disposal of qualifying holdings in credit institutions (except in the case of a bank resolution).[24] A further exception to the significant/less significant division of tasks can be found in Article 6(5) of the SSM Regulation, under which certain powers remain with the ECB, such as, for example, issuing guidelines, regulations, or general instructions to national competent authorities so as to ensure the consistency of supervisory outcomes.

In carrying out their respective tasks under the SSM Regulation, the relationship between the ECB and national competent authorities is one of cooperation in good faith and continuous exchange of relevant information.[25] The relationship of cooperation between the ECB and national competent authorities is designed in an especially interesting way[26] under the SSM

[22] Case C-450/17 P *Landeskreditbank* EU:C:2019:372 [38]–[41]. I will come back to this decision in more detail in Section 5.3.2.

[23] Defined in Article 14 and reserved to the ECB under Article 6(4) of the SSM Regulation.

[24] Defined in Article 15 and reserved to the ECB under Article 6(4) of the SSM Regulation. See also Article 6(6) of the SSM Regulation.

[25] Article 6(2) of the SSM Regulation.

[26] To be clear, I am merely a fish in the vast sea of legal commentators writing about this novel solution. For a few examples, see A Witte, 'The Application of National Banking Supervision Law by the ECB: Three Parallel Modes of Executing EU Law?' (2014) 21 *Maastricht Journal of European and Comparative Law* 89; L Boucon and D Jaros, 'The Application of National Law by the European Central Bank within the EU Banking Union's Single Supervisory Mechanism: A New Mode of European Integration?' (2018) 10 *European Journal of Legal Studies* 155; F Coman-Kund and F Amtenbrink, 'On the Scope and Limits of the Application of National Law by the European Central Bank within the Single Supervisory Mechanism' (2018) 33 *Banking & Finance Law Review* 133; E Gagliardi and L Wissink, 'Ensuring Effective Judicial Protection in Case of ECB Decisions Based on National Law' (2020) 13 *Review of European Administrative Law* 13; A Biondi and A Spano, 'The ECB and the Application of National Law in the SSM: New Yet Old . . .' (2020) 31 *European Business Law Review* 1023; F Hernández Fernández, 'The Application of National Law and Composite Procedures in the Single Supervisory Mechanism: Did the Court of Justice of the EU Find a New Van Gend en Loos?' (2021) 14(3) *Review of European Administrative Law* 5. By contrast, the novel character of this composite construct was downplayed in the Opinion of Advocate General Campos Sánchez-Bordona in Case C-219/17 *Berlusconi* EU:C:2018:502 [58]–[59].

Regulation: it is not only that these institutions share and divide supervisory and other tasks under the SSM Regulation. They also share the applicable law. This means that national competent authorities apply EU and national law, as does the ECB. Under Article 4(3) of the SSM Regulation, the ECB applies all the relevant Union law. However, given that all the relevant Union law also consists of national law implementing directives and exercising options granted by regulations, the ECB also applies that national law. Under Article 9(1), third subparagraph of the SSM Regulation, when necessary for the exercise of its supervisory tasks, the ECB will issue instructions to competent national authorities to make use of relevant powers under national law.

The ECB's need to apply and take into account national law is particularly manifest in areas where it is exclusively competent to exercise supervisory tasks regardless of the significant/less significant division. The first such situation is issuing and withdrawing authorisations to credit institutions:[27] here the ECB depends entirely on national law regulating the procedure and requirements for granting and withdrawing authorisations. The competent national authority draws up the draft decision proposing to the ECB to grant the authorisation (in the event of a negative assessment, the national authority merely submits its appraisal to the ECB). The ECB is equally dependent on national law when it comes to the assessment of qualifying holdings under Article 15 of the SSM Regulation.

This enmeshment of EU and national law within banking supervision brought about further innovations in judicial review. In the standard division of tasks between EU and national courts, the former are competent to interpret (and possibly invalidate) EU law and the same powers pertain to the latter in respect of national law. Yet, what happens when the ECB makes a decision based on the preparatory national act of the competent national authority? To complicate matters further, what if that national preparatory act is in parallel subject to judicial review at the national level, or further still, survived judicial review at the national level and the matter is considered *res judicata*? A simple conclusion answers all these questions simultaneously: the national preparatory act forms part of the final ECB decision and the consequences of this are not difficult to fathom: EU courts are exclusively competent to interpret and possibly invalidate such acts, while national courts are prevented from doing so.[28]

[27] Article 14 of the SSM Regulation.
[28] Case C-219/17 *Berlusconi* (n 10) [43]–[44], [47]–[51].

It is no wonder that legal accountability in the SSM framework deserves a case study of the EU and national judicial review given this rollercoaster of regulatory solutions. In the coming section, I will analyse decisions of the General Court and the Court of Justice, following their approach to access, remedies, and the interpretation of the principles of solidarity and equality.

5.3 JUDICIAL REVIEW AT THE EU LEVEL

5.3.1 *Access and Remedies*

The preliminary reference procedure, the foremost method of access to EU courts (or more precisely, the Court of Justice) in the area of monetary policy and financial assistance, does not dominate prudential supervision, where instead direct actions take centre stage.[29] This is, of course, resulting from the set-up of prudential supervision as described in the previous section: the ECB is centrally responsible for the supervision of significant entities and maintains the exclusive power to characterise an entity as such. These decisions necessarily then address the credit institution itself and the decision of the ECB is a challengeable act under Article 263(1) TFEU. Challenging these decisions, therefore, usually takes place before the General Court, possibly followed by an appeal before the Court of Justice.

Normally, ECB's decisions in the area of prudential supervision concern a specific entity. For example, the ECB may decide on the characterisation of an entity as significant or less significant (as in *Landeskreditbank*);[30] it may grant or revoke an authorisation to a credit institution (as in *Trasta Komercbanka*);[31] or it may approve or block the acquisition of a qualifying holding in a credit institution (as in *Berlusconi*).[32] Seeking annulment of such decisions under Article 263(4) TFEU[33] is fairly straightforward: the entity in

[29] At the time of writing, the SSM Regulation was the central subject matter of nine judgments before the Court of Justice (in others, the SSM Regulation was merely mentioned in other relevant provisions). Four of those were the result of preliminary references. In addition, the General Court dealt with twenty-six SSM cases. Of those, twenty-three deal with SSM proper (nine are currently under appeal), and three with access to documents in prudential supervision (one is currently under appeal).

[30] Case C-450/17 P *Landeskreditbank* (n 22).

[31] Joined Cases C-663/17 P, C-665/17 P and C-669/17 P *Trasta Komercbanka* EU:C:2019:923.

[32] Case C-219/17 *Berlusconi* (n 10).

[33] For an overview of the case law on direct and individual concern and its appraisal in the context of the SSM, see M Lamandini, D Ramos and J Solana, 'The European Central Bank (ECB) Powers as a Catalyst for Change in EU Law. Part 2: SSM, SRM and Fundamental Rights' (2017) 23 *Columbia Journal of European Law* 199, 248–250.

question is most certainly directly and individually concerned and will have no difficulty in triggering judicial review against such decisions of the ECB before the EU courts.[34]

The situation of less significant institutions is somewhat more complicated: while supervised by the national competent authority, as we have seen in the preceding section, some supervisory powers remain with the ECB. Either of these institutions, in addition, may be deciding on the basis of EU or national law (depending on the specific situation under the SSM Regulation). It is also often possible that such decisions are based on instructions or preparatory acts of the institution not making the final decision. A final twist comes also from the possibility that the decision of either of the institutions involves different degrees of discretion in enacting preparatory acts or instructions for the other institution. Depending on the combination of each of these factors, less significant institutions may find themselves before the national or EU courts.

Access to EU courts becomes progressively more difficult the more the powers of the ECB and national competent authorities intertwine.[35] Such are, for example, situations in which Member States implement directives or use the options offered by regulations.[36] Using options may involve supervisory or instruction powers for the ECB, which may issue such instructions to competent national authorities. It is also possible that under national law the national competent authorities retain some discretion in making decisions that

34 Türk and Xanthoulis call these the 'straightforward cases' in terms of achieving legal accountability in the SSM. They also provide a list of further administrative decisions of the ECB that pertain to this category. See A H Türk and N Xanthoulis, 'Legal Accountability of European Central Bank in Bank Supervision: A Case Study in Conceptualizing the Legal Effects of Union Acts' (2019) 26(1) *Maastricht Journal of European and Comparative Law* 151, 156.

35 What Türk and Xanthoulis label as 'hard cases'. See Türk and Xanthoulis (n 34) 159–164.

36 The regulatory framework in the area of banking regulation is the Single Rulebook, the aim of which is to 'strengthen the resilience of the banking sector across the European Union (EU) so it would be better placed to absorb economic shocks while ensuring that banks continue to finance economic activity and growth. The European Banking Authority (EBA) plays a key role in the implementation of the new Basel 3 regulatory framework in the European Union'. In respect of prudential supervision, the relevant rules are set out in the Regulation (EU) No 575/2013 of the European Parliament and of the Council of 26 June 2013 on prudential requirements for credit institutions and investment firms and amending Regulation (EU) No 648/2012 (OJ 2013 L 176) 1 and Directive 2013/36/EU of the European Parliament and of the Council of 26 June 2013 on access to the activity of credit institutions and the prudential supervision of credit institutions and investment firms, amending Directive 2002/87/EC and repealing Directives 2006/48/EC and 2006/49/EC (OJ 2013 L 176) 338. These are accompanied by a number of implementing acts. See also <www.eba.europa.eu/regulation-and-policy/implementing-basel-iii-europe>.

influence rights or obligations of credit institutions.[37] In this scenario, the threshold of Article 263(4) TFEU would not be met: the entity in question would need to turn to the national court instead. Whether the Court of Justice would assume jurisdiction to decide on the preliminary reference to review an ECB instruction or preparatory act has not yet been explicitly addressed.[38] However, it is possible to assume the answer would be yes. Let us then have a look at *Berlusconi* and *Balgarska Narodna Banka*.[39]

In *Berlusconi*, the central issue was the status of national preparatory acts that served as the basis for the ECB to block the acquisition of a qualifying holding under Article 15 of the SSM Regulation. The power of the ECB under this provision is exclusive regardless of the significance of a credit institution. Yet, the decision to oppose or not an acquisition of a qualifying holding is not possible without the use of national law following Article 4(3) of the SSM Regulation. More specifically, the requirements attached to such acquisitions are set out in national law and any such acquisition should be notified to the national competent authority.[40] The national competent authority then forwards the notification to the ECB and prepares a proposal for a decision to oppose the acquisition or not. It also assists the ECB in this process in any other way necessary.

Based on the proposal of the Italian competent authority (the Bank of Italy), the ECB decided to oppose the acquisition of a qualifying holding in a credit institution by Silvio Berlusconi. He was, prior to this acquisition attempt, found guilty of tax fraud and thus did not meet the reputation requirement required under the Italian law for acquiring qualifying holdings. In turn, this cast serious doubts with regard to the sound and prudential management of the credit institution in the future and formed the basis for the proposal of the Bank of Italy and the resulting decision of the ECB. Berlusconi challenged the national and ECB's decisions before all conceivable avenues. First, the decision of the Bank of Italy was challenged for breach of non-retroactivity, given that the requirement of good reputation entered into force after the criminal conviction and, according to Berlusconi, it should not have been taken into account. This action was successful in the second instance before the Italian Council of State.[41] Second, Berlusconi also challenged the ECB's

[37] See also Lamandini, Ramos and Solana (n 33) 250.

[38] This would also arguably depend on the interpretation of the option in question.

[39] Case C-501/18 *Balgarska Narodna Banka* EU:C:2021:249. These findings were confirmed by the Court subsequently in Case C-911/19 *Fédération bancaire française* EU:C:2021:599 [56].

[40] See Articles 85–87 of the SSM Framework Regulation for more detail.

[41] This circumstance further complicated matters for the preliminary reference procedure submitted by the Council of State, as we will see.

decision before the General Court.[42] Third, Berlusconi initiated an action for annulment of the Bank of Italy's decision before a regional administrative court. Finally, again before the Council of State, Berlusconi initiated an *azione di ottemperanza*,[43] demanding the Bank of Italy to comply with the abovementioned judgment concerning the breach of non-retroactivity.

Complexity reached its peak in this fourth procedure. At its centre were two issues: first, the relationship between decisions and procedures before the Bank of Italy and the ECB, and second, the role the Council of State's earlier judgment concerning the breach of non-retroactivity by the Bank of Italy. The matter reached the Court of Justice by way of a preliminary reference. First, the Council of State asked whether Article 263 TFEU may be used to challenge procedures, preparatory acts, and non-binding proposals of the national competent authorities in the area of prudential supervision. Next, if such jurisdiction is established, what role, if any, does the previous final judgment of a national court play?

The Advocate General, relying on the Court's previous decisions in *Borelli*[44] and *Sweden v Commission*,[45] found that the relevant criterion for determining jurisdiction to review national preparatory acts corresponds to the location of the final decision-making power. In other words, what is relevant is whether the national preparatory act is binding on the EU authority making the final decision. Given that the approval of acquisition of qualifying holdings belongs finally and exclusively to the ECB, the Advocate General concluded that the jurisdiction for review of such decisions accordingly 'must lie with the General Court and the Court of Justice'.[46] This, according to the Advocate General, includes the power to review both the decision of the ECB and the national preparatory act.[47] The proper place for this review is thus the annulment action against the ECB's decision (pending on appeal before the Court of Justice).[48] This finding then directly answers the second question of

[42] The action was rejected in Case T-913/16 *Fininvest and Berlusconi v ECB* EU:T:2022:279. That decision has been appealed and is currently pending before the Court of Justice in Case C-512/22 P *Fininvest v ECB*.

[43] A procedure in Italian law seeking to oblige an administrative authority to comply with previous final judgments.

[44] Case C-97/91 *Borelli* EU:C:1992:491. In that case, the EU institution had no discretion and was bound by the national preparatory act.

[45] Case C-64/05 P *Sweden v Commission* EU:C:2007:802. By contrast, in that case the final decision-making power was with the EU institution (the Commission).

[46] Opinion of Advocate General Campos Sánchez-Bordona in Case C-219/17 *Berlusconi* (n 26) [105].

[47] ibid [107].

[48] See n 42.

the Council of State: a national remedy cannot have any bearing on the exclusive jurisdiction of EU courts to review national preparatory acts and the ECB decision concerning the acquisition of qualifying holdings in credit institutions.[49]

The Court followed the Advocate General *en grandes lignes* when it comes to the *Borelli/Sweden v Commission* division of jurisdiction in composite procedures. Yet, establishing exclusive jurisdiction of EU courts was grounded in the exclusive power of the ECB to make a decision on the acquisition of qualifying holdings, thereby ensuring effective judicial protection of the persons concerned.[50] As a consequence, Article 263 TFEU, read in light of the principle of sincere cooperation in Article 4(3) TEU, prevents the national courts from conducting judicial review of the final decision of the ECB, but also of national preparatory acts.[51] This renders the cooperation mechanism between the EU and national authorities effective, preventing the risk of divergent assessments by the EU and national courts.[52] The necessary consequence of this finding is then also the inability of the national court to entertain the *azione di ottemporanza*.[53]

The clear division of jurisdiction between EU and national courts in this area and the explicit prohibition for the national courts to review national preparatory acts where the final word pertains to an EU institution is a major novelty in the case law of the Court.[54] The Court placed great emphasis on the specific cooperation mechanism that underlies the SSM as a manifestation of sincere cooperation from Article 4(3) TEU. From the perspective of evaluating access to legal accountability in the SSM, clarifying the division of jurisdiction (or to be precise, expanding it)[55] in complex institutional and legal situations contributes to legal certainty and legitimate expectations of individuals. Certainly, that comes at the expense of the jurisdiction of the national courts reviewing the acts of *national* institutions applying *national*

49 Opinion of Advocate General Campos Sánchez-Bordona in Case C-219/17 *Berlusconi* (n 26) [116]–[119].

50 Case C-219/17 *Berlusconi* (n 10) [44].

51 ibid [47].

52 ibid [49]–[50]. For a criticism of divergences in interpretation as a justification of the Court to assume exclusive jurisdiction in situations of overlapping competences, see Opinion of Advocate General Ćapeta in Case C-721/20 *DB Station & Service* EU:C:2022:288 [64]–[73].

53 Case C-219/17 *Berlusconi* (n 10) [57]–[59]. As a consequence, a national rule concerning *res judicata* was to be disapplied by the referring court.

54 F Brito Bastos, 'Judicial Review of Composite Administrative Procedures in the Single Supervisory Mechanism: *Berlusconi*' (2019) 56 *Common Market Law Review* 1355, 1372.

55 Opinion of Advocate General Campos Sánchez-Bordona in Case C-219/17 *Berlusconi* (n 26) [114].

law.[56] However, following up on the finding in *Landeskreditbank* that the power of the ECB in prudential supervision is exclusive in nature,[57] the decision of the Court is in no way surprising. A more sober reading of this decision would be to confine its effects only to those situations under the SSM where the ECB has full discretion to make the final decision (such as was the one in *Berlusconi*, and when it comes to the authorisation of credit institutions).

One question concerning the legal accountability of the ECB in a *Berlusconi* situation remains unanswered: what happens if the national preparatory act under review by EU courts is illegal as a matter of national law? This problem has, after the *Borelli* judgment, been termed as 'derivative illegality' in the literature: can the illegal national preparatory act contaminate the legality of an EU act? In a *Borelli* situation, where the EU decision-maker *does not* have discretion and is bound by the national preparatory act, the persons concerned are to seek redress before national courts.[58] This is so because first, EU courts do not have the competence to review national law, and second, because national acts cannot influence the legality of EU acts, as this would infringe the autonomy of EU law.[59]

However, if the ECB based its final decision on such an act, while having discretion, the EU courts would be able to review the exercise of this discretion as a matter of EU law. But of what use then is the power of EU courts to review the preparatory acts themselves? And against what standards would they be reviewed? It would appear that effective judicial protection (to have the national preparatory act reviewed against the standards of national law) is here sacrificed for the benefit of sincere cooperation in the 'specific cooperation mechanism' in prudential supervision. Still, the obligation of the ECB to apply national law under the SSM Regulation, coupled with the general obligation of cooperation and assistance with the national competent authorities, allows the EU courts to review the duty of care applied by the ECB in exercising its discretion. So ultimately, it may be said that the ECB's decision

[56] This more generally puts into question the strict dividing lines between the jurisdiction of EU and national courts. Brito Bastos (n 54) 1376.

[57] See also P Dermine and M Eliantonio, 'Case Note: CJEU (Grand Chamber), Judgment of 19 December 2018, C-219/17, Silvio Berlusconi and Finanziaria d'investimento Fininvest SpA (Fininvest) v Banca d'Italia and Istituto per la Vigilanza Sulle Assicurazioni (IVASS)' (2019) 12(2) *Review of European Administrative Law* 237, 244.

[58] See also Case C-785/18 *Jeanningross* EU:C:2020:46 [25]–[27].

[59] On the discussion of these points, see Brito Bastos (n 54) 1370–1372; Dermine and Eliantonio (n 57) 245.

would be controlled for mistakes in the national preparatory acts.[60] Accountability of national authorities in that process, however, seems to remain without redress. We have seen in Chapter 2 that preparatory acts are in principle not subject to a direct action before the EU courts (unlike in a preliminary reference procedure).[61] In theory, however, it is possible to imagine that national courts may subsequently entertain actions seeking responsibility of the national authority under national law, and it is by extension also possible to expect preliminary references in this area.

Thus we have learned about the organisation of judicial review for situations when the ECB makes a final decision based on a non-binding national preparatory act in accordance with national law. What about the reverse situation: a national competent authority makes a final decision based on non-binding guidance or instruction of the ECB? The Court has not, to my knowledge, addressed this point specifically in respect of the ECB. However, it has done so in the broader context of prudential supervision, concerning the guidelines issued by the European Banking Authority (EBA), which were then taken up by the competent national authority and influenced the rights and obligations of credit institutions. In *Balgarska Narodna Banka*, the Court took an approach that at first glance comes across as counter-intuitive:[62] non-binding acts of EU institutions cannot be subject to direct action under Article 263 TFEU, but the question of their validity may be submitted to the Court by way of a preliminary reference from a national court.[63] What is more, standing in such situations is covered by national procedural autonomy and does not depend on the standing threshold from Article 263 TFEU.[64]

This outcome makes perfect sense, specifically considering the challenges left from *Berlusconi* and the exclusive jurisdiction of the EU courts to review the national preparatory acts that were not binding upon the ECB. First, if we take up the traditional division of tasks between EU and national courts complemented by *Berlusconi*, we may conclude that the final decision based on a non-binding act of another institution should be reviewed by the court of the institution making the final decision. Simply put, EU courts will review

60 A further twist in this scenario is when the national law itself arguably wrongly implements EU law.

61 Chapter 2, Section 2.2.3.

62 This was certainly the view of Advocate General Bobek. See Opinion of Advocate General Bobek in Case C-911/19 *Fédération bancaire française* EU:C:2021:294 [141]–[142], [144], [149]–[155].

63 Case C-501/18 *Balgarska Narodna Banka* (n 39) [82]. On this point, see also Chapter 2, Section 2.2.3.

64 Case C-911/19 *Fédération bancaire française* (n 39) [62]–[65].

the final decisions of the ECB; national courts will review the final decisions of national competent authorities.

This division of tasks then translates into the relationship between Article 263 TFEU and Article 267 TFEU. As regards the former, the Court of Justice explained in *Fédération bancaire française* that non-binding acts cannot be subject to direct actions under Article 263 TFEU as they do not produce binding legal effects.[65] Indeed, in the language of *Berlusconi*, there is no decision of an EU institution that is binding as a matter of EU law. Subsequently, then, if a national competent authority follows the non-binding act, the content of such an act produces effects between private parties not merely by the authority of national law, but also as a matter of EU law. Hence, a preliminary reference on the interpretation or validity of such a non-binding act should be allowed to help the national court resolve the dispute before it. If we compare this situation to a Member State taking up an option provided by a directive, once it uses such an option, it will operate in the national legal system also as a matter of EU law.

Effective judicial protection here demands that a change in the legal position of an individual, which finds its source in EU law, be reviewed by a court.[66] This could not be the national court, as it would go against the *Foto-Frost* doctrine, which prohibits national courts to review the validity of EU law, as well as against Article 19(1) TEU, according to which it is the exclusive jurisdiction of the Court of Justice to interpret EU law. Still, the national court, to review comprehensively the national act based on the non-binding EU act, must know whether the latter is valid as a matter of EU law. In respecting the autonomy of EU law, then, it can achieve this result only through the preliminary reference procedure.

A final note concerning non-binding acts by EU institutions is due. Such acts are, as a general rule (repeated in *Balgarska Narodna Banka* and *Fédération bancaire française*), not subject to direct actions under Article 263 TFEU.[67] However, we now know from *Poggiolini* that preparatory acts of EU institutions are not entirely outside the scope of the Court's jurisdiction in direct actions. When preparatory acts do create an immediate change in the legal position of the person concerned (what the Court termed 'independent legal effects'), those acts are susceptible to judicial review under Article 263

65 ibid [37].

66 Opinion of Advocate General Bobek in Case C-911/19 *Fédération bancaire française* (n 62) [140].

67 This was recently confirmed by the General Court in Case T-709/21 *WhatsApp Ireland Ltd* EU:T:2022:783 [42], [45], in a case concerning the protection of personal data.

TFEU.[68] The Court's justification lies in effective judicial protection, which would be jeopardised if a direct action against a final decision would not be able to remedy the immediate (independent legal) effects of a preparatory act. For the purposes of prudential supervision, this means that we can expect the Court to entertain an assessment of independent legal effects of a preparatory act.

We have up to now dealt with situations in which the parties to the case did not struggle with meeting the standing threshold, either at the national level that triggered the preliminary reference procedure, or by way of a direct action. Yet, the threshold for direct and individual concern has been a hurdle for applicants beyond those individually named by the decision in question. Are shareholders also subjects that can meet the threshold of direct and individual concern when national law makes them the only actors effectively able to initiate judicial review? This question was raised before the Court of Justice in respect of an ECB decision withdrawing the authorisation to Trasta Komercbanka under Article 4(1)(a) and Article 14(5) of the SSM Regulation.[69] The context behind this action can also be neatly connected to the above discussion on the division of tasks between national and EU courts and in particular whether access to judicial review in prudential supervision is a matter of EU or national law. As we will see, *Trasta Komercbanka* depicts very well the clashes that can occur when national law is applied to the consequences of a final ECB decision in prudential supervision. Here, national law created a de facto limit to the legal accountability of the ECB in respect of its authorisation withdrawal.

Specifically, Latvian law determined that upon the withdrawal of an authorisation, the bank in question goes into automatic liquidation. For this purpose, a liquidator is appointed by the competent national authority that recommended the withdrawal to the ECB. In that case, the legal representative of the bank submitted an action before the General Court to challenge the ECB's decision concerning the withdrawal of the authorisation. However, because the liquidator withdrew the power of attorney to the legal representative, the General Court found this action inadmissible for lack of legal representation.[70] Instead, given that shareholders also challenged the ECB decision, claiming that their economic interests have been significantly

[68] Case C-408/20 P *Poggiolini* EU:C:2021:806 [39]–[42].
[69] Joined Cases C-663/17 P, C-665/17 P and C-669/17 P *Trasta Komercbanka* (n 31).
[70] Order T-247/16 *Fursin and Others v ECB* EU:T:2017:623 [49].

affected by the authorisation withdrawal, the General Court found they were directly and individually concerned and allowed their appeal.[71]

On appeal, both Advocate General Kokott and the Court of Justice endorsed the opposite finding. The Advocate General Opinion is particularly instructive when it comes to the consequences that national law may have on the right to an effective judicial remedy against EU acts. Specifically, the Opinion analyses the effect that the appointment of the liquidator under Latvian law had on the ability of Trasta Komercbanka to challenge the withdrawal decision of the ECB before the EU courts. The withdrawal decision was based on the recommendation of the Latvian competent authority, as was the appointment of the liquidator. The Latvian authority also had the power to discharge the liquidator of his or her function in case of loss of confidence. While formally it was at the disposal of the liquidator to initiate legal proceedings before the General Court, in fact, the liquidator would be in a conflict of interest and judicial protection would as a consequence not be effective.[72] This would mean, according to the Advocate General, that effective legal protection against an EU act would depend on national law, which cannot be upheld.[73]

The Court of Justice took up this point further: the withdrawal decision of the ECB resulted, under Latvian law, in mandatory liquidation. The Court considered it clear that the interests of the competent authority and the liquidator coincide,[74] making the conflict of interest, as the Advocate General put it, 'obvious'.[75] Both the Advocate General and the Court therefore agreed that the General Court should have disregarded the liquidator's decision to withdraw the power of attorney to the legal representative of the bank. Instead, for the purposes of effective legal protection, continuity of the previous legal representation should have been recognised by the General Court.[76] The mistake of the General Court was then to accept the rules of national law on representation to the detriment of effective judicial protection. This approach of the Court of Justice is both novel and extremely traditional.

[71] ibid [63], [69].

[72] Opinion of Advocate General Kokott in Joined Cases C-663/17 P, C-665/17 P and C-669/17 P *Trasta Komercbanka* EU:C:2019:323 [79].

[73] ibid [56].

[74] Joined Cases C-663/17 P, C-665/17 P and C-669/17 P *Trasta Komercbanka* (n 31) [73]–[78].

[75] Opinion of Advocate General Kokott in Joined Cases C-663/17 P, C-665/17 P and C-669/17 P *Trasta Komercbanka* (n 75) [75].

[76] Opinion of Advocate General Kokott in Joined Cases C-663/17 P, C-665/17 P and C-669/17 P *Trasta Komercbanka* (n 75) [100], [128]; Joined Cases C-663/17 P, C-665/17 P and C-669/17 P *Trasta Komercbanka* (n 31) [78].

It is novel because it asks of EU courts to disapply rules of representation in national law and depart from the general approach according to which the concept of a 'lawyer' for the purposes of representation is a matter of national law.[77] It is extremely traditional because the Court of Justice uses the route of effective judicial protection as a wild card whenever no other option seems available. In other words, without exploring further the specific enmeshment of EU and national law under the SSM and its obviously new consequences, the Court of Justice chose the well-travelled road of effective judicial protection.

Against this background, the Advocate General and the Court also agreed that the General Court erred in establishing direct and individual concern of the shareholders who challenged the decision of the ECB.[78] Both agreed that while there certainly exists an effect on the economic position of shareholders as a consequence of the withdrawal of the authorisation and the mandatory liquidation,[79] neither of these meet the standard of direct concern under EU law. In essence, then, had the General Court correctly treated the question of legal representation and disregarded the dismissal by the liquidator, effective judicial protection would have been safeguarded without distorting the concepts of direct and individual concern under Article 263(4) TFEU.

Is this a satisfactory solution? Discerning the actual representation and legal continuity in a case such as *Trasta Komercbanka* involves a certain degree of flexibility by the EU courts, including looking further into national law and its consequences for the purposes of effective judicial protection.[80] EU courts should in my view be able to surpass the rigidity of formal legal representation, which is ultimately a matter of national law.[81] This is so because national

[77] See also Article 44 of the Rules of Procedure of the Court of Justice and Article 39 of the Rules of Procedure of the General Court. Further on the treatment of this type of national law reference before EU courts, see M Prek and S Lefèvre, 'The EU Courts as "National Courts": National Law in the EU Judicial Process' (2017) 54 *Common Market Law Review* 369, 382.

[78] Opinion of Advocate General Kokott in Joined Cases C-663/17 P, C-665/17 P and C-669/17 P *Trasta Komercbanka* (n 75) [114]–[122]; Joined Cases C-663/17 P, C-665/17 P and C-669/17 P *Trasta Komercbanka* (n 31) [107]–[115].

[79] The Court underlined that this consequence is in any event stemming from national law, which thus represents an 'intermediate rule', precluding the existence of direct concern by an EU act. Joined Cases C-663/17 P, C-665/17 P and C-669/17 P *Trasta Komercbanka* (n 31) [114].

[80] The concern for effective judicial protection was, according to Simoncini, selective, given that it broadened the approach to legal representation while at the same time narrowing direct and individual concern for shareholders. M Simoncini, 'Different Shades of Legal Standing and the Right to Judicial Protection of Private Parties in the Banking Union: *Trasta Komercbanka*' (2020) 57 *Common Market Law Review* 1867, 1878.

[81] Joined Cases C-663/17 P, C-665/17 P and C-669/17 P *Trasta Komercbanka* (n 31) [58]–[59].

procedural autonomy yields before the right to an effective remedy[82] and it is for EU courts to move beyond a formal reading of national rules and ensure that this right is effectively safeguarded. This is particularly pressing in the context of *Berlusconi*: national courts are prevented from any judicial review in areas where the ECB has exclusive powers under the SSM Regulation, such as the authorisation withdrawal, as was the case in *Trasta Komercbanka*. We know that this also includes national preparatory acts. National acts dealing with the aftermath of such decisions should accordingly also not stand in the way of legal accountability of the ECB. It is certainly possible that the finding of EU courts concerning the legality of the ECB decision has an influence on subsequent legal developments at the national level.

The area of prudential supervision is, ultimately, not one where we were able to witness any creativity on behalf of EU courts when it comes to remedies themselves.[83] However, given the extensive changes that took place in terms of the division of jurisdiction between EU and national courts as well as the interpretation of access to judicial review, EU courts have indeed shown a degree of flexibility[84] to ensure legal accountability of decisions in prudential supervision. Procedurally, thus, a wide enough understanding of access can ensure that remedies are used to enforce legal accountability in prudential supervision. Next, I will turn to the substantive side of ensuring legal accountability.

5.3.2 *Solidarity and Equality*

The principal aim of the SSM more generally is to ensure the safety and soundness of credit institutions and the stability of the financial system of the Union and individual Member States. The system as a whole, and also its component parts, therefore, tell us something about the common interest as the guiding principle in the SSM. The criterion of significance of an entity is, as we have seen, at the centre of division of supervisory tasks between the ECB and national competent authorities. Article 6(4) of the SSM Regulation lays down what significance means more specifically. Without getting into listing

82 Case C-243/15 *Lesoochranáske zoskupenie* EU:C:2016:838 [65].

83 In Chapter 4, Section 4.3.1, we have seen that the Court of Justice, based on the special nature of the European System of Central Banks, for the first time annulled a national measure in Joined Cases C-202/18 and C-238/18 *Rimšēvičs* EU:2019:139.

84 G Marafioti, 'The *Trasta Komercbanka* Cases: Withdrawals of Banking Licences and *locus standi*' in C Zilioli and K-P Wojcik (eds), *Judicial Review in the European Banking Union* (Edward Elgar 2021) 528.

the individual criteria, what brings them together is the possibility that should such entities not be run in a prudential manner, consequences would be felt on a systemic level, or at least beyond a single Member State. In addition, the ECB supervises, for example, the three largest entities in each Member State, as well as those for which ESM or EFSF funding has been granted or requested. Ultimately, the ECB also has discretion in defining any entity as significant, should it consider that its cross-border assets and activities so warrant.

The nature of ECB's powers was clarified by the Court of Justice when Landeskreditbank disputed the decision of the ECB by which it refused to classify it as less significant (and by consequence place it under the supervision of the German competent authority). The General Court dismissed the action, and the Court of Justice dismissed the appeal against that judgment. Both courts found that the ECB gained by the SSM Regulation the exclusive competence to determine what are 'particular circumstances'[85] for characterising an entity as (less) significant. Are there any limits to ECB action here, such as the principle of proportionality? The Court found that the principle is embedded in the legislative framework and the ECB is not required to demonstrate how it is being met on a case-by-case basis.[86] In addition, the Court established that the SSM Regulation conferred an exclusive competence to the ECB to supervise all credit institutions, whereas given its decentralised implementation, the national authorities carry out and are responsible for less significant institutions.[87]

Landeskreditbank also argued that the General Court distorted the decision of the ECB, as it incorrectly represented it and added its own reasoning. This is of relevance for the type of judicial review that courts should perform in the EMU as proposed in Chapter 2: the duty to state reasons should be extensive and sufficient to allow for a meaningful review. Yet, the Court of Justice referred to its well-known discretion case law: the ECB has broad discretion in matters of supervision.[88] In addition, the Administrative Board of Review (ABoR) also carried out an internal administrative review of the ECB's decision, and the reasoning in that decision, according to the Court, also forms

[85] Case T-122/15 *Landeskreditbank* EU:T:2017:337 [54], [63], [72]; Case C-450/17 P *Landeskreditbank* (n 22) [49].

[86] Case C-450/17 P *Landeskreditbank* (n 22) [58]–[59].

[87] ibid [38]–[41], [49]. For a presentation of diverging views in the literature on how this division of tasks is to operate in practice, see F Annunziata, 'European Banking Supervision in the Age of the ECB: Landeskreditbank Baden-Württemberg-Förderbank v ECB' (2020) 21 *European Business Organization Law Review* 545, 555–556.

[88] Case C-450/17 P *Landeskreditbank* (n 22) [86].

part of the statement of reasons.[89] This could, in principle, be justified by the fact that credit institutions have the option to seek an internal review of ECB decisions by ABoR,[90] and once they have done so, cannot be unaware of the reasoning provided in that procedure. It should not go unmentioned, however, that the decision of ABoR is not subject to judicial review, but only the decision of the ECB.[91] It is thus not only desirable, but necessary, for full judicial protection, that the reasoning of ABoR also be subject to judicial review indirectly: when the original ECB decision is under review.

The division of tasks endorsed by the Court of Justice in *Landeskreditbank* opened a number of new questions. What is the role of systemic risk in terms of safeguarding the common interest? What interests are represented and considered by the ECB in making the decision concerning the significance of an entity? In controlling the ECB in its activities, how do EU courts interpret the ECB's assessment of significance in relation to the principles of equality and/or solidarity? Finally, does the SSM Regulation impose any conditions on the national law regulating the functioning of credit institutions? In other words, the ECB is to grant or withdraw an authorisation based on the entity meeting or failing to meet the requirements set out in national law – but is that very national law in some way restrained by the SSM Regulation in turn?

Supervisory powers of the ECB and national competent authorities are designed to overcome individual interests of Member States, for the greater good of safeguarding the stability of the system as a whole. The decision in *Landeskreditbank* illustrates this vividly: regardless of the historical or financial relevance of individual large credit institutions for the Member State concerned, their supervision is transferred exclusively to the ECB. This then tells us something about safeguarding the common interest: controlling the systemic risk that significant credit institutions may bring about is prioritised over a formal demand for equality of Member States in safeguarding their financial interests.

Member States and the EU have, for better or worse, been put in a position to bail-in a number of large credit institutions to assuage the consequences of the crisis.[92] While the events in *Kotnik* took place just as the SSM was entering into force, the findings of the Court in the area of state aid and bail-ins are helpful in understanding the approach to the common interest in

89 ibid [92].
90 Article 24(5) of the SSM Regulation.
91 Annunziata (n 87) 563.
92 See Opinion of Advocate General Wahl in Case C-526/14 *Kotnik* EU:C:2016:102 [2].

respect of bearing the burdens of the financial crisis. Specifically, bailing-in banks to preserve the stability of the system as a whole is a perfect example of increased solidarity demands. The Court in *Kotnik* addressed the issue of whether additional conditions of burden-sharing by shareholders and subordinated creditors may be attached to a bail-in measure intended to maintain the viability of banks.[93] Bail-ins of banks were in that case state aid that was notified to and approved by the Commission. In its Banking Communication,[94] that guided the design of national bail-in measures,[95] the Commission stated: 'State support can create moral hazard and undermine market discipline. To reduce moral hazard, aid should only be granted on terms which involve adequate burden-sharing by existing investors.'[96] Advocate General Wahl explained the tensions that brought about the need for burden-sharing:

> [F]inancial services play a very distinct role in modern economic systems. Banks and other credit institutions are a vital source of finance for (most) undertakings active on any given market. Furthermore, banks are often closely interconnected and many of them operate at an international level. That is why the crisis of one or more banks risks quickly spreading to other banks (both in the home State and in other Member States) and that, in turn, risks producing negative spill-over effects in other sectors of the economy (often referred to as the 'real economy'). This effect of contagion is liable, ultimately, to severely affect the lives of private individuals.[97]

Bailing-in banks thus carries significant benefits and risks. To balance these out, the Advocate General found nothing problematic in attaching the demands of burden-sharing to state support.[98] The Court agreed:

> [. . .] the burden-sharing measures involving both shareholders and subordinated creditors constitute, when they are imposed by the national authorities, exceptional measures. They can be adopted only in the context of there

[93] Case C-526/14 *Kotnik* EU:C:2016:570.

[94] Communication from the Commission on the application, from 1 August 2013, of State aid rules to support measures in favour of banks in the context of the financial crisis (OJ 2013 C 216) 1. Its aim was to provide guidance on the criteria for the compatibility of State aid with the internal market pursuant to Article 107(3)(b) TFEU for the financial sector during that crisis.

[95] It should be stated that the Court found that the Communication was not binding on Member States, but rather only on the Commission when assessing notified State aid. Case C-526/14 *Kotnik* (n 93) [44]–[45].

[96] Section 3.1.2, point 40 of the Banking Communication (n 94).

[97] Opinion of Advocate General Wahl in Case C-526/14 *Kotnik* (n 92) [59].

[98] ibid [59]–[63].

> being a serious disturbance of the economy of a Member State and with the objective of preventing a systemic risk and ensuring the stability of the financial system.[99]

The stability of the entire financial system of the Union may easily be translated to the common interest: banks that are too big to fail risk, causing further disturbances to the entire system and thus may be subject to exceptional selective measures. The Court confirmed, agreeing with the Advocate General, that burden-sharing in this scenario represents an overriding public interest.[100] Property rights of the shareholders and subordinate creditors can on this basis be restricted by the requirement of burden-sharing.[101] We therefore move to the area of prudential supervision already knowing that the stability of the system as a whole may involve exceptional and asymmetrical measures.

Although neither the Advocate General nor the Court mentioned the principle of solidarity specifically, the findings in *Kotnik* align with the theoretical understanding of solidarity presented in Chapter 1. Preventing systemic risk from materialising, or turned around, the preservation of the financial stability of the entire system, is the guiding justification of differentiated measures. In addition, it also guides the division of tasks between the ECB and the national competent authorities: Member States have, for this common interest, given up their own supervisory powers of significant credit institutions.

5.4 JUDICIAL REVIEW AT THE NATIONAL LEVEL

5.4.1 *Access and Remedies*

The regulatory choice of mixing national and EU law obligations in prudential management complicated the respective tasks of national and EU courts, as did the separation of different preparatory and final decision-making powers between the ECB and national supervisory authorities. The 'usual' division of tasks according to which each court applies its own law is becoming increasingly difficult to sustain. In addition to this, the nature of supervisory powers granted to the ECB and national authorities remains contested, or at the very least, disagreements about it persist between national and EU courts. Before

99 Case C-526/14 *Kotnik* (n 93) [88]. See also Case C-686/18 *OC and Others v Banca d'Italia and Others* EU:C:2020:567 [92].

100 Case C-526/14 *Kotnik* (n 93) [69].

101 ibid [80].

delving into more detail on access and remedies under the SSM Regulation, I will first turn to the judicial review of its implementation at the national level, challenged in Germany before the Bundesverfassungsgericht.

Mirroring the subject matter of the *Landeskreditbank* decision of the Court of Justice, the Bundesverfassungsgericht decided in 2019 that the SSM Regulation is compliant with the German Basic Law. Unlike the Court of Justice, the German court did not wholeheartedly subscribe to the idea that the ECB gained exclusive competence in banking supervision. The judgment is interesting in two ways: the first relates to access; the second to submitting a preliminary reference to the Court of Justice. In terms of access, the threshold for initiating a constitutional complaint in Germany against an act implementing EU legislation is wide. Individuals have the right to challenge such acts if they have sufficiently asserted and substantiated a possible violation of their right to democratic self-determination and demonstrated that they are individually, presently, and directly affected.[102] Forming part of the national procedural autonomy, wide standing rules are always welcome to counterbalance the narrow rules on access before the Court of Justice.

The second aspect relates to the Bundesverfassungsgericht deciding not to submit a preliminary reference to the Court of Justice on the interpretation of Article 127(6) TFEU. According to the Bundesverfassungsgericht, the interpretation of Article 127(6) TFEU is not necessary because 'it cannot be assumed that the CJEU might interpret Art. 127(6) TFEU, which governs the allocation of competences in this case, more narrowly than the Federal Constitutional Court'.[103] The German court appears to misunderstand entirely the purpose of the preliminary reference procedure: it treats it as a procedural device of use only to justify a possible *ultra vires* finding. In the eyes of the Bundesverfassungsgericht, it seems irrelevant that its own interpretation, albeit permissive, might not be the same as that of the Court of Justice.[104] In fact, we will see in the next section that this is exactly what

[102] On this point, see Chapter 4, Section 4.4.1, as well as Epilogue, section 'Judicial Review at the National Level'.

[103] Cases 2 BvR 1685/14 and 2 BvR 2631/14 *Banking Union* Judgment of the Second Senate of 30 July 2019 [317]. See Epilogue, section 'Judicial Review at the National Level', where the Bundesverfassungsgericht used the same justification for not submitting a reference on the interpretation of Articles 122 and 311(2) TFEU when reviewing the ratification of the Own Resources Decision.

[104] See also P Faraguna and D Messineo, 'Light and Shadows in the Bundesverfassungsgericht's Decision Upholding the European Banking Union' (2020) 57 *Common Market Law Review* 1629, 1636.

happened: the nature of ECB's competence in banking supervision was interpreted differently by the two courts. A sincere use of the preliminary reference procedure would mean genuinely seeking the interpretation of an EU norm, instead of instrumentalising the procedure for the narrow purpose of a possible *ultra vires* finding.

This development also goes against the approach taken in respect of other courts in Germany: under the case law of the Bundesverfassungsgericht, the submission of a preliminary reference to the Court of Justice forms part of the right to a lawful judge under Article 101(1) of the Basic Law.[105] It does so when the national court commits a fundamental disregard of the obligation to make a reference; when there is a deliberate deviation without a willingness to make a submission; and if there are other possibilities of interpretation of a certain provision without it being *acte eclairé* under the case law of the Court of Justice.[106] The German court was open about the fact that it was its own interpretation that sufficed for the purposes of the constitutional complaint, regardless of possible differences that might have arisen had the reference been submitted. Such a reasoning makes it possible that at least some of the situations entailing a breach of the right to a lawful judge is engaged. Broad access to a national court should include all the benefits that entails, the preliminary reference procedure being one of them. Maintaining this review process in-house deprives not only the Court of Justice of providing an interpretation with Union-wide relevance, but also preventively shields the Bundesverfassungsgericht from any possible external input that might interfere with a purely national interpretation of the norm in question. As we will see in the next section, a Germany-oriented approach is widely present also when it comes to the substantive interpretation of Article 127(6) TFEU and the SSM Regulation.

Apart from this *ex ante* review, judicial review at the national level will more prominently develop in the actual application of supervisory functions by the national authorities and the ECB. National law should provide access to judicial review and appropriate remedies when the national supervisory authority makes a final decision in which the ECB is not subsequently involved. This is, for example, the first stage of the process of granting an authorisation to a credit institution.[107] National supervisory authorities are

[105] For example, in Cases 2 BvR 615/09 and 2 BvR 535/09 Judgment of the Second Senate of 21 November 2011.

[106] Further on this, see R Valutytė, 'Legal Consequences for the Infringement of the Obligation to Make a Reference for a Preliminary Ruling under Constitutional Law' (2012) 19(3) *Jurisprudencija/Jurisprudence* 1171, 1175.

[107] Article 4(1)(a) of the SSM Regulation.

included in the process at different stages: at the outset they have the power to reject the application for an authorisation if it does not meet the substantive requirements in national law.[108] Here, the rejection is only forwarded to the ECB, who has no power to act further. Under the second sentence of Article 19(1) TEU, sufficient remedies should be provided to ensure effective legal protection, as this is a field regulated by EU law.[109] The concrete modalities of access and remedies in this context are of course subject to choices that remain within national procedural autonomy.[110]

Another role for national courts is the authorisation of on-site inspections, when such authorisation is required by national law.[111] In such cases national courts control the authenticity of the ECB's decision, the arbitrariness or excessiveness of coercive measures, and may demand from the ECB detailed explanations relating to the on-site inspection. National courts are prevented, however, from reviewing the necessity for the inspection and from demanding to see the ECB's case file. Finally, the lawfulness of the ECB's decision may only be reviewed by the Court of Justice. This provision causes some confusion as to who does what: if national courts are prevented from examining the necessity of the inspection, it is unclear what exactly they would examine when it comes to the excessiveness of that same measure. This becomes clear when it comes to remedies, because if a national court can block a measure due to its excessiveness, the ECB's defence of the measure will intuitively be focused on the necessity of the measure.

Arguably, national courts would be able to submit a preliminary reference to the Court of Justice to interpret this provision of the SSM Regulation,[112] but it seems to me that the Court would not be able to provide all the answers. The SSM Regulation refers specifically to the national law requiring a judicial authorisation, and it would be logical to assume that if a national law requires it, it also regulates what is to be assessed in this process. A legal accountability perspective of this matter would require a solution where national courts broadly use their power to demand of the ECB extensive explanations to

108 Article 75 of the SSM Framework Regulation.

109 See also Article 47(1) of the Charter.

110 Limited by the principles of effectiveness and equivalence, national rules for enforcing EU law rights: '... must not be less favourable than those concerning similar claims based on provisions of national law or arranged in such a way as to make the exercise of rights conferred by the EU legal order practically impossible'. See, for example, Case C-397/21 *HUMDA* EU:C:2022:790 [33].

111 Article 13 of the SSM Regulation.

112 D Segoin, 'The Investigation Powers, Including On-Site Inspections, of the ECB, and Their Judicial Control' in Zilioli and Wojcik (n 84) 293.

ensure that on-site inspections respect fundamental rights of all those subject to or affected by such a measure.

5.4.2 *Solidarity and Equality*

As in the previous section, here I will also first focus on the decision of the Bundesverfassungsgericht reviewing the SSM Regulation, after which I will turn to how judicial review at the national level can contribute to legal accountability in respect of achieving the common interest. In the ESM, we have seen that achieving the common interest, and by extension the political equality of all EU citizens, faced the tension between the interest of different socioeconomic groups across the EU and nationally oriented aims that creditors and debtor states, respectively, were trying to protect. In monetary policy, the focus was on how the ECB balances different interests that hinge upon the common interest when making decisions with high redistributive effects. In the SSM, the emphasis is on how national courts balance national interests behind banking supervision with what the EU-wide common interest demands.

First, then, to the review of the SSM Regulation against the German Basic Law. There are two takeaways relevant for our thinking about legal accountability and achieving the common interest. First, the Bundesverfassungsgericht repeatedly emphasised that the ECB must be subject to different mechanisms of accountability, which is the only way to ensure it complies with its mandate in supervision. Second, as a consequence of that nature of the ECB's mandate in supervision, the German court provided an interpretation of the SSM Regulation at odds with that of the Court of Justice in *Landeskreditbank*, by taking a highly Germany-oriented approach. From the common interest perspective, the first point can be read as positive, and the second negative.

A holistic approach to accountability was at the centre of finding that the supervisory mandate given to the ECB does not exceed the transfer of competences to the EU level under Article 127(6) TFEU. The ECB holds considerable discretion and independence in its supervisory activities,[113] and the analysis of the Bundesverfassungsgericht focused on the multitude of legal and political accountability mechanisms designed to keep the ECB in check.[114] This included references to both EU and national judicial review,

[113] K Alexander, 'The European Central Bank and Banking Supervision: The Regulatory Limits of the Single Supervisory Mechanism' (2016) 13 *European Company and Financial Law Review* 467.

[114] Cases 2 BvR 1685/14 and 2 BvR 2631/14 *Banking Union* (n 103) [209]–[218].

as well as parliamentary oversight. A similar holistic analysis of accountability in the SSM has shown that numerous accountability mechanisms in store are individually superficial, thus resulting in an overall weak accountability of the ECB.[115] This is not to suggest that the Bundesverfassungsgericht should have annulled the German implementation of the SSM Regulation but rather that a genuine analysis of accountability needs to go further than a formal box-ticking exercise. The positive impression nevertheless remains in terms of promoting a message that the ECB should be held under strict scrutiny in conducting its supervisory activities.

The problematic part of the decision, in my view, is the Bundesverfassungsgericht's purely national interpretation of the SSM. It insisted on a reading according to which the ECB's powers are strictly limited to 'specific tasks', while all other tasks remain for national supervisors.[116] Although the finding of significance of a credit institution is for the ECB to decide, the German court made it seem as if this is an objectively discernible fact.[117] Yet, Article 6(4), third sentence, gives the ECB considerable discretion in determining the concept of significance.[118] The same was confirmed by the Court of Justice in *Landeskreditbank*.[119] The Bundesverfassungsgericht also underlined that the activities of the Federal Financial Supervisory Authority and the Bundesbank are subject to judicial review at the national level, stating that such review is 'generally comprehensive and addresses factual and legal aspects'.[120] This approach, however, disregards the diminished role for national courts under the SSM Regulation, in particular when the final decision lies with the ECB. By focusing only on what the German Basic Law would allow,[121] and

[115] M Dawson, A Maricut-Akbik and A Bobić, 'Reconciling Independence and Accountability at the European Central Bank: The False Promise of Proceduralism' (2019) 25(1) *European Law Journal* 75; A-L Högenauer, 'Paper 7: The ECB as a Banking Supervisor: Transparent Compared to What?' (2023) 45(1) *Journal of European Integration* 121. For a positive assessment of the responsiveness of the ECB as an accountability mechanism in the SSM, see P Nicolaides, 'Accountability of the ECB's Supervisory Activities (SSM): Evolving and Responsive' (2019) 26(1) *Maastricht Journal of European and Comparative Law* 136.

[116] Cases 2 BvR 1685/14 and 2 BvR 2631/14 *Banking Union* (n 103) [160], [167], [171]–[172].

[117] '... it depends on the significance of the credit institution whether the ECB of a national supervisory authority is competent.' ibid [174]. See also [176].

[118] 'The ECB may also, on its own initiative, consider an institution to be of significant relevance where it has established banking subsidiaries in more than one participating Member States and its cross-border assets or liabilities represent a significant part of its total assets or liabilities subject to the conditions laid down in the methodology.'

[119] Case C-450/17 P *Landeskreditbank* (n 22) [56].

[120] Cases 2 BvR 1685/14 and 2 BvR 2631/14 *Banking Union* (n 103) [229].

[121] Faraguna and Messineo (n 104) 1641.

ignoring the interpretation of the Court of Justice,[122] it made it more difficult for national courts to focus on the common interest.

Options for judicial review in the actual operation of the SSM also display a tendency for a more pronounced safeguarding of national over the common interest.[123] This, however, is the result of banking regulation, which remains outside the SSM. The basics are contained in the Basel III Framework, a set of internationally agreed rules developed by the Basel Committee on Banking Supervision in response to the financial crisis.[124] To harmonise compliance with these standards in the EU, the European Banking Authority issues standards, guidelines, recommendations, and the like under the Single Rulebook. The Basel III Framework rules are also reflected in the Capital Requirements Directive[125] and the Capital Requirements Regulation.[126] As instruments striving for exhaustive regulation, they leave predetermined options and discretions for national legislation. Arguably due to a shift towards maximum harmonisation in these instruments, options and discretions at the national level are increasing fragmentation[127] and are a method for national authorities to protect their policy choices.[128] Banking regulation thus forms an important part of the SSM context, given that prudential management of credit institutions assumes a continuing compliance with capital requirements and its other elements. These are mostly found in national law, and although they are implementing EU law, considerable leeway remains for national supervisors and courts alike.

Within the SSM Regulation, these national particularities may come to the fore, for example, when it comes to granting authorisations to credit institutions. As already mentioned, under Article 4(3) of the SSM Regulation, even when decision-making power lies with the ECB, it may happen that it applies the relevant national law. Still, national courts are not the ones who review those decisions: review of ECB decisions is the task of EU courts. Given that EU jurisprudence tackling this conundrum is barely nascent, one can only speculate about the methods of interpretation and sources that will

[122] See also A L Riso, 'A Prime for the SSM before the Court: The *L-Bank* Case' in Zilioli and Wojcik (n 84) 497.

[123] See also Boucon and Jaros (n 26) 159.

[124] For more information, see <www.bis.org/bcbs/basel3.htm?m=2572>.

[125] See n 36.

[126] ibid.

[127] Z Kudrna and S Puntscher Riekmann, 'Harmonizing National Options and Discretions in the EU Banking Regulation' (2018) 21(2) *Journal of Economic Policy Reform* 144.

[128] Boucon and Jaros (n 26) 186.

be considered when deciding how the ECB interpreted and applied national law.

It is also important to consider how the ECB will in fact apply this national law. Arguably, when applying national law that implements options and discretions, the ECB is by extension necessarily promoting the national interests behind them, rather than pursuing the common interest of the entire system.[129] This opposes the traditional wisdom according to which the task of EU institutions and legislation is to safeguard the common interest.[130] A mitigating factor comes from research on systemic risk: here it was established that by preserving the diversity of national banking systems, chances of systemic risks are decreased, thereby resulting in benefits for the sustainability of the system as a whole.[131] By taking into account national peculiarities in the banking system, the ECB can indeed thus also safeguard the common interest.[132]

In the judicial review at the EU level, to ensure that national banking regulation of highly diverse systems[133] is not taken out of context but is properly applied, it would in my view be necessary to include in the procedure at least the national supervisory authority. Of course, the shortcoming is that the national authority would likely share the interest of the ECB and thus merely echo the latter's position on how to interpret the relevant national law. Still, it seems problematic that EU courts should be left to their own devices when interpreting national law,[134] for which they do not have jurisdiction (under Article 19 TEU), nor the requisite knowledge. In opposition to this view, Advocate General Mengozzi was more optimistic and argued, in the context of public contracts where national law may also be of relevance, that it sometimes cannot be avoided that national law forms part of the relevant legal

[129] ibid.

[130] For example, see Case C-128/89 *Commission v Italy* EU:C:1990:311 [14] and Case C-282/90 *Vreugdenhil v Commission* EU:C:1992:124 [24].

[131] O Butzbach, 'Systemic Risk, Macro-Prudential Regulation and Organizational Diversity in Banking' (2016) 35 *Policy and Society* 239, 247–248. See also in the UK context, J Michie, 'Promoting Corporate Diversity in the Financial Services Sector' (2011) 32(4) *Policy Studies* 309.

[132] In *Landeskreditbank* analysed above, the bank argued that due to its specificity, it would be more efficient had supervision been left to the national authorities. The Court of Justice, however, dismissed this argument (albeit without much explanation). It is to be expected, nevertheless, that the ECB, operating through the aid of Joint Supervisory Teams, would conduct its supervision considering institutional and regulatory particularities of credit institutions. See Case C-450/17 P *Landeskreditbank* (n 22) [112].

[133] T Beck, O De Jonghe and G Schepens, 'Bank Competition and Stability: Cross-country Heterogeneity' (2013) 22(2) *Journal of Financial Intermediation* 218.

[134] On this problem more generally, see Prek and Lefèvre (n 77).

framework before the EU courts, which should be approached 'with all due caution'.[135]

This problem arose in *Corneli v ECB*,[136] decided by the General Court and currently under appeal before the Court of Justice.[137] Here, Ms Corneli, a minority shareholder of Banca Carige, challenged the decision of the ECB to put the bank under temporary administration.[138] Banca Carige is considered a significant institution and is thus subject to direct supervision by the ECB. The ECB here had to apply the national law that implemented the Resolution Directive,[139] which provides that before putting a bank under temporary administration, the competent authority can remove senior management or the management body of the bank. The Italian law, however, only provided for the temporary administration decision. In a situation of a bank deteriorating at great speed, the ECB conducted what might be termed a conform interpretation of the national law and opted for the temporary administration measure. The General Court disagreed that the conform interpretation of national law was possible in that situation because it would amount to a *contra legem* interpretation.[140] It thus annulled the ECB's decision.[141] The Court of

[135] Opinion of Advocate General Mengozzi in Case C-401/09 P *Evropaïki Dynamiki v ECB* EU:C:2011:31 [71].

[136] Case T-502/19 *Corneli v ECB* EU:T:2022:627.

[137] Case C-777/22 P *ECB v Corneli* and Case C-789/22 P *Commission v Corneli*.

[138] In terms of standing, it would appear, following the findings in *Trasta Komercbanka*, that Ms Corneli as a shareholder would not have standing to challenge the decision of the ECB. However, the General Court used that judgment to distinguish it from the situation of Ms Corneli: because *Trasta Komercbanka* concerned the withdrawal of an authorisation of a credit institution and its subsequent liquidation, the ceasing of its operation concerned directly not the shareholders but the credit institution itself. That decision on liquidation was, however, not a decision of the ECB. Here, on the contrary, Banca Carige was put under temporary administration by a decision of the ECB and is different from the situation in *Trasta Komercbanka*. Case T-502/19 *Corneli v ECB* (n 136) [47]–[53]. Whether the Court of Justice will agree with this distinction remains to be seen.

[139] Directive 2014/59/EU of the European Parliament and of the Council of 15 May 2014 establishing a framework for the recovery and resolution of credit institutions and investment firms and amending Council Directive 82/891/EEC, and Directives 2001/24/EC, 2002/47/EC, 2004/25/EC, 2005/56/EC, 2007/36/EC, 2011/35/EU, 2012/30/EU and 2013/36/EU, and Regulations (EU) No 1093/2010 and (EU) No 648/2012, of the European Parliament and of the Council (OJ 2014 L 173) 190.

[140] Case T-502/19 *Corneli v ECB* (n 136) [106]–[108].

[141] For a criticism directed to the General Court concerning its misunderstanding of the case law on the effects of directives in national law, see D Sarmiento, 'Setting the Limits of Implementation of National Law by EU Institutions: The *Corneli v ECB* Case (T-502/19)' *EU Law Live* October 2022. Available at <https://eulawlive.com/op-ed-setting-the-limits-of-implementation-of-national-law-by-eu-institutions-the-corneli-v-ecb-case-t-502-19-by-daniel-sarmiento/>.

Justice is thus faced with an appeal on how properly to interpret national law in relation to a directive. In another recent case, the Court of Justice did indeed refer to the national case law when interpreting a provision of national law.[142]

Could there be a role in such and similar cases for national courts? Given that actions against the ECB will be direct, there is no possibility for national courts to participate in the procedure (and which national court would this be in the first place?). Yet, it would be incumbent on EU courts to ensure that all relevant case law from the national level is considered when making a decision. In the context of public procurement, the General Court stated that while EU courts have no power to interpret national law, the institutions are, 'in accordance with the principles of sound administration and solidarity', to ensure that national law is complied with.[143] Whether the EU courts will take up this duty of care remains to be seen in the litigation to come.

5.5 ON JUDICIAL INTERACTIONS

The judicial review in the SSM raised novel and unique challenges for judicial interactions, and by extension, for legal accountability. There are two essential characteristics of this area relevant for judicial interactions. The first concerns the division of competences between EU and national courts resulting from the composite nature of the SSM, and the second the dominance of direct actions. Each of these produce important consequences for the legal accountability of decision-makers in the SSM, and by extension, the achievement of the common interest.

The question of who does what and on the basis on which law is a pressing one. We have seen in Section 5.2 that the SSM is organised as a composite structure: supervision of financial institutions is shared between the ECB and national supervisory authorities. In Section 5.3, it was further established that for those competences where the final decision lies with the ECB,[144] national courts are prevented, under *Berlusconi*, from reviewing the national preparatory acts. Finally, for those supervisory competences that remain with the national authorities, judicial review is conducted at the national level in line

[142] Joined Cases C-152/18 P and C-153/18 P *Crédit Mutuel Arkéa* EU:C:2019:810 [99]–[109].
[143] Case T-139/99 *AICS v Parliament* EU:T:2000:182 [41].
[144] See also L Wissink, T Duijkersloot and R Widdershoven, 'Shifts in Competences between Member States and the EU in the New Supervisory System for Credit Institutions and Their Consequences for Judicial Protection' (2014) 10(5) *Utrecht Law Review* 92, 96–100.

with national procedural rules on access and remedies. What about non-binding preparatory acts or guidelines of the ECB when the national supervisory authority issues the final decision?[145] This should arguably be the competence of national courts,[146] although EU courts have not yet expressed their position on this point. To resolve these uncertainties, I consider it crucial that national courts remain as active as possible in prudential supervision and use the preliminary reference procedure extensively (unlike the approach of the Bundesverfassungsgericht in the *Banking Union* decision). These judicial interactions ought to promote clarity and refinement of the case law of EU courts and provide broader access to legal accountability for individuals.

The second characteristic of the SSM is the dominance of direct actions over preliminary rulings at the EU level. This is the result of the powers of the ECB as a supervisor in respect of significant credit institutions as well as of its exclusive powers in select tasks concerning all credit institutions. While it is intuitive that the EU courts should be the ones reviewing the ECB's final decisions under the SSM Regulation, after *Berlusconi*, they now also have the power to review national preparatory acts leading to the ECB's final decision. National courts are left to review only the final national acts. This is problematic as it removes the central role that national courts have as interlocutors of the Court of Justice, the role in which they can keep the Court of Justice in check by either challenging its decisions when important countervailing constitutional concerns arise, or simply when it is necessary to point out inconsistencies in its case law.

Another weakness of direct actions pervading the SSM is the relationship between the General Court and the Court of Justice. In this context, legal accountability does not benefit from the broad input that national courts can provide but instead remains in-house. In preliminary references, national courts are the ones ultimately deciding the case. While the Court of Justice emphasises the binding nature of its rulings,[147] there is little it can do to ensure that the national courts abide by its rulings. For its judgments to be accepted by the national courts, the Court of Justice needs to work on its

[145] See Article 9(1) of the SSM Regulation, on instructions of the ECB to national authorities to use the powers they have available under national law, and Article 18(5) of the SSM Regulation, on the ECB requiring the national authorities to initiate proceedings under national law which may result in administrative penalties.

[146] C Brescia Morra, 'The Interplay between the ECB and NCAs in the "Common Procedures" under the SSM Regulation: Are There Gaps in Legal Protection?' (2018) 84 *Quaderni di Ricerca Giuridica della Consulenza Legale* 81, 84.

[147] Case C-62/14 *Gauweiler* EU:C:2015:400 [16].

judgments being persuasive, coherent, consistent, and mindful of possible consequences that might arise in the national context. None of these constraints exist when it is deciding on appeals against the decisions of the General Court.

What is more, the General Court cannot challenge the Court of Justice in the same way that national courts can: the latter has appellate jurisdiction and is undoubtedly in a superior position, which prevents a more significant influence of the General Court. Several examples illustrate the inherent subordination of the General Court when it comes to pushing legal accountability forward. In *Trasta Komercbanka*, the General Court attempted to expand access to judicial review by also including shareholders of a bank that underwent mandatory liquidation – the Court of Justice disagreed. In *Corneli v ECB*, the General Court persisted in finding another way of justifying standing for the shareholders. It remains to be seen how the appeal will be decided, but there is no incentive for the Court of Justice to change course.[148] In *Crédit lyonnais v ECB*,[149] the General Court conducted an intense judicial review of ECB's discretion. Currently pending on appeal, Advocate General Emiliou suggested to the Court to annul the decision of the General Court for too intrusive a review of ECB's discretion.[150]

The SSM thus displays a worrying lack of judicial interactions and little hope that this might change. The General Court cannot be left alone to bear the burden of keeping the Court of Justice in check, something it is procedurally not equipped to do in the first place. It is precisely the other way around: as the appellate jurisdiction, it is the task of the Court of Justice to control the General Court and keep it in check. National courts should maintain their presence in the SSM as important actors in legal accountability, something that might require a departure from the prohibition of review of national preparatory acts. Using the preliminary reference procedure as a platform, they too can contribute to the political equality of citizens in achieving the common interest.

[148] Another example was mentioned in Chapter 3 concerning the accountability of the Euro Group. The General Court attempted to find a way to make the Euro Group accountable in Case T-680/13 *Chrysostomides* EU:T:2018:486, but the Court of Justice refused to follow this innovation in Joined Cases C-597/18 P, C-598/18 P, C-603/18 P and C-604/18 P *Chrysostomides* EU:C:2020:1028. See further, Chapter 3, Section 3.4.1.

[149] Case T-504/19 *Crédit lyonnais v ECB* EU:T:2021:185. Pending on appeal in Case C-389/21 P *ECB v Crédit lyonnais.*

[150] Opinion of Advocate General Emiliou in Case C-389/21 P *ECB v Crédit lyonnais* EU:C:2022:844.

Conclusion

C.1 INTRODUCTION

Whenever I explained to other people what my book will be about, I always visualised a Greek pensioner who voted for Syriza in the January 2015 elections, hopeful that it will make good on its anti-austerity promises (outlined in the Thessaloniki Programme). The Syriza government was formed, promises were broken, and Memoranda of Understanding were signed. Tsipras resigned as Prime Minister on 20 August 2015. Devastating consequences materialised and fundamentally transformed the Greek social fabric. What was that Greek pensioner able to do? In other words, was there a space for the individual to hold decision-makers in EU economic governance to account before courts, where political actions fail? Across theory and practice, my aim was to reconceptualise legal accountability in a way that replaces the individual at the heart of all activities in the Economic and Monetary Union.

For this purpose, I proposed a framework of legal accountability for EU's economic governance that reasserts the centrality of the individual in its institutional framework. The equal ability of all EU citizens to hold decision-makers in the EMU accountable, I argued, can be achieved through a balanced application of the principles of equality and solidarity. From this perspective, accountability is the glue that binds the public institution to the common interest. To achieve it, these institutions have a duty to maintain a balance between the principles of equality and solidarity. Seen in this way, all institutions are under an obligation to consider the interests involved in a way that best serves the common interest.

Because of deficiencies in political and other forms of accountability in the EMU, the focus of this book was on courts. I proposed a new framework of judicial review designed to enforce a high duty of care by decision-makers towards the common interest, and an extensive duty to state reasons on how this was done. Decisions in the EMU carry high redistributive effects, which should be an important concern in judicial scrutiny. The burden then shifts to the parties to demonstrate not only who should win the case, but also, preliminarily, what the appropriate standard of review and all the necessary evidence should be. The parties in the litigation thus carry the responsibility to present a rich evidentiary basis that serves as ammunition aimed at endorsing or rebutting the presumption of full judicial review. In this way, courts become the public platform for discussing the extent of power given to an institution and deciding on the way it has contributed to the common interest.

The exploration of legal accountability in this book spanned across three case studies, each of which brought to light different challenges for the individual in holding decision-makers to account. In the European Stability Mechanism and other instruments of financial assistance, issues for accountability were caused by the nature of the legal acts in question, and the lack of connection between the decision-makers and those affected. Here, the major socioeconomic effects in debtor states were the result of decisions without democratic input either on the creditor side (led by the Troika) or on the debtor side (due to the urgency of accepting the conditions of financial assistance). Courts barely intervened, and changes, for example by expanding the scope of the Charter of Fundamental Rights by the Court of Justice, were slow and with little practical effect.

In monetary policy, the puzzle was finding out the proper intensity of review that courts should apply when controlling the action of an independent central bank. Thus, the main challenge was to reconcile the high level of independence of the European Central Bank in making its decisions with the need to subject it to any sort of accountability. Given that political accountability is difficult to achieve against a highly independent institution, the thrust of the matter here was the extent of judicial review and the degree of deference that courts should exhibit. The Court of Justice and the German Bundesverfassungsgericht engaged in a tumultuous exchange on the proper duty to state reasons and balancing the different interests in monetary policy decisions.

Finally, the central question in the Single Supervisory Mechanism was who does what and based on which law? Banking supervision is the task of the ECB, but it conducts it by sharing its tasks with national supervisors. In so doing, it also often applies national law. Which courts review which decisions here, and based on which law? This area is thus characterised by a shift in the traditional division of competences between EU and national courts, because now the Court of Justice is the one to review also the national preparatory acts against the standards of national law.

The aim of the conclusion is to offer some final thoughts on the role that the common interest played in judicial review and with what intensity the courts reviewed the duties of decision-makers to achieve it across the three case studies.

C.2 FINANCIAL ASSISTANCE MECHANISMS

> 'They work in the port,' said he after a pause. 'Do you know what we call them? Structural reforms.'(. . .)
>
> 'Every day, there are more people. Yesterday, I had another meeting with them in the office. I have meetings all the time. First with the World Bank, then with them, then again with the World Bank. Take a look at these people, standing there. They think it depends on me. They think I can do something. I do not know what to say to them. There are new rules now. Things work differently, companies are run differently. Parts of the port will need to be privatized. Someone has to do it. It just happens to be me, but if it wasn't me, it would have to be someone else, whoever, does not matter who, someone has to do it.'[1]

The powerlessness of national political actors in the process of negotiating the desperately needed financial assistance deprived them of responsiveness to their citizens. Structural reforms were imposed and, as we have seen in Chapters 2 and 3, hardly any questions were asked about the social impacts of such reforms. The legal nature of financial assistance exacerbated this dire situation: EU courts would not review non-EU law. Intuitively we might have expected that judicial review in this area would dominantly take place at the national level, given that financial assistance mechanisms were mainly created outside EU law and carried out at the national level. Alas, we have seen in Chapter 3 that the urgency of the situation and the superior position of creditors placed the national political institutions between a rock and a hard place, making democratic input virtually inexistent. Courts were also in an extremely delicate position, juggling between constitutional protections in the socioeconomic sphere and external demands for reforms that focused only on financial stabilisation and debt restructuring.

The crux of national judicial review of measures implementing individual reforms, similarly to the review of the ESM Treaty ratification process, was on

[1] L Ypi, *Free: Coming of Age at the End of History* (Penguin Books 2022) 242, 244.

justifying such reforms by compelling public interest, which in some cases (such as Greece) included a reference to the common interest of the Eurozone. Save for the case of Portugal, where the Constitutional Tribunal attempted to safeguard social protection standards (albeit with limited success), it is difficult to conclude that national courts had any significance in contesting measures of post-crisis governance. The common interest, instead of being conceptually aligned with the aims of Article 3 TEU by providing a space for socioeconomic considerations to come to the fore, was reduced to mere survival, epitomised through the restructuring of public debt. The intensity of review was low, where the duty to state reasons and possible alternatives were not explored in depth. That was, of course, the result of strict conditionality of financial assistance terms: national decision-makers had limited leeway in implementing what was required of them and less still were they able to show that they carried out a thorough examination of socioeconomic effects that would arise as a result.

The Irish Supreme Court was the lone institution to submit a preliminary reference to the Court of Justice to determine the compliance of the ESM Treaty with EU law. A perhaps more optimistic remark should be made about the national review of the ESM Treaty. The courts mostly referred to each other's jurisprudence in supporting their findings. In that sense, Austrian, Polish, and Estonian decisions cite earlier German findings, and the German final decision on the ESM[2] in turn cites the Estonian and French decisions. While the courts did not cite each other on questions of solidarity or the common interest, this does leave us with the impression of their awareness of a shared project, which may in the future pave the way for a more coordinated approach towards judicial review of economic governance.

As mentioned, the contribution of EU courts grew over time. The initial resistance to admit cases concerning Memoranda of Understanding eventually changed. The Court of Justice also extended the applicability of the Charter to those instruments. As regards Memoranda under the ESM assistance, the Court of Justice expanded the applicability of EU law, and consequently the Charter, to EU institutions when acting within the ESM framework.[3] These are important developments that pave way for the common interest to take up

[2] Case 2 BvR 1390/12 *ESM Treaty II* Judgment of the Second Senate of 12 September 2012, citing the Estonian decision in [211], [220], and the French decision in [244].

[3] Case C-258/14 *Florescu* EU:C:2017:448.

a more prominent role. It is also possible to say that the Court of Justice is bringing closer together the myriad sources of law regulating financial assistance and drawing them nearer to traditional EU judicial review. We can thus conclude that the Court of Justice has changed its approach to expand judicial protection. However, only to a limited extent.

The ability of individuals to seek direct recourse against Memoranda of Understanding under the ESM is restricted solely to action for damages, which remains problematic.[4] It does not result in more general accountability of the European Central Bank and the Commission for their conduct within the ESM. It also requires the individual to construct indirect routes to hold these institutions to account and this will only be successful if she is able to prove that a sufficiently serious breach has occurred, as explicitly reasserted by the Court of Justice in *Chrysostomides*. None of the applicants in the cases analysed were able to meet this threshold. In addition, the Court of Justice made no mention of the principle of solidarity and we can consequently see little to no concrete use of it in the area of financial assistance. But given that incremental change did take place, why not expect the same for the common interest? It is thus possible to argue for a more prominent role of the principle of solidarity in the interpretation of the common interest in the area of financial assistance.

One can, however, hardly be optimistic about the standard of justification that was required from EU institutions in this area of review. The duty to state reasons and the information required from decision-makers was incommensurate with the severe redistributive effects their decisions brought about. It is interesting to see the General Court attempting to improve this limited reach of judicial review. This is visible in its more substantive approach to judicial review and broadening of access to individuals. Yet, the Court of Justice disagreed with the General Court and little progress appears to be on the horizon.

A final note is due on the reform of the ESM Treaty that is currently awaiting Italy's ratification. Its main novelty is the possibility of demanding from the country in trouble to implement a preliminary restructuring of debt as a precondition of receiving aid.[5] The current Italian government is opposed

4 See also F Pennesi, 'The Accountability of the European Stability Mechanism and the European Monetary Fund: Who Should Answer for Conditionality Measures?' (2018) 3(2) *European Papers* 511, 528–529.

5 For an overview, see M Messori, 'The Flexibility Game Is Not Worth the New ESM' Luiss SEP Working Paper 15/2019, 4.

to the introduction of such a possibility because, as economists explain (although this view is not unanimous among experts), the Italian debt is held mainly by its residents (unlike the Greek debt, which was mainly held by foreign banks and wealthy individuals).[6] Restructuring such debt would have devastating consequences for domestic consumption and would lead to a major recession.[7] The dispute among experts is anchored in opposing economic philosophies of the EU's North and South,[8] and this tells us something about the common interest: insistence on formal equality of Member States results in uniform macroeconomic solutions across Member States based on a single economic philosophy.

The common interest demands of decision-makers to look beyond these constraints and take due care of the heterogeneous conditions across different socioeconomic groups within and across the Member States. The financial assistance mechanisms that were analysed in Chapter 3 were arguably a victim of urgency, where quick and (financially) efficient solutions needed to be put in place. We are now in a better position to approach the design of future emergency solutions that would account for differences among Member States, improve the democratic participation of both national decision-makers and EU citizens, and protect the social and equality aims in Article 3 TEU and Articles 8 and 9 TFEU. This, with the aim of avoiding the painful socioeconomic effects we witnessed in debtor Member States.

C.3 MONETARY POLICY OF THE EUROPEAN CENTRAL BANK

Was the individual able to ensure that the common interest is served in the monetary policy field? The short answer is: not quite. Here, the main hurdle to overcome was the ECB's high level of independence in achieving its price stability mandate. Overall, as presented in Chapter 4, we have witnessed the Court of Justice and the Bundesverfassungsgericht disagreeing over the appropriate intensity of review of ECB's decisions and the extent to which it should justify how it balanced the different interests affected. What does this mean for the common interest?

From the perspective of the Court of Justice, the ECB is shielded by its independence and expertise. The Court of Justice accepted as admissible

6 G Galli, 'The Reform of the ESM and Why It Is So Controversial in Italy' (2020) 15(3) *Capital Markets Law Journal* 262, 270.

7 ibid 271.

8 ibid 267.

questions on the interpretation and validity of even a Press Release of the ECB, thus arguably providing broad access to justice with EU-wide effects. However, in terms of the common interest, we are left with the impression that objectives from Article 3 TEU (and Articles 8 and 9 TFEU) did not influence how the ECB achieves its primary mandate of price stability. This can best be illustrated if we compare what took place before the Court of Justice with my proposal for the type of judicial review[9] that should ideally be carried out against decisions with high redistributive effects.

Ideally the Court of Justice should begin with a presumption of a full review and hold the ECB to a high standard of a duty to state reasons. The ECB should, in response, provide the Court with the full material that led to its decision, including a detailed explanation of the possible directions it could have taken, how each of these options would materialise in the redistributive field, what socioeconomic interests would be affected, and how it ultimately balanced those interests in reaching its decision. If possible, the Court of Justice should also include in its review other experts that might contradict or support the claims of the ECB in that respect. Regrettably, that is not what happened. The Court of Justice, instead, both in *Gauweiler* and *Weiss*, accepted the ECB's argument that the decisions it made were the only possible course of action it had before it. This may well be the case, but there was insufficient evidentiary material presented to the Court for it to be absolutely certain that the ECB acted with a proper duty of care.

What about the parallel review that took place before the Bundesverfassungsgericht? First, to the common interest. The biggest weakness of that court's approach was its sole focus on Germany. German pensioners, German savers, and German prices of assets were the considerations of relevance in its review of ECB's quantitative easing programmes. Let us now imagine courts in all Member States doing the same. Would this increase the accountability of the ECB in respect of the common interest? Most certainly not. The ECB's decisions need to cater to the entire Eurozone, ensuring that their effects account for the possibility of contagion, cross-border shocks, and socioeconomic groups across the Eurozone. These decisions should also cater to considerations of the common interest, such as balanced economic growth and price stability, social justice and protection, and the combat against social exclusion. If we follow the logic of the German court, the ECB should arguably issue a different decision for each

9 See Chapter 2, Section 2.3.3.

Eurozone member to ensure that only national interests are protected. I consider this highly problematic.

What of the intensity of judicial review? In this respect, the Bundesverfassungsgericht's approach does hold lessons that are more generally valuable for reviewing ECB's decisions. Specifically, to achieve objectives in the common interest, the ECB should be subject to a high duty of justifying its decisions. Of course, it is not necessary that this exercise follows the rigid steps of the proportionality test of the German court. Nevertheless, preparing a highly specific evidentiary basis for the decisions that it makes, an analysis of the redistributive effects, and more generally macroeconomic effects that can be expected is something that should not be seen as a burden on the ECB's operational independence. Another lesson from the German review is the inclusion of a broader pool of experts in the field, which would make judicial review a public forum for assessing how the ECB used its expertise and are there any deficiencies or inconsistencies in how it reached its conclusions on the best course of action. In the context where the ECB makes its decisions in a highly independent, and thus publicly unavailable process, unveiling them before the courts is in my opinion a benefit for the individual. Her ability to enforce the common interest through this process counterbalances the lack of ECB's accountability in the political sphere.

Finally, can we make any conclusions on the benefits of the preliminary reference procedure as it played out in *Gauweiler* and *Weiss*? The preliminary reference has important benefits in the context of a highly independent ECB. National courts should be seen as agents promoting contestation with effects for the entire Eurozone. Although this book was critical of the deferential approach of the Court of Justice to the ECB, it should be said that problems with ECB's accountability would likely have remained obscured had it not been for the two preliminary references that forced the Court of Justice to engage in the review of quantitative easing in the first place. In that sense, national courts also enhance the common interest, by acting on behalf of EU citizens in triggering the preliminary reference procedure, the result of which is binding on all EU Member States.

In addition, submitting a preliminary reference may assuage some of the drawbacks related to access to review at the national level. Namely, access to constitutional review on the national level is most commonly guaranteed only to privileged applicants. Lower courts, where access is broader, may contribute to the creation of EU-wide legal solutions by potentially accessing the Court of Justice through the preliminary reference procedure. This procedure has the additional benefit of holding the Court of Justice itself to account by incentivising it to create and maintain consistent standards of review and use its privileged position to grant an EU-wide authority to the application of those standards.

C.4 THE SINGLE SUPERVISORY MECHANISM

The last case study in this book analysed legal accountability in the Single Supervisory Mechanism, which again demonstrated its own specific challenges. As a tool aimed at preventing future banking crises from developing, the ECB and national competent authorities supervise credit institutions to ensure that they comply with the requirements of prudential management in a composite setting. This means that both the ECB and national authorities apply EU and national law, which, as Chapter 5 has shown, created novel challenges for the judicial review done by EU and national courts. In a nutshell, the question is which court reviews what and based on which law (EU or national)? A second challenge in the SSM concerns the dominance of direct actions. Both of these have specific outcomes when it comes to the duty of decision-makers to act in the common interest and the intensity of judicial review that the courts perform in ensuring that duty.

In respect of the division of tasks between national and EU courts in reviewing decisions made in a composite procedure, the Court of Justice reserved for the EU level the review of decisions of the ECB, but also of national decisions that lead to a final decision of the ECB when the latter has discretion. This means that the traditional organisation of judicial review is somewhat distorted because EU courts gained the power also to review national decisions based on national law. Here the question of the common interest then becomes central: the national preparatory act is most commonly the result of national law, which was in turn enacted by the legislator in pursuit of national interests. The same may be said of a situation in which the ECB acts on the basis of national law, and it remains unclear whether the ECB then has the obligation to promote the national interest underlying that law, or is it supposed to adjust its decisions also in the pursuit of the common interest.

Two considerations are relevant here. First, by reserving the review on the EU level whenever the ECB is making the final decision by using discretion, it may be said that the involvement of EU courts ensures that the common interest is taken into account. As was done in the context of state aid in bailing-in banks in *Kotnik*, considerations such as a fair sharing of burden among shareholders and creditors of a troubled bank were given a prominent position.[10] However, as we have seen that systemic risk can be prevented by preserving the diversity of the banking systems across Member States, EU courts should always ensure that the heterogeneity of banking systems, including national interests in preserving them, is safeguarded and that an extensive examination of expert opinions in these situations is of essence.

The second consideration to keep in mind is how EU courts interpret national law that the ECB applies. With the aim of remaining within their sphere of competence under Article 19(1) TEU, EU courts should pay great attention to relevant national case law and involve as much as possible national authorities in procedures before them. This aligns with my proposal for a thorough and extensive examination of the duty to state reasons by the institution whose decision is under review. In the SSM context, this approach would impose on the ECB and the opposing party a high burden of showing how relevant national law should be interpreted, what normative considerations can be found in that national law, and whether the common interest should have any influence in this process.

Access to justice for individuals who are in one way or another affected by supervisory decisions should not suffer, however, due to this novel division of tasks. Under the current case law of the Court of Justice, these concerns are not entirely dispelled. For example, it is unclear how effective judicial protection can be ensured for those individuals who do not meet the standing threshold of Article 263(4) TFEU, and yet are affected by the national preparatory act where the ECB enacts the final decision. Such national acts may have ancillary effects not only on the credit institution supervised, but also, for example, on individuals whose fundamental rights might be affected during the search of premises or other investigation powers of national authorities. The Court of Justice did demonstrate a degree of flexibility in *Trasta Komercbanka* when standing is affected by national rules on legal representation. However, it does not appear that the position of shareholders (especially minority ones) will improve.[11]

To assuage these deficiencies, national rules of standing traditionally act as a counterforce to rigid standing requirements in EU law. We have seen how

[10] See, in the context of the troubles of Credit Suisse, 'SRB, EBA and ECB Banking Supervision Statement on the Announcement on 19 March 2023 by Swiss Authorities' Press Release of 20 March 2023. Available at <www.srb.europa.eu/en/content/srb-eba-and-ecb-banking-supervision-statement-announcement-19-march-2023-swiss-authorities#:~:text=The%20Single%20Resolution%20Board%2C%20the,order%20to%20ensure%20financial%20stability>.

[11] This issue is, after *Trasta Komercbanka*, now again pending before the Court of Justice in Case C-777/22 P *ECB v Corneli* and Case C-789/22 P *Commission v Corneli*.

the implementation of the SSM in Germany triggered a constitutional complaint under the same conditions as in other areas of EU law. Yet, we have also seen in *Berlusconi* that national remedies cannot interfere with the exclusive jurisdiction of EU courts to also review national preparatory acts. Procedurally, thus, national courts are cornered and have few other options but to assume jurisdiction nevertheless, if effective judicial protection would otherwise be jeopardised. In a way, that would follow the logic of the Court of Justice in *Trasta Komercbanka* when it admitted legal representation contrary to national law. Of course, this strategy for national courts would also mean departing from the Court's findings in *Berlusconi*. Still, my view is that they should in those situations submit a preliminary reference. The double benefit here would be that the Court of Justice would remain involved, and yet, the ownership of the main proceedings and the final outcome would remain in the hands of the national court.

This disobedience is necessary to combat the downsides of direct actions dominating the SSM. It was already emphasised in Chapter 5 that in such a constellation the Court of Justice loses national courts as important interlocutors. Their continued interaction is crucial for the management of national and common interests that come into play when the ECB and national authorities apply both EU and national law. In other words, composite procedures require composite judicial review. The General Court cannot substitute that role as it is inherently subordinate to the Court of Justice. Lastly, by holding the Court of Justice to its standards, national courts are able to create long-term legitimate expectations, and ultimately, contribute to the uniformity and coherence of EU law.

C.5 THE COMMON INTEREST BEFORE COURTS AND BEYOND

That was what courts could or should have done. But they cannot do everything. I would like to close this book by underlining that courts, as important as they are in ensuring after-the-fact accountability to individuals, are not the platform where democratic deliberation and participation should take place. In an ideal world, highly redistributive decisions in the EMU should be taken after ample democratic input by those affected. Regrettably, that is not how the EMU is designed, but instead displays grave deficiencies that result in political inequality of EU citizens. This book thus started from the premise that in the absence of a radical overhaul of how EMU decisions are made, courts can improve the position of the individual in holding EMU decision-makers to account. It should also be said that another benefit of judicial involvement in this area is that it can create change in the behaviour of decision-makers themselves. In other words, when enacting decisions in the EMU, the relevant institutions will rectify their previous behaviour due to their knowledge of the standards of review that await them before courts. While writing this book, the Next Generation EU package saw the light of day. The Epilogue that follows will analyse it from the perspective of legal accountability as conceived of in this book and offer some final thoughts on what awaits individuals in its rollout.

Epilogue

The adoption at the European Council of 10 and 11 December 2020 of the Multiannual Financial Framework 2021–2027 and the European Union Recovery Facility (Next Generation EU) is arguably the biggest step forward in terms of solidarity which the European Union has taken in its history.[1]

The NGEU entails a substantial reinterpretation of what is possible under the Treaties.[2]

The Next Generation EU (NGEU) certainly made a big splash. It is a package of instruments that essentially allow the EU, for the very first time, to borrow money on capital markets in unprecedented amounts and use portions of it for transfers to Member States in the form of non-refundable grants.[3] Developing from the momentous Franco-German Initiative to institute a Recovery Fund with an ambitious €500 billion envelope,[4] the rationale behind the NGEU is to address the consequences of the COVID-19 crisis by supporting the recovery of Member States and improving their resilience for the future.

In this epilogue, my aim is to test the NGEU against the benchmarks of legal accountability as laid out in Chapter 1. While much ink has already dried concerning how the political institutions made use of the Treaties to justify the

1 Opinion of Advocate General Campos Sánchez-Bordona in Case C-848/19 P *Germany v Poland* [2021] EU:C:2021:218 [61], footnote43.

2 P Leino-Sandberg and M Ruffert, 'Next Generation EU and Its Constitutional Ramifications: A Critical Assessment' (2022) 59(2) *Common Market Law Review* 433, 437.

3 Of the €723.8 billion, €385.8 billion pertain to loans, and €338 billion to grants. See <https://ec.europa.eu/info/strategy/recovery-plan-europe_en#documents>.

4 See Bundesregierung, Pressemitteilung Nummer 173/20 vom 18. Mai 2020. Available at <www.bundesregierung.de/resource/blob/974430/1753772/414a4b5a1ca91d4f7146eeb2b39ee72b/2020-05-18-deutsch-franzoesischer-erklaerung-eng-data.pdf?download=1>.

novel elements of NGEU,[5] very little has happened before the courts. This makes the NGEU the perfect guinea pig for testing the framework of legal accountability aiming to ensure the political equality of citizens. In other words, I will explore what judicial avenues remain available to individuals, should they, alongside the academic community, harbour doubts as to the compatibility of the NGEU with what the Treaties and/or national constitutions allow.

To do so, I will start by presenting the legal framework of the NGEU and how it has been grounded in the Treaties by the Council and the Commission. Turning to the national level, I will present judicial developments that accompanied the ratification of the Own Resources Decision, one of NGEU's components. Third, I will look into the possible avenues of judicial review at the EU level. In the last part, I will offer some concluding thoughts on what awaits individuals in holding decision-makers in the EMU to account before courts.

THE NGEU: STRUCTURE AND CONSTITUTIONAL ISSUES

The NGEU is an umbrella term for three instruments, each of which has sparked discussions on the appropriateness of their respective legal bases. Essentially, the question is: has the EU acquired or is it on its way to acquire its own fiscal capacity that will transform it into a transfer union, in contradiction to what the Treaties currently allow? I will outline each of the instruments' main features, legal basis, and the conflicting views on their compliance with the Treaties. The focus on judicial review in subsequent sections will take as its focus precisely these debates.

The mother instrument of the NGEU is the EURI Regulation,[6] which introduced borrowing for spending based on Article 122 TFEU.[7] Thus, 'in a

[5] In addition to the critical stance taken by Leino-Sandberg and Ruffert (n 2), for a supportive analysis see B de Witte, 'The European Union's COVID-19 Recovery Plan: The Legal Engineering of an Economic Policy Shift' (2021) 58(3) *Common Market Law Review* 635. For a middle ground approach, see P Dermine, *The New Economic Governance of the Eurozone: A Rule of Law Analysis* (Cambridge University Press 2022) chapter 3.

[6] Council Regulation (EU) 2020/2094 of 14 December 2020 establishing a European Union Recovery Instrument to support the recovery in the aftermath of the COVID-19 crisis (OJ L 433 I/23). For a presentation of the political process leading to its enactment, see de Witte (n 5) 638–644.

[7] '1. Without prejudice to any other procedures provided for in the Treaties, the Council, on a proposal from the Commission, may decide, in a spirit of solidarity between Member States, upon the measures appropriate to the economic situation, in particular if severe difficulties arise in the supply of certain products, notably in the area of energy.

2. Where a Member State is in difficulties or is seriously threatened with severe difficulties caused by natural disasters or exceptional occurrences beyond its control, the Council, on a

spirit of solidarity between Member States, in particular for those Member States that have been particularly hard hit',[8] coherent and unified measures are exceptionally necessary to address the 'significant disturbances to economic activity which are reflected in a steep decline in gross domestic product and have a significant impact on employment, social conditions, poverty and inequalities'.[9] The Council has obscured which paragraph of Article 122 TFEU specifically allowed for such an instrument, given that each of the two paragraphs has its own requirements: the first pertaining to financial assistance generally, and the second regulating assistance to individual Member States.[10] This approach has been touted as obfuscating and instrumentalist by some,[11] and as readily justified by others.[12] Thus the first point of contention.

The other two instruments deal respectively with borrowing and spending. Based on Article 311(3) TFEU,[13] the former is regulated in more detail by the Own Resources Decision,[14] which for the first time, exceptionally, allows the Commission temporarily to borrow on capital markets up to €750 billion,[15] which must be returned by 31 December 2058.[16] The original Commission proposal envisaged €500 billion for grants and €250 billion for loans, which was in the negotiations reduced to €390 billion for the former and increased to €360 billion for the latter. A second novelty of the Own Resources Decision was the increase in own resources ceiling, by 0.6 per cent, to ensure the

proposal from the Commission, may grant, under certain conditions, Union financial assistance to the Member State concerned. The President of the Council shall inform the European Parliament of the decision taken.'

8 EURI Regulation, Recital 5.

9 EURI Regulation, Recital 2.

10 For an interpretation of the two different paragraphs of Article 122 TFEU, see Case C-370/12 *Pringle* EU:C:2012:756 [115]–[122].

11 Leino-Sandberg and Ruffert (n 2) 445–446.

12 de Witte (n 5) 655.

13 'The Council, acting in accordance with a special legislative procedure, shall unanimously and after consulting the European Parliament adopt a decision laying down the provisions relating to the system of own resources of the Union. In this context it may establish new categories of own resources or abolish an existing category. That decision shall not enter into force until it is approved by the Member States in accordance with their respective constitutional requirements.'

14 Council Decision (EU, Euratom) 2020/2053 of 14 December 2020 on the system of own resources of the European Union and repealing Decision 2014/335/EU, Euratom (OJ L 424/1). The Own Resources Decision required, under Article 311 TFEU, ratification in all Member States in line with their respective constitutional requirements. This process was completed on 31 May 2021 (in five and a half months). By way of comparison, it took two years and four months to ratify the Own Resources Decision from 2014.

15 Own Resources Decision, Recital 14 and Article 5.

16 Own Resources Decision, Article 6.

coverage of the newly introduced borrowing liabilities of the Union (to the exclusion of all other liabilities).[17] No additional guarantees from the Member States for meeting these liabilities were required. Should the exceptional situation arise that the liabilities from these borrowings cannot be serviced, as a last resort, Member States can be called upon to provide the necessary resources in proportion to the estimated budget revenue.[18]

More generally, the resources necessary for eventually repaying new borrowings are, in large part, yet to be established,[19] aside from the newly established own resource of a uniform call rate to the weight of non-recycled plastic packaging waste generated in each Member State[20] and a new simplified calculation of VAT.[21] The lack of a precise assignment of income to cover the liabilities for borrowing has been seen as a breach of the balanced budget rule set out in the third sentence of Article 310(1) TFEU, which states that '[the] revenue and expenditure shown in the budget shall be in balance'. In that respect, the commentary is in dispute whether this provision outright prohibits the EU to finance its policies by incurring debt, given that each item of expenditure must have its counterpart in the income section.[22]

The debate further turned to the EU's Financial Regulation.[23] Despite being an act of secondary law, the financial regulation under Article 322(1)(a) TFEU sets out the 'procedure to be adopted for establishing and implementing the budget and for presenting and auditing accounts'. Consequently, de Witte suggests it has a higher rank in relation to all other rules concerning the organisation and implementation of the budget.[24] Yet, different provisions of the Financial Regulation have been used to determine whether the EU can use loans to cover its expenditure. While de Witte recalls its Article 220(1), which provides for a possibility of the Commission to raise loans to provide financial assistance,[25] de Gregorio Merino resorts to its Article 17(2), which prohibits Union institutions and bodies to raise loans within the framework of

17 Own Resources Decision, Articles 3 and 6.
18 Own Resources Decision, Recital 23 and Article 9.
19 Interinstitutional Agreement (IIA) of 16 December 2020 between the EP, the Council and the Commission on budgetary discipline, on cooperation in budgetary matters and on sound financial management, as well as on new own resources, including a roadmap towards the introduction of new own resources (OJ L 433I) 28, Annex II.
20 Own Resources Decision, Article 2(1)(c).
21 Own Resources Decision, Article 2(1)(b).
22 Compare Leino-Sandberg and Ruffert (n 2) 451 with de Witte (n 5) 660.
23 Regulation (EU, Euratom) 2018/1046 of the European Parliament and of the Council of 18 July 2018 on the financial rules applicable to the general budget of the Union (OJ L 193/1).
24 de Witte (n 5) 661.
25 ibid.

the budget.[26] Proceeds from loans are in the Own Resources Decision labelled as 'external assigned revenue', an item that does not pertain to the budget, nor is it shown in the budget or subject to the rules on enacting the budget.[27] However, in order to prevent a formalistic abuse of the balanced budget rule by labelling debts as external revenue, de Gregorio Merino underlines that the increase of the ceilings of Member State contributions in effect represents the asset side of the equation and ensures that the budget remains balanced.[28] The definitive meaning of the balanced budget rule in the Treaties remains yet to be elucidated. Thus the second point of contention.

On the spending side of the equation,[29] the Recovery and Resilience Facility (RRF)[30] is based on Article 175(3) TFEU,[31] forming part of Cohesion Policy. The choice of legal basis equally sparked a debate. If the purpose of the RRF is exceptionally to address the consequences of the COVID-19 crisis, as the NGEU itself emphasises, what exactly should be funded to achieve this aim? The Commission itself appears to send mixed signals, stating simultaneously that '[the] Facility is a temporary recovery instrument'[32] and that it is 'more than a recovery plan'.[33] Article 3 of the RRF Regulation defines its scope in six pillars,[34] only two of which mention cohesion.

26 A de Gregorio Merino, 'The Recovery Plan: Solidarity and the Living Constitution' EU Law Live Weekend Edition, No. 50, 6 March 2021, 6. This provision is also referred to by the Bundesverfassungsgericht in its decision on the constitutionality of the Own Resources Decision. Cases 2 BvR 547/21 and 2 BvR 798/21 *Own Resources Decision* Judgment of 6 December 2022 [151].

27 de Gregorio Merino (n 26) 7.

28 ibid.

29 The RRF takes up roughly 90 per cent of the total NGEU budget, the remainder pertaining to pre-existing EU funding programmes, such as ReactEU, Horizon Europe, and the Just Transition Fund. See Conclusions of the Special meeting of the European Council (17 to 21 July 2020) para A14. Available at <www.consilium.europa.eu/media/45109/210720-euco-final-conclusions-en.pdf>.

30 Regulation (EU) 2021/241 of the European Parliament and of the council of 12 February 2021 establishing the Recovery and Resilience Facility (OJ L57/17).

31 'If specific actions prove necessary outside the Funds and without prejudice to the measures decided upon within the framework of the other Union policies, such actions may be adopted by the European Parliament and the Council acting in accordance with the ordinary legislative procedure and after consulting the Economic and Social Committee and the Committee of the Regions.'

32 European Commission website on the RRF. Available at <https://ec.europa.eu/info/business-economy-euro/recovery-coronavirus/recovery-and-resilience-facility_en>.

33 Website of the European Commission. Available at <https://ec.europa.eu/info/strategy/recovery-plan-europe_en>. The original Franco-German proposal calls it a 'Recovery Fund', describing it as 'ambitious, temporary and targeted'. See above n 4.

34 'The scope of application of the Facility shall refer to policy areas of European relevance structured in six pillars: (a) green transition; (b) digital transformation; (c) smart, sustainable

Leino-Sandberg and Ruffert find that, with the exception of security and defence or financial market policies, plans in any and all other policy areas seem susceptible to funding under the RRF.[35] De Witte also finds the scope of the RRF broader than what might previously have been regarded as traditional cohesion policy, thus bringing about a new understanding of cohesion focused on resilience rather than recovery.[36] This debate is well-illustrated by the following example. The German plan under the RRF accords the largest part of the funding (37 per cent) to 'Climate policy and energy transition'. Even more interesting is that 22.1 per cent of that share pertains to 'Building renovation: federal funding for energy efficient buildings'. How this aim contributes to recovery from the COVID-19 pandemic remains entirely unclear, likewise its connection to cohesion.[37] This third point of contention is equally still in need of a resolution.

There is finally something to be said on the relationship between solidarity and equality in the way these three instruments are organised. That the disbursement of non-refundable grants to Member States represents an expression of solidarity and a break from the traditional forms of conditionality is certainly evident, both in its logic and public statements surrounding it.[38] The NGEU is no longer about helping an individual Member State in need, who will in return comply with conditions to ensure it continues to conduct a sound budgetary policy. Rather, the diversity of policy areas eligible for RRF funding allows us to consider it a set of 'macro-economic policy measures aiming at improving the overall balance of economic development within the territory of the European Union'.[39] A focus on the common interest, to be

and inclusive growth, including economic cohesion, jobs, productivity, competitiveness, research, development and innovation, and a well-functioning internal market with strong SMEs; (d) social and territorial cohesion; (e) health, and economic, social and institutional resilience, with the aim of, inter alia, increasing crisis preparedness and crisis response capacity; and (f) policies for the next generation, children and the youth, such as education and skills.'

35 Leino-Sandberg and Ruffert (n 2) 449.

36 de Witte (n 5) 679.

37 European Parliament Briefing, 'Germany's National Recovery and Resilience Plan: Latest State of Play'. Available at <www.europarl.europa.eu/RegData/etudes/BRIE/2021/698849/EPRS_BRI(2021)698849_EN.pdf>.

38 R Crowe, 'An EU Budget of States and Citizens' (2020) 36 *European Law Journal* 331, 340; de Gregorio Merino (n 26) 10. See also, as part of the ECB Economic Bulletin (2022) 1, M Freier, C Grynberg, M O'Connell, M Rodríguez-Vives and N Zorell, 'Next Generation EU: A Euro Area Perspective', available at <www.ecb.europa.eu/pub/economic-bulletin/articles/2022/html/ecb.ebart202201_02~318271f6cb.en.html>; Presentation by Commissioner Hahn of the NextGenerationEU, 14 April 2021, available at <https://ec.europa.eu/commission/presscorner/detail/en/speech_21_1743>.

39 de Witte (n 5) 658.

achieved even by non-repayable, possibly asymmetrically awarded grants, moves the NGEU closer to the solidarity framework proposed in Chapter 1.

Yet, there is much to be desired when it comes to more than paying lip service to solidarity that we witnessed in the context of financial assistance. The RRF Regulation refers to Articles 120 and 121 TFEU, thereby indirectly including the obligation to achieve the objectives set out in Article 3 TEU. Yet, a more specific surpassing of the narrow view of solidarity as money being transferred to the national level is missing. Equally, conditionality has not entirely disappeared from the radar, although it has metamorphosed somewhat in the process. Dermine argues that conditionality acquired an entirely new, systemic dimension that permeates the entire NGEU logic, and in particular the RRF.[40] On this view, the logic of 'cash against reforms' is exacerbated through the requirement for the Member States to submit their National Recovery and Resilience Plans to the Commission, who assesses and then accepts or rejects these plans in advance of the disbursement of funds. In addition, national plans must be in line with the country-specific recommendations made under the European Semester and other pre-existing plans and requirements.[41] Once submitted to the Commission for assessment, the national plans are checked against the standards of relevance, effectiveness, efficiency, and coherence.[42] If the Commission finds them satisfactory according to these elements, they are submitted to the Council for approval by qualified majority.[43] Finally, the implementation of all plans and financing under the RRF Regulation is, among others, subject to the newly established Rule of Law Conditionality Regulation.[44]

Overall, the constitutional footing of the NGEU laid bare debates, old and new, on the flexibility of Treaty rules as well as possible new directions in which the EU may be headed after this exceptional, and at present temporary, experiment. In what comes next, my aim is to explore the way these debates have or might in the future play out before national and EU courts.

JUDICIAL REVIEW AT THE NATIONAL LEVEL

Previous chapters dealing with judicial review at the national level showed that at the outcome level, EU measures and their national implementation

40 Dermine (n 5) 91–94.

41 RRF Regulation, Article 17(3).

42 RRF Regulation, Articles 18 and 19.

43 RRF Regulation, Recital 48 and Article 20.

44 RRF Regulation, Article 8. See also Regulation (EU, Euratom) 2020/2092 of the European Parliament and of the Council of 16 December 2020 on a general regime of conditionality for the protection of the Union budget (OJ L 433I/1).

dealing with the crisis have, for the most part, been found in line with what national constitutions allow. Among the instruments of the NGEU package, only the Own Resources Decision required unanimous ratification of the Member States, in line with national constitutional requirements: a perfect occasion for judicial review.

The only national court asked to review the constitutionality of the act ratifying the Own Resources Decision was, lo and behold, the Bundesverfassungsgericht.[45] The applicants were arguing that the NGEU, and the Own Resources Decision in specific, breach Germany's constitutional identity under Article 79(3) of the Basic Law (concerning the Bundestag's overall budgetary responsibility). They claimed furthermore that it amounted to an *ultra vires* act in contravention of Article 23(1) of the Basic Law, given that the programme and its financing exceed the applicable EU integration agenda in a manifest and structurally significant manner.

We have already seen in Chapter 4 that when it comes to challenging the activities of constitutional organs for their European integration obligations, standing rules before the Bundesverfassungsgericht are fairly generous. This is evidenced also by the Own Resources Decision ratification challenge, which was initiated by 2,279 applicants no less. They have, according to the Bundesverfassungsgericht, 'sufficiently asserted and substantiated a possible violation of their right to democratic self-determination and have demonstrated that they are individually, presently and directly affected'.[46]

Primarily, the applicants sought a preliminary injunction to prevent the president from certifying the ratification. On this, the standard employed for awarding an injunction is 'if this is urgently required to avert severe disadvantage, prevent imminent violence or for other important reasons in the interest of the common good'.[47] On 26 March 2021, the Bundesverfassungsgericht issued an order that the ratification is not to be certified until the preliminary injunction is decided upon.[48] With the wounds inflicted by *Weiss* still healing, the order that included but one sentence ('Die Begründung wird nachgereicht')[49] instilled fears of yet another 'Nein'.[50] Still, there was no need to hold

[45] More information on the initiative behind the constitutional complaint is available at <https://buendnis-buergerwille.de/verfassungsbeschwerde/>.
[46] Cases 2 BvR 547/21 and 2 BvR 798/21 *Own Resources Decision* (n 26) [105].
[47] Case 2 BvR 547/21 Order of the Second Senate of 15 April 2021 [65].
[48] Case 2 BvR 547/21 Decision of the Second Senate of 26 March 2021.
[49] 'The justification will be given later' (Free translation by the author).
[50] See R Repasi, 'Karlsruhe, Again: The Interim-Interim Relief of the German Constitutional Court regarding Next Generation EU', EU Law Live, 29 March 2021. Available at <https://eulawlive.com/analysis-karlsruhe-again-the-interim-interim-relief-of-the-german-constitutional-court-regarding-next-generation-eu-by-rene-repasi/>.

one's breath for too long. On 15 April 2021, the preliminary injunction was rejected,[51] and the final judgment on 6 December 2022 rejected the challenge as unfounded, which will be the focus of the paragraphs ahead. I will specifically look at the three points of contention discussed above: Article 122 TFEU, Article 175(3) TFEU, and the balanced budget rule.

First, is the NGEU (and the Own Resources Decision forming its part) an emergency measure? In the preliminary injunction decision, the German court did not interpret Article 122 TFEU. Upon the summary examination in the preliminary injunction decision, it was of central importance that obligations arising from the Own Resources Decision are temporary in nature without containing any provisions on additional borrowing, which would in any event require an amendment of that decision.[52] It is only if the Own Resources Decision would lead to the creation of a permanent instrument (whereby Germany would assume liability for decisions of other Member States) that constitutional identity would be engaged.[53] In the final judgment, however, the Bundesverfassungsgericht, without batting an eyelid, took up the interpretation of Article 122 TFEU.

In the course of fifteen paragraphs, the German court analysed the relationship between the two paragraphs of Article 122 TFEU, offered their narrow interpretation, found that aims such as digital transformation, climate neutrality, and financing of existing programmes of the EU are difficult to reconcile with the aims of the NGEU.[54] It nevertheless concluded that, first, the exact contents of this provision have not been settled,[55] and second, the Council and the Commission have a wide margin of discretion in interpreting Article 122 TFEU[56] – both conclusions that would pertain to the Court of Justice to make – and this was enough for the Own Resources Decision to survive.

In close connection is the analysis that might shed further light on the question of Cohesion Policy and more generally the debate regarding the relationship between recovery and resilience in the NGEU package. For the Bundesverfassungsgericht, the situation could not be simpler: 'The funds in question are to be used exclusively to address the aftermath of the COVID-19 crisis.'[57] In another passage, the German court emphasised again that this is

51 Case 2 BvR 547/21 Order of 15 April 2021 (n 47).
52 ibid [101].
53 ibid [103].
54 Cases 2 BvR 547/21 and 2 BvR 798/21 *Own Resources Decision* (n 26) [172]–[187].
55 ibid [174].
56 ibid [183].
57 Case 2 BvR 547/21 Order of 15 April 2021 (n 47) [100]. See also Cases 2 BvR 547/21 and 2 BvR 798/21 *Own Resources Decision* (n 26) [214].

specifically aimed at the consequences of the pandemic that are to be taken in a relatively short period of time.[58] In respect of this question, then, the arguments from academia on the use of cohesion did not reach Karlsruhe.

Finally, the applicants argued that the Own Resources Decision breaches the balanced budget rule as well as the prohibition of monetary financing under Article 125(1) TFEU, by empowering the Commission, should any of the Member States not be able to honour a call on time, to borrow additional funds or call on other Member States. This was the first time that the Bundesverfassungsgericht would decide on the 'justiciable limits regarding the assumption of payment obligations or commitments to accept liability'.[59] In *Weiss*, debt-sharing was excluded from what is currently possible under the Treaties and instituting it would amount to a breach of Germany's constitutional identity. We also know that to reach that level of a breach, the budgetary autonomy of the Bundestag must be essentially negated for an appreciable period of time.

In response, the German court offered a wide reading of the balanced budget rule: 'under exceptional circumstance, it does not appear (completely) implausible that the measure could be based on Art. 311(2) TFEU, with the borrowed funds constituting a category of "other revenue" within the meaning of that provision'.[60] Without submitting a preliminary reference, the Bundesverfassungsgericht itself interpreted the balanced budget rule, stating that it includes the following requirements:[61]

> [...] it sets out an authorisation to borrow on behalf of the European Union; it ensures that the financial means obtained be used exclusively for tasks for which the EU has competence in accordance with the principle of conferral; it subjects the borrowing to limits as to the duration and the amount of the commitments assumed; and it requires that the amount of other revenue not exceed the total amount of own resources.[62]

58 Case 2 BvR 547/21 Order of 15 April 2021 (n 47) [106]; Cases 2 BvR 547/21 and 2 BvR 798/21 *Own Resources Decision* (n 26) [215].

59 Case 2 BvR 547/21 Order of 15 April 2021 (n 47) [96].

60 Cases 2 BvR 547/21 and 2 BvR 798/21 *Own Resources Decision* (n 26) [149]. It is interesting to read also how the German court understands the nature of the EU in terms of its budgetary powers: 'Over time, the European Union has transitioned from the classic model of financing international organisations, which rely on state party contributions, to a financial architecture based on own resources – although it is submitted that, in terms of financial economics, the EU's own resources are basically still 'camouflaged member contributions' ([...]).' [166].

61 It is unclear where the inspiration for these requirements comes from.

62 ibid [149].

Although the German court could not reach a definitive conclusion that these conditions are met in the Own Resources Decision, it refrained from concluding that the chosen Treaty legal basis is manifestly insufficient. This was grounded in its temporary nature,[63] that borrowing for this purpose is, although contested, not outright prohibited, so long as it does not fund the general EU budget[64] and finally that the volume and duration of the NGEU is limited.[65] The NGEU would also not amount to a circumvention of Article 125(1) TFEU because the values underpinning Article 122 TFEU do not go against the no-bailout logic.[66]

From the point of view of access and remedies, the need for the Own Resources Decision to be ratified by all Member States, and therefore possibly be subject to constitutional review, is in my view a good thing. Access to judicial review is in the first place easier at the national level, at least in the context of the German constitutional complaint, but it may be presumed that other Member States' standing requirements are lower than those under Article 263(4) TFEU.[67] In that respect, when national courts see possible issues with the provisions of primary EU law involved, we may expect the submission of a preliminary reference to the Court of Justice. This by extension means opening up an EU-wide discussion of these matters that may otherwise not be possible due to the high threshold of direct actions before EU courts. For a programme of a magnitude such as the NGEU, access to legal accountability by all EU citizens is from a democratic legitimacy point of view a crucial necessity.

Against this view, two counter-arguments arise. First, one criticism pertains to the realities of the use of constitutional review at the national level: while the preliminary reference procedure is open to all national courts, it is the loud minority that grabs all the attention and dominates the discourse.[68] Here, of course, we cannot but think of the Bundesverfassungsgericht and its imposition of a certain understanding of EMU law.[69] From the perspective of the interpretation of the common interest, the preliminary injunction and

63 ibid [135], [152].
64 ibid [155]–[161].
65 ibid [162].
66 ibid [210].
67 On that point, see Chapter 3, Section 3.3.1.
68 In a similar vein, see A Guazzarotti, '"It's the (Asymmetric) Economy, Stupid!" Some Remarks on the Weiss Case of the Bundesverfassungsgericht' (2020) 6 *Italian Law Journal* 655, 664–667.
69 With thanks to Paul Dermine for raising this point.

the judgment show reason for optimism that the German court might take a step back from the limelight: in the preliminary injunction, it stated that 'the Federal Republic of Germany cannot unilaterally shape foreign relations and related courses of events'.[70] Without reading too much between the lines, it is undeniable that the Bundesverfassungsgericht's viewpoint surpasses that of Germany alone, and it grants the Federal Government a wide margin of discretion.

This matters for two reasons. First, it promotes a reserved approach by the German court, therefore countering the criticism that courts should not be the ones meddling into the decisions of economic governance that pertain to experts or those with a more direct democratic legitimation. Second, in the full analysis in the main proceedings, considerations of solidarity under Article 122 TFEU were given more importance than Article 125(1) TFEU considerations. In other words, the post-pandemic recovery context provided the leeway necessary in achieving the common interest and somewhat reduced the equality of Member States as the guiding logic of EU action. This is not to say that a more permanent debt-sharing would be something acceptable for the German court (as the judgment itself makes clear), but rather that the financial assistance type of conditionality is no longer the only acceptable option for EU action in economic governance.

The second criticism concerns the German court not submitting a preliminary reference. It is most certainly the last instance court for the purposes of Article 267(3) TFEU and it without a doubt engaged in the interpretation of EU law, a prerogative of the Court of Justice. According to the Bundesverfassungsgericht, its interpretation of Articles 122 and 311 TFEU was generous enough to prevent the submission of a preliminary reference: 'There is no reason to assume that the Court of Justice of the European Union would interpret the competences in Art. 122 and 311(2) TFEU more narrowly'.[71] This entirely misunderstands the purpose of the preliminary reference procedure as a device ensuring the uniform interpretation of EU law: just because the Own Resources Decision did not breach those articles, a reference would help us better understand what these articles, in fact, allow.[72] Given that the NGEU is now in full motion, the preliminary reference

[70] Case 2 BvR 547/21 Order of 15 April 2021 (n 47) [107].

[71] Cases 2 BvR 547/21 and 2 BvR 798/21 *Own Resources Decision* (n 26) [236]. The same was stated by the German court in its review of the SSM and the SRM. See Cases 2 BvR 1685/14 and 2 BvR 2631/14 *Banking Union* Judgment of 30 July 2019 [317]. See also Chapter 5, Section 5.4.2.

[72] As the Bundesverfassungsgericht itself recognises in respect of Article 122 TFEU. ibid [176].

procedure should be used profusely by national courts with the aim of achieving the common interest.

JUDICIAL REVIEW AT THE EU LEVEL

As things stand, the Court of Justice has been at the margins of the NGEU developments, with only indirectly touching upon its novelties when deciding on the validity of the Rule of Law Conditionality Regulation.[73] The lack of litigation before the Court appears as both a blessing and a curse. The emergency package proceeded without judicial interference that may have thwarted the immediate economic benefits of the package, to echo the Bundesverfassungsgericht. The curse, however, is that a silence on the points of contention concerning the interpretation of the Treaties leaves open the possibility of further cavalier uses of their provisions. In this section, I reflect on the way in which the Court might resolve them in the future, given the constellations of judicial review and the existing case law in respect of the three points of contention.

Two avenues of judicial review at the EU level seem possible. First, the Council has approved all national recovery and resilience plans. In the category of 'what could have been', there is the now withdrawn action of the Parliament against the Commission for the failure to act.[74] Here, the Parliament argued that the Commission infringed the Treaties by failing fully and immediately to apply the Rule of Law Conditionality Regulation against Poland and Hungary in the process of approving their recovery and resilience plans. In a category of 'what might be' are the four actions for annulment initiated by associations of national judges against the decision of the Council on the approval of the recovery and resilience plan for Poland.[75] The trouble with this set of actions is admissibility, given that the applicants are associations of judges from other Member States, thus facing an uphill battle in proving direct and individual concern under Article 263(4) TFEU.

The second, and a more realistic, avenue for judicial review at the EU level may result from the management of funding under the national plans. What

[73] Case C-156/21 *Hungary v Parliament and Council* EU:C:2022:97 and Case C-157/21 *Poland v Parliament and Council* EU:C:2022:98.

[74] Case C-657/21 *Parliament v Commission* Order of the President of the Court of 8 June 2022 of the Removal from the Register.

[75] T-530/22 *Medel v Council*; T-531/22 *International Association of Judges v Council*; T-532/22 *Association of European Administrative Judges v Council*; T-533/22 *Rechters voor Rechters v Council*. For more information on the actions, see <www.thegoodlobby.eu/wp-content/uploads/2022/08/TGL-Profs-Press-Release-28-Aug-2022-.pdf>.

I mean by this is that Member States may, in the years to come, challenge the Commission's assessment of milestones being reached or not and the RRF funds (not) being released accordingly. On a further micro level still, it is possible to imagine individual operators carrying out specific items in the national plans and challenging the decisions of the Commission on payments and accounts. It is unlikely though that this latter option would raise fundamental issues of Treaty compliance. What is likelier is that it will further test how rigid (or flexible) is access for individuals under Article 263(4) TFEU. A possible issue in this area will concern the nature of acts by which the Commission will assess the milestones and decide on requests for disbursement: it is likely these will fall in the category of preparatory or similar types of soft law acts. We have seen in Chapter 2[76] that challenging such acts poses a particular difficulty at the EU level and is more likely to succeed through a preliminary reference.

Another point of interest will be the implementation of national plans. We have learned in Chapter 5 that EU and national institutions operating in a composite structure brings about novel solutions in the division of work between EU and national courts. The cooperative and multilevel nature of the implementation of national recovery and resilience plans, not unlike the one in cohesion policy, will in my opinion resemble litigation in that area of EU law: the Commission will possibly participate in proceedings at the national level, and the Court of Justice will intervene to ensure compliance with the principle of sound financial management. For example, both the Commission and the national authorities are under an obligation to respect the principle of sound financial management in cohesion policy, and these are, in the absence of explicit EU rules, to be decided on before national courts in accordance with their national law.[77]

Turning to the three points of contention concerning the NGEU's constitutional backing, I will begin by looking at how the Court interpreted Article 122 TFEU up to now and how these findings may possibly be applied to the EURI Regulation. Following *Pringle*, we know, first, that Article 122(1) TFEU does not regulate the power of the Council to grant financial assistance from the Union to a Member State; and second, that Article 122(2) TFEU is not the exclusive way for granting financial assistance to an individual Member State.[78]

Article 122 TFEU was further interpreted on the occasion of the Commission's rejection to register the proposal for a European citizens'

76 Section 2.2.3.
77 For example, in Case C-443/21 *Avicarvil Farms* EU:C:2022:899 [32], [37].
78 Case C-370/12 *Pringle* EU:C:2012:756 [116], [118]–[120].

initiative 'One million signatures for a Europe of solidarity', which triggered litigation before the General Court[79] and, on appeal, before the Court of Justice, in *Anagnostakis*.[80] The proposed ECI sought to introduce in EU law the principle of 'the state of necessity, in accordance with which, when the financial and political existence of a Member State is threatened by the servicing of abhorrent debt, the refusal to repay that debt is necessary and justifiable', grounding it in Article 122 TFEU. The General Court sided with the Commission and in the process provided a further interpretation of that article. The Court of Justice agreed.

As regards the first paragraph, both courts recalled *Pringle* in confirming that it cannot serve as the legal basis for financial assistance to a Member State nor for a unilateral decision of a Member State not to repay its debt.[81] The interpretation of Article 122(2) TFEU in both judgments concerned the permanent nature of the proposed ECI. Specifically, a permanent instrument based on the state of necessity could not be based on Article 122(2) TFEU.[82] Likewise, that provision could only be used for the assistance granted by the Union, but not debts owed to legal and natural persons, neither public or private.[83] Against this background, would the EURI Regulation pass muster if analysed in respect of Article 122 TFEU?

Let us begin with the first paragraph of Article 122 TFEU. The NGEU package could indeed be characterised as an EU-wide measure taken in the spirit of solidarity between Member States. But does it address a situation whereby 'severe difficulties arise in the supply of certain products, notably in the area of energy'?[84] The EURI Regulation defines its targets in such a broad manner ('significant disturbances to economic activity') that a generous reading of Article 122(1) TFEU may well turn it into a universal emergency clause in EU law.[85] In addition, given the broad reach of areas that can be financed

[79] Case T-450/12 *Anagnostakis v Commission* EU:T:2015:739.

[80] Case C-589/15 P *Anagnostakis* EU:C:2017:663.

[81] ibid [70]–[71].

[82] ibid [75]. See also Opinion of Advocate General Mengozzi in Case C-589/15 P *Anagnostakis* EU:C:2017:175 [42]–[43].

[83] Case C-589/15 P *Anagnostakis* (n 80) [76]–[77].

[84] According to the Bundesverfassungsgericht, the Commission at the hearing in the Own Resources Decision procedure argued that this reference is an illustration of 'one typical example falling within the scope of this treaty competence'. Cases 2 BvR 547/21 and 2 BvR 798/21 *Own Resources Decision* (n 26) [184].

[85] On a critique of 'elastic formats of EU emergency rule', see J White, 'Constitutionalizing the EU in an Age of Emergencies' (2022) *Journal of Common Market Studies* 1, 4. See also B de Witte, 'EU Emergency Law and Its Impact on the EU Legal Order' Guest Editorial (2022) 59 (1) *Common Market Law Review* 3.

through the NGEU, it is further unclear whether it in fact addresses only the broad 'significant disturbances to economic activity' or goes beyond them. Support for the latter conclusion can be found in the use of Article 175(3) TFEU as the legal basis for the RRF (regulating specifically how funds are distributed). As the abovementioned German recovery and resilience plan illustrated, projects with little connection to COVID-19 consequences were accepted for RRF funding. Put simply, even a generous reading of Article 122 (1) TFEU, going beyond 'severe difficulties in the supply of certain products, notably in the area of energy', may not be enough to capture the funding of national projects currently approved.[86]

The second paragraph of Article 122 TFEU focuses on assistance to individual Member States 'experiencing difficulties or a serious threat of severe difficulties caused by natural disasters or exceptional occurrences beyond its control'. Given that Article 122(1) TFEU, following the Court in *Pringle* and *Anagnostakis*, cannot be used for financial assistance to Member States, one might see the need to include also the second paragraph. The COVID-19 crisis may be interpreted as an exceptional occurrence beyond the control of a Member State without engaging in unnecessary legal acrobatics. What remains unclear, however, is the connection between the root cause (the COVID-19 crisis) and the way in which it is granted (loans and grants for an open-ended range of national projects). In sum, it appears that the NGEU is simply too big of a pot of money to be disbursed and thus sits uneasily with the rationale of Article 122(2) TFEU.

We have thus seen that the use of Article 122 TFEU is at least potentially problematic. What about Article 175(3) TFEU? Although the Court did not, to the best of my knowledge, interpret this provision after the Lisbon Treaty entered into force, it did have the chance to say something about its predecessor, Article 159(3) EC. I will therefore present that case law to offer some conclusions on how the Court might assess the legal basis of the RRF in the context of the NGEU.

In 1986, the Governments of Ireland and the United Kingdom established the International Fund for Ireland, with the aim of promoting economic and social advance and encouraging contact, dialogue, and reconciliation between nationalists and unionists. In 2006, the (then) Community enacted a regulation, based on Article 308 EC[87] (now Article 352 TFEU), to regulate

[86] de Witte argues that the inclusion of Article 122(1) TFEU was necessary given the unprecedented amounts of borrowing on capital markets granted to the Commission in the Own Resources Decision. See de Witte (n 5) 655.

[87] 'If action by the Community should prove necessary to attain, in the course of the operation of the common market, one of the objectives of the Community, and this Treaty has not provided the necessary powers, the Council shall, acting unanimously on a proposal from the Commission and after consulting the European Parliament, take the appropriate measures.'

its financial contributions to that fund between 2007 and 2010. The European Parliament initiated an action for annulment, arguing the regulation should have been adopted based on Article 159(3) EC. The practical consequence of the choice of the legal basis was whether an ordinary legislative procedure (co-decision) should have been used, as opposed to the Council acting unanimously after consulting the European Parliament. To determine which legal basis is appropriate in that case, it was necessary to establish the aims and scope of Community action in cohesion policy.

In his Opinion, Advocate General Bot sided with the European Parliament. To reach that point, he offered a useful recap of the creation and meaning of cohesion policy: inserted into the Single European Act in 1987, its aim was to promote the overall harmonious development of the Community. An expression of solidarity between Member States, cohesion policy is a tool for restoring balance and redistribution.[88] But what exactly does it cover?

> The protean nature of economic and social cohesion and the general nature of the tasks given to that policy mean that it is difficult to define it exactly. It thus proves difficult to lay down the limits of the area covered by the policy because economic and social cohesion emerges as a broad overall concept with imprecise contours. The Court's case-law offers no decisive guidance in that connection.[89]

Well. Despite the opaque diagnosis, the Advocate General ultimately found that the contested regulation required a legal basis in cohesion policy, as it selectively focused on a region that manifested 'certain economic and social imbalances'.[90] The Court disagreed with this approach and concluded that it should have been adopted based on both Article 159(3) and 308 EC. Without entering into the discussion on institutional balance,[91] the Court stated that Article 159 EC 'covers only independent action by the Community carried out in accordance with the Community regulatory framework and whose content does not extend beyond the scope of the Community's policy on economic and social cohesion'.[92] The Advocate General and the Court did share the same elusive approach to defining cohesion policy, leaving a broad margin of manoeuvre to the co-legislators in the ordinary legislative procedure.

88 Opinion of Advocate General Bot in Case C-166/07 *Parliament v Council* EU:C:2009:213 [85].

89 ibid [82] (footnotes omitted).

90 ibid [92].

91 On this, see T Corthaut, 'Case C-166/07, *European Parliament v. Council of the European Union* Judgment of the Court of Justice (Grand Chamber) of 3 September 2009, [2009] ECR I-7135. Institutional pragmatism or constitutional mayhem?' (2011) 48 *Common Market Law Review* 1271.

92 Case C-166/07 *Parliament v Council* EU:C:2009:499 [64].

What does that tell us about the legal basis of the RRF Regulation? If the underlying rationale of cohesion is levelling the playing field between Member States, it seems to me that the debate on the ratio between recovery and resilience in the RRF does not affect the choice of its legal basis.[93] My view is that the RRF Regulation is mainly the collateral victim of the arguments against borrowing, not spending. Cohesion policy as such regularly consists of non-refundable grants, because those are sourced in Member States' contributions to the EU's budget.[94] In that area of EU law, then, there is in a way a perfect overlap between financial input and output.[95] The RRF is instead financed through borrowing, without a final decision on how this money will be returned by 2058.[96]

This brings me to the last point of contention when it comes to the NGEU package: did the Own Resources Decision breach the balanced budget rule in Article 310(1) TFEU? In addition, given the prohibition for the Union to finance itself through loans,[97] is borrowing for spending compliant with the Treaties? There are several principles governing the management of the EU budget throughout Article 310 TFEU that are of relevance for the assessment of the NGEU's compliance with the Treaties.

First, the principle of unity of the budget means that the EU's budget ought to be one document presenting all the expenditure and revenue for a given financial year.[98] This principle prevents the establishment of different budgets within the realm of EU spending and serves to protect the institutional

93 The European Court of Auditors's report on the proposed RRF Regulation found that it does not clearly define how the funding will address precisely the consequences of COVID-19 as they have materialised in each Member State, but rather presumes economic conditions from 2018 to guide the allocation of funding. This element remained in the final RRF Regulation and may be seen as a weakness in respect of its legal basis. See Opinion No 6/2020 concerning the proposal for a regulation of the European Parliament and of the Council establishing a Recovery and Resilience Facility (COM(2020) 408) (OJ C 350/1) [17], [25].

94 The Member States and the Commission then manage the spending of funds. For an analysis of the multilevel nature of such management, its reforms, and challenges, see J Bachtler and C Mendez, 'Who Governs EU Cohesion Policy? Deconstructing the Reforms of the Structural Funds' (2007) 45(3) *Journal of Common Market Studies* 535.

95 By this, I mean that the total amount of money received through Member States' contributions is then redistributed through Cohesion Policy. This of course does not mean that the redistributed amounts match the original contributions of each Member State (which would be precisely opposite to the logic of cohesion funds as a programme intended to level the playing field across the EU).

96 See above n 19.

97 Article 17(2) of the 2018 Financial Regulation (n 23). See also Opinion of Advocate General Trstenjak in Case C-539/09 *Commission v Germany* EU:C:2011:345 [54].

98 The first sentence of Article 310(1) TFEU states: 'All items of revenue and expenditure of the Union shall be included in estimates to be drawn up for each financial year and shall be shown in the budget.' See also Article 7(1) of the 2018 Financial Regulation (n 23).

prerogatives of the co-legislators in the enactment of the budget under Article 314 TFEU.[99] The Court of Justice is entitled to review the proper involvement of the relevant institutions in this process.[100] Next comes the principle of budget universality reflected again in Article 310(1) TFEU,[101] requiring that all items of revenue and expenditure be made visible in the budget. Lastly comes the principle of budgetary balance of income and expenditure.[102]

The criticism directed to the Own Resources Decision, was that it does away with the balanced budget rule. This is so because it allows borrowing operations without assigning specific revenue to offset the expenditure that returning those loans will entail.[103] Another criticism concerns labelling the loans as 'external assigned revenue', which therefore does not feature in the budget itself and possibly circumvents the principle of budget universality. It also excludes the European Parliament from decision-making that it would otherwise participate in as a co-legislator.[104]

FINAL THOUGHTS

Where does this leave the individual in her quest of achieving legal accountability in the EMU? As regards the NGEU, providing an answer would require too much time spent staring into a crystal bowl. Learning from experience in financial assistance, monetary policy, and the SSM, however, some trends are visible. First, we know that national courts will not and generally do not wait for EU courts to step in before taking initiative in protecting the constitutional rights of individuals. We have witnessed wider access to national judicial review in the area of financial assistance and national courts did not shy away from awarding remedies to individuals that would not be possible before the EU courts. The preliminary reference procedure has equally produced a number of important decisions at the EU level and prompted solutions in the SSM. In some ways, one of the central findings of this book seems to me to be that individuals do not see Luxembourg as the go-to place to seek accountability of those making decisions in the EMU.

[99] See also R Repasi, 'Legal Options for an Additional EMU Fiscal Capacity' (2013) Note for the European Parliament Directorate General of Internal Policies, Citizens' Rights and Constitutional Affairs, 13.

[100] Case 34/86 *Council v Parliament* EU:C:1986:291 [12].

[101] See also Article 20 of the 2018 Financial Regulation (n 23).

[102] Article 17(1) of the 2018 Financial Regulation (n 23). See also Case C-392/02 *Commission v Denmark* EU:C:2005:683 [54].

[103] On this point, see n 19 above.

[104] In specific on this point, see Leino-Sandberg and Ruffert (n 2) 454.

Another lesson from the NGEU may be that decisive steps do not take place before courts, and are a result of political, rather than legal empowerment. In a way, the NGEU is a development that runs counter to the traditional 'integration through law' paradigm, and instead appears to be a demonstration of integration *despite* the law: the text of the Treaties was stretched to accommodate what was politically and economically seen as a sheer necessity. Paradoxically, this in the long run may grant it stronger democratic legitimacy: ratification by all Member States, who now take ownership of its implementation, may be seen as a shift from the top-down approach through which EU law usually moves forward. This dynamic also disincentivises any challenge to the NGEU to come from its political creators at either the EU or the national level.

From the perspective of the political equality of individuals and achieving the common interest, I should like to close this book with two final remarks. First, the bottom-up creation and design of national recovery and resilience plans promotes their democratic ownership, which inevitably encouraged citizens' participation and voice in defining the common interest behind the NGEU. This helps legitimise the NGEU on a more fundamental level: the selection of priorities and the design of national plans helped shape and concretise the common interest. Their subsequent approval by the Commission and the Council had a double function. In respect of the Council, it allowed for all Member States to be brought together, who then jointly learn of the various asymmetries across the EU, as well as of the interests and needs of different socioeconomic groups across the EU. For the Commission, these priorities should be an important consideration when determining the benchmarks to be met and how to assess them. Through this, national and EU institutions take up a duty towards all EU citizens to achieve the common interest.

Second, one may expect an important contribution from national and EU courts in ensuring that these institutions meet their duty of achieving the common interest. Precisely due to the multilevel nature of the NGEU's implementation, it is crucial that both national and EU courts take part in this activity. In this way, political empowerment buttresses legal empowerment. Because citizens, in their quest for legal accountability, are to access national courts first and foremost, access to justice and possible redress is more direct and possibly more efficient. The Court of Justice is in that sense a secondary actor: through the preliminary reference procedure, it ensures that the EU-wide common interest is not hampered, that EU institutions comply with the basic principles of the EU legal order, and ensures a connection between different national plans by standardising the conditions of their realisation. All the while, its duty is to ensure that the common interest as expressed in the Treaties is adhered to by those shaping public policy.

Bibliography

Adam K and Tzamourani P, 'Distributional Consequences of Asset Price Inflation in the Euro Area' (2016) 89 *European Economic Review* 172

Adamski D, *Redefining European Economic Integration* (Cambridge University Press 2018)

Alexander K, 'The European Central Bank and Banking Supervision: The Regulatory Limits of the Single Supervisory Mechanism' (2016) 13 *European Company and Financial Law Review* 467

Almeida Ribeiro G, 'Judicial Review of Legislation in Portugal: A Brief Genealogy' in F Biagi, J O Frosini and J Mazzone (eds), *Constitutional History: Comparative Perspectives* (Brill 2020)

Alter K, *Establishing the Supremacy of European Law: The Making of an International Rule of Law in Europe* (Oxford University Press 2003)

Amtenbrink F, 'The European Central Bank's Intricate Independence versus Accountability Conundrum in the Post-crisis Governance Framework' (2019) 26(1) *Maastricht Journal of European and Comparative Law* 165

Amtenbrink F and van Duin K, 'The European Central Bank before the European Parliament: Theory and Practice after Ten Years of Monetary Dialogue' (2009) 34 (3) *European Law Review* 561

Anagnostaras G, 'Activation of the *ultra vires* Review: The *Slovak Pensions* Judgment of the Czech Constitutional Court' (2013) 14(7) *German Law Journal* 959

Andolfato D and Li L, 'Quantitative Easing in Japan: Past and Present' (2014) 1 *Economic Synopses* 1

Annunziata F, 'European Banking Supervision in the Age of the ECB: *Landeskreditbank Baden-Württemberg-Förderbank v ECB*' (2020) 21 *European Business Organization Law Review* 545

Arena A, 'Exercise of EU Competences and Pre-emption of Member States' Powers in the Internal and the External Sphere: Towards "Grand Unification"?' (2016) 35 (1) *Yearbook of European Law* 28

Argyroulis D and Vagdoutis N, 'Tackling Economic Inequality: Reorienting ECB's Role?' (manuscript)

Arnull A, 'EU Recommendations and Judicial Review' (2018) 14 *European Constitutional Law Review* 609

'Private Applicants and the Action for Annulment under Article 173 of the EC Treaty' (1995) 32(1) *Common Market Law Review* 7

Arnull A and Wincott D, *Accountability and Legitimacy in the European Union* (Oxford University Press 2013)

Auel K and Höing O, 'National Parliaments and the Eurozone Crisis: Taking Ownership in Difficult Times?' (2015) 38(2) *West European Politics* 375

Azoulai L, Barbou des Places S and Pataut E, 'Being a Person in the European Union' in L Azoulai, S Barbou des Places and E Pataut (eds), *Constructing the Person in EU Law: Rights, Roles, Identities* (Hart 2016)

Bachtler J and Mendez C, 'Who Governs EU Cohesion Policy? Deconstructing the Reforms of the Structural Funds' (2007) 45(3) *Journal of Common Market Studies* 535

Baldwin R, *Rules and Government* (Clarendon Press 1995)

Bardutzky S and Fahey E, 'Who Got to Adjudicate the EU's Financial Crisis and Why? Judicial Review of the Legal Instruments of the Eurozone' in M Adams, F Fabbrini and P Larouche (eds), *The Constitutionalization of European Budgetary Constraints* (Hart 2014)

Barnard C, 'EU Citizenship and the Principle of Solidarity' in E Spaventa and M Dougan (eds), *Social Welfare and EU Law* (Hart 2005)

Bauer M W and Becker S, 'The Unexpected Winner of the Crisis: The European Commission's Strengthened Role in Economic Governance' (2014) 36(3) *Journal of European Integration* 213

Beck T, De Jonghe O and Schepens G, 'Bank Competition and Stability: Cross-Country Heterogeneity' (2013) 22(2) *Journal of Financial Intermediation* 218

Bergstrom C F, 'Defending Restricted Standing for Individuals to Bring Direct Actions against Legislative Measures: Court of Justice of the European Union Decision of 3 October 2013 in Case C-583/11 P' (2014) 10 *European Constitutional Law Review* 481

Beukers T, 'The New ECB and Its Relationship with the Eurozone Member States: Between Central Bank Independence and Central Bank Intervention' (2013) 50 *Common Market Law Review* 1579

Bickel A M, *The Least Dangerous Branch: The Supreme Court at the Bar of Politics* (Yale University Press 1986)

Bickerton C J, Hodson D and Puetter U, 'The New Intergovernmentalism: European Integration in the Post-Maastricht Era' (2015) 53(4) *Journal of Common Market Studies* 703

Biondi A and Spano A, 'The ECB and the Application of National Law in the SSM: New Yet Old...' (2020) 31 *European Business Law Review* 1023

Black J, 'Constructing and Contesting Legitimacy and Accountability in Polycentric Regulatory Regimes' (2008) 2 *Regulation & Governance* 137

Bobić A, 'Constitutional Pluralism Is Not Dead: An Analysis of Interactions between Constitutional Courts of Member States and the European Court of Justice' (2017) 18(6) *German Law Journal* 1395

'Constructive versus Destructive Conflict: Taking Stock of the Recent Constitutional Jurisprudence in the EU' (2020) 22 *Cambridge Yearbook of European Legal Studies* 60

The Jurisprudence of Constitutional Conflict in the European Union (Oxford University Press 2022)

Bobić A and Dawson M, 'How Can Law Contribute to Accountability in EU Monetary Policy?' in D Adamski, F Amtenbrink and J de Haan (eds), *The Cambridge Handbook on European Monetary, Economic and Financial Market Integration* (Cambridge University Press 2023)

'Making Sense of the "Incomprehensible": The PSPP Judgment of the German Federal Constitutional Court' (2020) 57(6) *Common Market Law Review* 1953

de Boer N and Van 't Klooster J, 'The ECB, the Courts and the Issue of Democratic Legitimacy after Weiss' (2020) 57(6) *Common Market Law Review* 1689

von Bogdandy A, 'The Democratic Legitimacy of International Courts: A Conceptual Framework' (2013) 14(2) *Theoretical Inquiries in Law* 361

Bonelli M and Claes M, 'Judicial Serendipity: How Portuguese Judges Came to the Rescue of the Polish Judiciary ECJ 27 February 2018, Case C-64/16, *Associação Sindical dos Juízes Portugueses*' (2018) 14 *European Constitutional Law Review* 622

Borger V, *The Currency of Solidarity: Constitutional Transformation during the Euro Crisis* (Cambridge University Press 2020)

'How the Debt Crisis Exposes the Development of Solidarity in the Euro Area' (2013) 9 *European Constitutional Law Review* 7

Boucon L and Jaros D, 'The Application of National Law by the European Central Bank within the EU Banking Union's Single Supervisory Mechanism: A New Mode of European Integration?' (2018) 10 *European Journal of Legal Studies* 155

Bovens M, 'Analysing and Assessing Accountability: A Conceptual Framework' (2007) 13(4) *European Law Journal* 447

'Two Concepts of Accountability: Accountability as a Virtue and as a Mechanism' (2010) 33(5) *West European Politics* 946

Bovens M, Curtin D and 't Hart P (eds), *The Real World of EU Accountability: What Deficit?* (Oxford University Press 2010)

Brandsma G J and Adriaensen J, 'The Principal-Agent Model, Accountability and Democratic Legitimacy' in T Delreux and J Adriaensen (eds), *The Principal Agent Model and the European Union* (Palgrave 2017)

Braun D and Guston D H, 'Principal-Agent Theory and Research Policy: An Introduction' (2003) 30(5) *Science and Public Policy* 302

Brescia Morra C, 'The Interplay between the ECB and NCAs in the "Common Procedures" under the SSM Regulation: Are There Gaps in Legal Protection?' (2018) 84 *Quaderni di Ricerca Giuridica della Consulenza Legale* 81

Brest P, 'The Puzzling Persistence of Process-Based Constitutional Theories' (1980) 89 *Yale Law Journal* 1063

van den Brink M, 'The Promises and Drawbacks of European Union Citizenship for a Polycentric Union' in J van Zeben and A Bobić, *Polycentricity in the European Union* (Cambridge University Press 2019)

Brito Bastos F, 'Judicial Review of Composite Administrative Procedures in the Single Supervisory Mechanism: *Berlusconi*' (2019) 56 *Common Market Law Review* 1355

De Brito Gião Hanek R and Gallo D, *Constitutional Change through Euro Crisis Law: Report of Portugal* (European University Institute 2015) <https://eurocrisislaw.eui.eu/wp-content/uploads/sites/44/2019/05/Portugal.pdf>

Brunkhorst H, *Solidarity: From Civic Friendship to a Global Legal Community* (MIT Press 2005)

Buchanan A, *Justice, Legitimacy, and Self-Determination: Moral Foundations for International Law* (Oxford University Press 2004)

de Búrca G, 'Developing Democracy beyond the State' (2008) 46(2) *Columbia Journal of Transnational Law* 101

Butzbach O, 'Systemic Risk, Macro-Prudential Regulation and Organizational Diversity in Banking' (2016) 35 *Policy and Society* 239

Canotilho M, Violante T and Lanceiro R, 'Austerity Measures under Judicial Scrutiny: The Portuguese Constitutional Case-Law' (2015) 11 *European Constitutional Law Review* 155

Cappelletti M, Seccombe M and Weiler J H H (eds), *Integration through Law: Europe and the American Federal Experience*, Book 1 (de Gruyter 1986)

Cappellina B, Ausfelder A, Eick A, Mespoulet R, Hartlapp M, Saurugger S and Terpan F, 'Ever More Soft Law? A Dataset to Compare Binding and Non-binding EU Law across Policy Areas and over Time (2004–2019)' (2022) 23(4) *European Union Politics* 741

Carmosino L, 'Direct Concern in State Aid Direct Actions: A Review of the Scuola Montessori Case' (2019) 2019 *European State Aid Law Quarterly* 71

Carroll L, *Through the Looking Glass* (Oxford World's Classics 2022)

Chalmers D, 'The European Redistributive State and a European Law of Struggle' (2012) 18(5) *European Law Journal* 667

Chandler D, 'New Rights for Old: Cosmopolitan Citizenship and the Critique of State Sovereignty' (2003) 51 *Political Studies* 332

Chang M, Howarth D and Pierret L, 'Unconventional Monetary Policies and Moral Hazard: Constructing or Deconstructing the Legitimacy of the European Central Bank's New Instruments?' (manuscript)

Chiti E and Teixeira P G, 'The Constitutional Implications of the European Responses to the Financial and Public Debt Crisis' (2013) 50 *Common Market Law Review* 683

Claes M, *The National Courts' Mandate in the European Constitution* (Hart 2006)

Claes M and Reestman J-H, 'The Protection of National Constitutional Identity and the Limits of European Integration at the Occasion of the Gauweiler Case' (2015) 16(4) *German Law Journal* 917

Cohen J and Sabel C F, 'Sovereignty and Solidarity: EU and US' in K H Ladeur (ed), *Public Governance in the Age of Globalization* (Routledge 2004)

Coman-Kund F and Amtenbrink F, 'On the Scope and Limits of the Application of National Law by the European Central Bank within the Single Supervisory Mechanism' (2018) 33 *Banking & Finance Law Review* 133

Conant L, Hofmann A, Soennecken D and Vanhala L, 'Mobilizing European Law' (2018) 25(9) *Journal of European Public Policy* 1376

Corthaut T, 'Case C-166/07, *European Parliament v. Council of the European Union*, Judgment of the Court of Justice (Grand Chamber) of 3 September 2009, [2009]

ECR I-7135. Institutional Pragmatism or Constitutional Mayhem?' (2011) 48 *Common Market Law Review* 1271
Craig P, *EU Administrative Law* (Oxford University Press 2012)
'The Eurogroup, Power and Accountability' (2017) 23 *European Law Journal* 234
Crowe R, 'An EU Budget of States and Citizens' (2020) 36 *European Law Journal* 331
Crum B, 'Parliamentary Accountability in Multilevel Governance: What Role for Parliaments in Post-crisis EU Economic Governance?' (2018) 25(2) *Journal of European Public Policy* 268
Crum B and Merlo S, 'Democratic Legitimacy in the Post-crisis EMU' (2020) 42(3) *Journal of European Integration* 399
Dahl R A, *Polyarchy: Participation and Opposition* (Yale University Press 1971)
Dani M, 'The Subjectification of the European Citizen' in L Azoulai, S Barbou des Places and E Pataut (eds), *Constructing the Person in EU Law: Rights, Roles, Identities* (Hart 2016)
Davies G, 'The German Constitutional Court Decides Price Stability May Not Be Worth Its Price' (European Law Blog, 20 May 2020) <https://europeanlawblog.eu/2020/05/21/the-german-federal-supreme-court-decides-price-stability-may-not-be-worth-its-price/>
Dawson M, 'The Legal and Political Accountability Structure of 'Post-crisis' EU Economic Governance' (2015) 53(5) *Journal of Common Market Studies* 976
New Governance and the Transformation of European Law: Coordinating EU Social Law and Policy (Cambridge University Press 2011)
Dawson M and Bobić A, 'Quantitative Easing at the Court of Justice – Doing Whatever It Takes to Save the Euro: *Weiss and Others*' (2019) 56(4) *Common Market Law Review* 1005
Dawson M and Maricut-Akbik A, 'Procedural vs Substantive Accountability in EMU Governance: Between Payoffs and Trade-offs (2021) 28(11) *Journal of European Public Policy* 1707
Dawson M, Maricut-Akbik A and Bobić A, 'Reconciling Independence and Accountability at the European Central Bank: The False Promise of Proceduralism' (2019) 25(1) *European Law Journal* 75
Dawson M and de Witte F, 'From Balance to Conflict: A New Constitution for the EU' (2016) 22(2) *European Law Journal* 204
Dehousse R, 'Delegation of Powers in the European Union: The Need for a Multi-principals Model' (2008) 31(4) *West European Politics* 789
Dermine P, 'The Instruments of Eurozone Fiscal Surveillance through the Lens of the Soft Law/Hard Law Dichotomy – Looking for a New Approach' (2021) 23(7) *Journal of Banking Regulation* 18
The New Economic Governance of the Eurozone: A Rule of Law Analysis (Cambridge University Press 2022)
'The Ruling of the Bundesverfassungsgericht in *PSPP* – An Inquiry into Its Repercussions on the Economic and Monetary Union' (2020) 16 *European Constitutional Law Review* 525
Dermine P and Eliantonio M, 'Case Note: CJEU (Grand Chamber), Judgment of 19 December 2018, C-219/17, Silvio Berlusconi and Finanziaria d'investimento Fininvest SpA (Fininvest) v Banca d'Italia and Istituto per la Vigilanza Sulle Assicurazioni (IVASS)' (2019) 12(2) *Review of European Administrative Law* 237

Domurath I, 'The Three Dimensions of Solidarity in the EU Legal Order: Limits of the Judicial and Legal Approach' (2013) 35(4) *Journal of European Integration* 459

Dougan M, *National Remedies before the Court of Justice Issues of Harmonisation and Differentiation* (Hart 2004)

Dragomir L, 'The ECB's Accountability: Adjusting Accountability Arrangements to the ECB's Evolving Roles' (2019) 26(1) *Maastricht Journal of European and Comparative Law* 35

Durkheim E, *The Division of Labour in Society* (1893; New York Free Press 1997)

Dworkin R, *Freedom's Law: The Moral Reading of the American Constitution* (Harvard University Press 1996)

'The Model of Rules' (1967) 35 *University of Chicago Law Review* 14

Taking Rights Seriously (Harvard University Press 1977; Bloomsbury Revelations reprint 2022)

Editorial Comments, 'Not Mastering the Treaties: The German Federal Constitutional Court's PSPP Judgment' (2020) 57 *Common Market Law Review* 965

Egidy S, 'Proportionality and Procedure of Monetary Policy-Making' (2021) 19(1) *International Journal of Constitutional Law* 285

Ekengren M, Matzén N, Rhinard M and Svantesson M, 'Solidarity or Sovereignty? EU Cooperation in Civil Protection' (2006) 28(5) *Journal of European Integration* 457

Eliantonio M and Korkea-aho E (eds), *EU Soft Law in the Member States: Theoretical Findings and Empirical Evidence* (Hart 2021)

Eliantonio M and Stefan O (eds), Special Section 'Soft Law in the EU Legal Order: Reflections and Contemporary Trends' (2018) 37 *Yearbook of European Law*

Ely J H, *Democracy and Distrust* (Harvard University Press 1981)

Eriksen E O, 'Structural Injustice: the Eurozone Crisis and the Duty of Solidarity' ARENA Working Paper 4/2017

European Parliamentary Research Service, 'Transnational Electoral Lists: Ways to Europeanise Elections to the European Parliament' (February 2021), <www.europarl.europa.eu/RegData/etudes/STUD/2021/679084/EPRS_STU(2021)679084_EN.pdf>

Fabbrini F, *Economic Governance in Europe: Comparative Paradoxes and Constitutional Challenges* (Oxford University Press 2016)

'After the OMT Case: The Supremacy of EU Law as the Guarantee of the Equality of Member States' (2015) 16 *German Law Journal* 1003

Fabbrini S, 'Intergovernmentalism and Its Limits' (2013) 46(9) *Comparative Political Studies* 1003

Faraguna P and Messineo D, 'Light and Shadows in the Bundesverfassungsgericht's Decision Upholding the European Banking Union' (2020) 57 *Common Market Law Review* 1629

Farahat A and Arzoz X (eds), *Contesting Austerity: A Socio-Legal Inquiry* (Bloomsbury 2021)

Fasone C, 'European Economic Governance and Parliamentary Representation: What Place for the European Parliament?' (2014) 20(2) *European Law Journal* 164

Fernandes S and Rubio E, 'Solidarity within the Eurozone: How Much, What for, for How Long?' Notre Europe Policy Paper 51 (2012)

Freier M, Grynberg C, O'Connell M, Rodríguez-Vives M and Zorell N, 'Next Generation EU: A Euro Area Perspective' (2022) ECB Economic Bulletin 1 <www.ecb.europa.eu/pub/economic-bulletin/articles/2022/html/ecb.ebart202201_02~318271f6cb.en.html>

Forst R, *Contexts of Justice: Political Philosophy beyond Liberalism and Communitarianism* (University of California Press 2002)

Forsthoff U and Aerts J, 'Financial Assistance to Euro Area Members (EFSF and ESM)' in F Amtenbrink and C Herrmann (eds), *The EU Law of Economic and Monetary Union* (Oxford University Press 2020)

Fritzsche A, 'Discretion, Scope of Judicial Review and Institutional Balance in European Law' (2010) 47 *Common Market Law Review* 361

Fromage D, 'The European Parliament in the Post-crisis Era: An Institution Empowered on Paper Only?' (2018) 40(3) *Journal of European Integration* 281

Gagliardi E and Wissink L, 'Ensuring Effective Judicial Protection in Case of ECB Decisions Based on National Law' (2020) 13 *Review of European Administrative Law* 13

Galli G, 'The Reform of the ESM and Why It Is So Controversial in Italy' (2020) 15(3) *Capital Markets Law Journal* 262

Galligan D J, 'Arbitrariness and Formal Justice in Discretionary Decisions' in D J Galligan (ed), *Essays in Legal Theory: A Collaborative Work* (Melbourne University Press 1984)

Discretionary Powers: A Legal Study of Official Discretion (Clarendon Press 1986, reprinted 2011)

Garben S, 'The Constitutional (Im)balance between 'the Market' and 'the Social' in the European Union' (2017) 13(1) *European Constitutional Law Review* 23

Gärditz K F, 'Beyond Symbolism: Towards a Constitutional Actio Popularis in EU Affairs? A Commentary on the OMT Decision of the Federal Constitutional Court' (2014) 15(2) *German Law Journal* 183

Genschel P and Jachtenfuchs M, 'More Integration, Less Federation: The European Integration of Core State Powers' (2016) 23(1) *Journal of European Public Policy* 42

Gentile G, 'Ensuring Effective Judicial Review of EU Soft Law via the Action for Annulment before the EU Courts: A Plea for a Liberal-Constitutional Approach' (2020) 16(3) *European Constitutional Law Review* 466

Goldmann M, 'Adjudicating Economics? Central Bank Independence and the Appropriate Standard of Judicial Review' (2014) 15(2) *German Law Journal* 265

'The Case for Intra-Executive Accountability in the Banking Union' in M Dawson (ed), *Towards Substantive Accountability in EU Economic Governance* (Cambridge University Press forthcoming)

'Constitutional Pluralism as Mutually Assured Discretion: The Court of Justice, the German Federal Constitutional Court, and the ECB' (2016) 23(1) *Maastricht Journal of European and Comparative Law* 119

Goldoni M, 'The Limits of Legal Accountability of the European Central Bank' (2017) 24 *George Mason Law Review* 595

Goodhart M, 'Democratic Accountability in Global Politics: Norms, Not Agents' (2011) 73(1) *The Journal of Politics* 45

de Gregorio Merino A, 'The Recovery Plan: Solidarity and the Living Constitution' EU Law Live Weekend Edition, No 50, 6 March 2021

Grimm D, 'A Long Time Coming' (2020) 21 *German Law Journal* 944

Grossman N, 'Legitimacy and International Adjudicative Bodies' (2009) 41 *George Washington International Law Review* 107

Grund S and Grle F, 'The European Central Bank's Public Sector Purchase Programme (PSPP), the Prohibition of Monetary Financing and Sovereign Debt Restructuring Scenarios' (2016) 41 *European Law Review* 781

Guazzarotti A, '"It's the (Asymmetric) Economy, Stupid!" Some Remarks on the Weiss Case of the Bundesverfassungsgericht' (2020) 6 *Italian Law Journal* 655

Habermas J, *Between Facts and Norms: Contributions to a Discourse Theory of Law and Democracy* (MIT Press 1996)

The Crisis of the European Union: A Response (Polity 2012)

'Democracy, Solidarity and the European Crisis' in A-M Grozelier, B Hacker, W Kowalsky, J Machnig, H Meyer and B Unger (eds), *Roadmap to a Social Europe* (Social Europe Report 2013)

Harbo T-I, 'The Function of the Proportionality Principle in EU Law' (2010) 16(2) *European Law Journal* 158

Harlow C, *Accountability in the European Union* (Oxford University Press 2002)

'Citizen Access to Political Power in the European Union' (1999) EUI Working Paper RSC No. 99/2

Harlow C and Rawlings R, 'Promoting Accountability in Multi-Level Governance: A Network Approach' (2006) *European Governance Papers* No. C-06-02

Hayek F A, *Law, Legislation and Liberty, Vol. 1 Rules and Order* (University Chicago Press 1978)

Heidelberg R L, 'Political Accountability and Spaces of Contestation' (2017) 49(10) *Administration & Society* 1379

Hernández Fernández F, 'The Application of National Law and Composite Procedures in the Single Supervisory Mechanism: Did the Court of Justice of the EU Find a New Van Gend en Loos?' (2021) 14(3) *Review of European Administrative Law* 5

Hildebrand M, 'Unravelling the Politicisation – Depoliticisation Nexus of Decontestatory Politics during the Euro-Crisis' in A Farahat and X Arzoz (eds), *Contesting Austerity: A Socio-Legal Inquiry* (Hart 2021)

Hilson C, 'Judicial Review, Policies and the Fettering of discretion' (2002) *Public Law* 111

Hinarejos A, 'The Court of Justice Annuls a National Measure Directly to Protect ECB Independence: *Rimšēvičs*' (2019) 56 *Common Market Law Review* 1649

'Economic and Monetary Union: Evolution and Conflict' in P Craig and G de Búrca (eds), *Evolution of EU Law* (Oxford University Press, 3rd ed. 2021)

'The Role of Courts in the Wake of the Eurozone Crisis' in M Dawson, H Enderlein and C Joerges (eds), *Beyond the Crisis: The Governance of Europe's Economic, Political, and Legal Transformation* (Oxford University Press 2019)

Hofmann A and Naurin D, 'Explaining Interest Group Litigation in Europe: Evidence from the Comparative Interest Group Survey' (2021) 34 *Governance* 1235

Högenauer A-L, 'Paper 7: The ECB as a Banking Supervisor: Transparent Compared to What?' (2023) 45(1) *Journal of European Integration* 121

Honneth A, *The Struggle for Recognition: The Moral Grammar of Social Conflicts* (MIT Press 1996)

Honneth A and Fraser N, *Redistribution or Recognition? A Political-Philosophical Exchange* (Verso 2003)

Howarth D and Quaglia L, 'Internationalised Banking, Alternative Banks and the Single Supervisory Mechanism' (2016) 39 *West European Politics* 438

Huber P, 'The Federal Constitutional Court and European Integration' (2015) 21(1) *European Public Law* 83

Isiksel T, *Europe's Functional Constitution* (Oxford University Press 2016)

Jančić D (ed), *National Parliaments after the Lisbon Treaty and the Euro Crisis: Resilience or Resignation?* (Oxford University Press 2017)

Joerges C, '"Brother, Can You Paradigm?"' (2014) 12(3) *International Journal of Constitutional Law* 772

Juul S, 'Solidarity and Social Cohesion in Late Modernity: A Question of Recognition, Justice and Judgement in Situation' (2010) 13(2) *European Journal of Social Theory* 253

Karagianni A and Scholten M, 'Accountability Gaps in the Single Supervisory Mechanism Framework' (2018) 34(2) *Utrecht Journal of International and European Law* 185

Kavanagh A, 'Deference or Defiance? The Limits of the Judicial Role in Constitutional Adjudication' in G Huscroft (ed), *Expounding the Constitution: Essays in Constitutional Theory* (Cambridge University Press 2008)

Kelemen R D, 'Suing for Europe: Adversarial Legalism and European Governance' (2006) 39(1) *Comparative Political Studies* 101

'On the Unsustainability of Constitutional Pluralism: European Supremacy and the Survival of the Eurozone' (2016) 23 *Maastricht Journal of European and Comparative Law* 136

Kilpatrick C, 'Are the Bailouts Immune to EU Social Challenge Because They Are Not EU Law?' (2014) 10 *European Constitutional Law Review* 393

'Constitutions, Social Rights and Sovereign Debt' in T Beukers, B de Witte and C Kilpatrick (eds), *Constitutional Change through Euro-Crisis Law* (Cambridge University Press 2017)

'On the Rule of Law and Economic Emergency: The Degradation of Basic Legal Values in Europe's Bailouts' (2015) 35(2) *Oxford Journal of Legal Studies* 325

Kokott J, 'Report on Germany' in A-M Slaughter, A Stone Sweet, J H H Weiler (eds), *The European Court and National Courts, Doctrine and Jurisprudence: Legal Change in Its Social Context* (Hart 1998)

Korkea-aho E, 'National Courts and European Soft Law: Is *Grimaldi* Still Good Law?' (2018) 37(1) *Yearbook of European Law* 470

Kotzur M, 'Solidarity as a Legal Concept' in A Grimmel and S My Giang (eds), *Solidarity in the European Union: A Fundamental Value in Crisis* (Springer 2017)

Koukiadaki A and Kretsos L, 'Opening Pandora's Box: The Sovereign Debt Crisis and Labour Market Regulation in Greece' (2012) 41(3) *Industrial Law Journal* 276

Krajewski M, *Relative Authority of Judicial and Extra-Judicial Review: EU Courts, Boards of Appeal, Ombudsman* (Hart 2021)

Krisch N, *Beyond Constitutionalism: The Pluralist Structure of Postnational Law* (Oxford University Press 2013)

'The Decay of Consent: International Law in an Age of Global Public Goods' (2014) 108(1) *The American Journal of International Law* 1

Kucko M, 'The Status of Natural or Legal Persons According to the Annulment Procedure Post-Lisbon' (2017) 2 *LSE Law Review* 101

Kudrna Z and Puntscher Riekmann S, 'Harmonizing National Options and Discretions in the EU Banking Regulation' (2018) 21(2) *Journal of Economic Policy Reform* 144

Lamandini M, Ramos D and Solana J, 'The European Central Bank (ECB) Powers as a Catalyst for Change in EU Law. Part 2: SSM, SRM and Fundamental Rights' (2017) 23 *Columbia Journal of European Law* 199

Lanceiro R, '*Dano* and *Alimanovic*: The Recent Evolution of CJEU Caselaw on EU Citizenship and Cross-border Access to Social benefits' (2017) 3(1) *UNIO – EU Law Journal* 63

Larsen S R, 'European Public Law after Empires' (2022) 1(1) *European Law Open* 6

Leino-Sandberg P and Ruffert M, 'Next Generation EU and Its Constitutional Ramifications: A Critical Assessment' (2022) 59(2) *Common Market Law Review* 433

Lenaerts K, 'The European Court of Justice and Process-Oriented Review' (2012) 31 (1) *Yearbook of European Law* 3

'The Rule of Law and the Coherence of the Judicial System of the European Union' (2007) 44 *Common Market Law Review* 1625

Leonelli G C, 'The Fine Line between Procedural and Substantive Review in Cases Involving Complex Technical-Scientific Evaluations: *Bilbaína*' (2018) 55(4) *Common Market Law Review* 1217

Lindeboom J, 'Is the Primacy of EU Law Based on the Equality of the Member States? A Comment on the CJEU's Press Release Following the PSPP Judgment' (2020) 21(5) *German Law Journal* 1032

Lister M, 'The Legitimating Role of Consent in International Law' (2011) 11(2) *Chicago Journal of International Law* 663

Losada F, 'Institutional Implications of the Rise of a Debt-Based Monetary Regime in Europe' (2016) 22(6) *European Law Journal* 822

Lupia A, 'Delegation and Its Perils' in K Strøm, W C Müller and T Bergman (eds), *Parliamentary Democracy: Promise and Problems* (Oxford University Press 2006)

Lynch G E, 'Democracy and Distrust: A Theory of Judicial Review' (1980) 80 *Columbia Law Review* 857

Maatsch A, *Parliaments and the Economic Governance of the European Union: Talking Shops or Deliberative Bodies?* (Routledge 2016)

MacCormick N, 'The Maastricht-Urteil: Sovereignty Now' (1995) 1(3) *European Law Journal* 259

Questioning Sovereignty (Oxford University Press 1999)

Maduro M P, 'EU Law and Sovereign Debt Relief' in K Lenaerts, J-C Bonichot, H Kanninen, C Naômé and P Pohjankoski (eds), *An Ever-Changing Union? Perspectives on the Future of EU Law in Honour of Allan Rosas* (Hart 2019)

Majone G, 'The Rise of the Regulatory State in Europe' (1994) 17(3) *West European Politics* 77

Marafioti G, 'The *Trasta Komercbanka* Cases: Withdrawals of Banking Licences and *locus standi*' in C Zilioli and K-P Wojcik (eds), *Judicial Review in the European Banking Union* (Edward Elgar 2021)

Maricut-Akbik A, 'EU Politicization beyond the Euro Crisis: Immigration Crises and the Politicization of Free Movement of People' (2019) 17 *Comparative European Politics* 380

The European Parliament as an Accountability Forum: Overseeing the Economic and Monetary Union (Cambridge University Press 2022)

Marjosola H, van Rijsbergen M and Scholten M, 'How to Exhort and to Persuade with(out Legal) Force: Challenging Soft Law after *Fédération bancaire française*. Case C-911/19, *Fédération bancaire française (FBF) v Autorité de contrôle prudential et de resolution (ACPR)*, Judgment of the Court (Grand Chamber) of 15 July 2021, EU:C:2021:559' (2022) 59 *Common Market Law Review* 1523

Markakis M, *Accountability in the Economic and Monetary Union: Foundations, Policy, and Governance* (Oxford University Press 2020)

Markakis M and Dermine P, 'Bailouts, the Legal Status of Memoranda of Understanding, and the Scope of Application of the EU Charter: *Florescu*' (2017) 55(2) *Common Market Law Review* 643

Marketou A I and Dekastros M, *Constitutional Change through Euro Crisis Law: Report of Greece* (European University Institute 2017) <https://eurocrisislaw.eui.eu/wp-content/uploads/sites/55/2019/05/Greece.pdf>

Martinico G, 'Judging in the Multilevel Legal Order: Exploring the Techniques of "Hidden Dialogue"' (2010) 21 *King's College Law Journal* 257

Marzal T, 'Is the BVerfG PSPP Decision "Simply Not Comprehensible"?' (Verfassungsblog, 9 May 2020) <https://verfassungsblog.de/is-the-bverfg-pspp-decision-simply-not-comprehensible/>

Matsaganis M, 'The Greek Crisis: Social Impact and Policy Responses' (Friedrich Ebert Stiftung, November 2013) <https://library.fes.de/pdf-files/id/10314.pdf>

Mayer F, 'Rashomon in Karlsruhe: A Reflection on Democracy and Identity in the European Union: The German Constitutional Court's Lisbon Decision and the Changing Landscape of European Constitutionalism' (2011) 9(3) *International Journal of Constitutional Law* 757

'To Boldly Go Where No Court Has Gone Before: The German Federal Constitutional Court's *ultra vires* decision of May 5, 2020' (2020) 21 *German Law Journal* 1116

McDonnell A, 'Solidarity, Flexibility and the Euro-Crisis: Where Do Principles Fit In?' in L S Rossi and F Casolari (eds), *The EU after Lisbon Amending or Coping with the Existing Treaties?* (Springer 2014)

Mendes J, 'Bounded Discretion in EU Law: A Limited Judicial Paradigm in a Changing EU' (2017) 80 *Modern Law Review* 443

'Constitutive Powers and Justification: The Duty to Give Reasons in EU Monetary Policy' in M Dawson (ed), *Towards Substantive Accountability in EU Economic Governance* (Cambridge University Press forthcoming)

'Constitutive Powers of Executive Bodies: A Functional Analysis of the Single Resolution Board' (2021) 84(6) *Modern Law Review* 1330

'The Foundations of the Duty to Give Reasons and a Normative Reconstruction' in E Fisher, J King and A Young (eds), *The Foundations and Future of Public Law: Essays in Honour of Paul Craig* (Oxford University Press 2020)

Menéndez A J, 'The Sinews of Peace: Rights to Solidarity in the Charter of Fundamental Rights of the European Union' (2003) 16(3) *Ratio Juris* 374

'Whose Citizenship? Whose Europe? – The Many Paradoxes of European Citizenship' (2014) 15(5) *German Law Journal* 907

Messori M, 'The Flexibility Game Is Not Worth the New ESM' Luiss SEP Working Paper 15/2019

Michie J, 'Promoting Corporate Diversity in the Financial Services Sector' (2011) 32 (4) *Policy Studies* 309

Michigan Law Review, 'Dworkin's "Rights Thesis"' (1976) 74(6) *Michigan Law Review* 1167

Mody A, *EuroTragedy: A Drama in Nine Acts* (Oxford University Press 2018)

Monnet E, 'The Democratic Challenge of Central Bank Credit Policies' (2023) *Accounting, Economics, and Law: A Convivium* 1

Morvillo M and Weimer M, 'Who Shapes the CJEU Regulatory Jurisprudence? On the Epistemic Power of Economic Actors and Ways to Counter It' (2022) 1 (3) *European Law Open* 510

Muir E, 'Drawing Positive Lessons from the Presence of "The Social" outside of EU Social Policy *Stricto Sensu*' (2018) 14(1) *European Constitutional Law Review* 81

Nehl H P, 'Judicial Review of Complex Socio-Economic, Technical, and Scientific Assessments in the European Union' in J Mendes (ed), *EU Executive Discretion and the Limits of Law* (Oxford University Press 2019)

Nicolaides P, 'Accountability of the ECB's Supervisory Activities (SSM): Evolving and Responsive' (2019) 26(1) *Maastricht Journal of European and Comparative Law* 136

Nowag J, 'EU Law, Constitutional Identity, and Human Dignity: A Toxic Mix? Bundesverfassungsgericht: *Mr R* 2 BvR 2735/14, *Mr R v. Order of the Oberlandesgericht Düsseldorf*, Order of the Bundesverfassungsgericht (Second Senate) of 15 December 2015, DE:BVerfG:2015:rs20151215.2bvr273514' (2016) 53(5) *Common Market Law Review* 1441

Oliver D, *Government in the United Kingdom: The Search for Accountability, Effectiveness and Citizenship* (Open University Press 1991)

Van Oorschot W and Komter A, 'What Is It That Ties ...? Theoretical Perspectives on Social Bond' (1998) 41(3) *Sociale Wetenschappen* 4

Ott A, 'A Flexible Future for the European Union: The Way Forward or a Way Out?' in S Blockmans and S Prechal (eds), *Reconciling the Deepening and Widening of the European Union* (TMC Asser Press 2007)

Papadopoulos Y, 'Accountability and Multi-level Governance: More Accountability, Less Democracy?' (2010) 33(5) *West European Politics* 1030

Pech L and Kochenov D, 'Respect for the Rule of Law in the Case Law of the European Court of Justice: A Casebook Overview of Key Judgments since the *Portuguese Judges* Case' SIEPS Report 2021

Pennesi F, 'The Accountability of the European Stability Mechanism and the European Monetary Fund: Who Should Answer for Conditionality Measures?' (2018) 3(2) *European Papers* 511

Pernice I, 'Multilevel Constitutionalism and the Crisis of Democracy in Europe' (2015) 11(3) *European Constitutional Law Review* 541

Pisani-Ferry J, 'Rebalancing the Governance of the Euro Area' in M Dawson, H Enderlein and C Joerges (eds), *Beyond the Crisis: The Governance of Europe's Economic, Political, and Legal Transformation* (Oxford University Press 2015)

Pollak J and Slominski P, 'The Representative Quality of EU Treaty Reform: A Comparison between the IGC and the Convention' (2004) 26(3) *Journal of European Integration* 201

Poulou A, 'Austerity and European Social Rights: How Can Courts Protect Europe's Lost Generation?' (2014) 15 *German Law Journal* 1145

'Financial Assistance Conditionality and Human Rights Protection: What Is the Role of the EU Charter of Fundamental Rights?' (2017) 54 *Common Market Law Review* 991

'Human Rights Accountability in European Financial Assistance' in M Dawson (ed), *Substantive Accountability in Europe's New Economic Governance* (Cambridge University Press forthcoming)

Prek M and Lefèvre S, 'The EU Courts as "National Courts": National Law in the EU Judicial Process' (2017) 54 *Common Market Law Review* 369

Ragnarsson K H, 'The Counter-Majoritarian Difficulty in a Neoliberal World: Socio-Economic Rights and Deference in Post-2008 Austerity Cases' (2019) 8 *Global Constitutionalism* 605

Ratner S R, *The Thin Justice of International Law* (Oxford University Press 2015)

Rawls J, *A Theory of Justice* (Harvard University Press 1971)

Repasi R, 'Judicial Protection against Austerity Measures in the Euro Area: Ledra and Mallis' (2017) 54 *Common Market Law Review* 1123

'Karlsruhe, Again: The Interim-Interim Relief of the German Constitutional Court Regarding Next Generation EU' (EU Law Live, 29 March 2021) <https://eulawlive.com/analysis-karlsruhe-again-the-interim-interim-relief-of-the-german-constitutional-court-regarding-next-generation-eu-by-rene-repasi/>

'Legal Options for an Additional EMU Fiscal Capacity' (2013) Note for the European Parliament Directorate General of Internal Policies, Citizens' Rights and Constitutional Affairs

Riso A L, 'A Prime for the SSM before the Court: The *L-Bank* Case' in C Zilioli and K-P Wojcik (eds), *Judicial Review in the European Banking Union* (Edward Elgar 2021)

Ritleng D, 'Judicial Review of EU Administration Discretion: How Far Does the Separation of Powers Matter?' in J Mendes and I Venzke (eds), *Allocating Authority: Who Should Do What in European and International Law?* (Hart 2018)

Ross M, 'Solidarity – A New Constitutional Paradigm for the EU?' in M Ross and Y Borgmann-Prebil (eds), *Promoting Solidarity in the European Union* (Oxford University Press 2010)

Rossi L S, 'The Principle of Equality among Member States of the European Union' in L S Rossi and F Casolari (eds), *The Principle of Equality in EU Law* (Springer 2017)

Salomon M E, 'Of Austerity, Human Rights and International Institutions' (2015) 21 (4) *European Law Journal* 521

Sandbu M, 'A Political Backlash against Monetary Policy Is Looming' (Financial Times, 23 October 2022) <www.ft.com/content/6f70bbcd-72b7-4518-be6b-401adba7cc34>

Sarmiento D, 'Setting the Limits of Implementation of National Law by EU Institutions: The *Corneli v ECB* Case (T-502/19)' (EU Law Live, October 2022) <https://eulawlive.com/op-ed-setting-the-limits-of-implementation-of-national-law-by-eu-institutions-the-corneli-v-ecb-case-t-502-19-by-daniel-sarmiento/>

Schacter J S, 'Ely and the Idea of Democracy' (2004) 57 *Stanford Law Review* 737

Schammo P, 'Institutional Change in the Banking Union: The Case of the Single Supervisory Mechanism' (2021) 40(1) *Yearbook of European Law* 265

Schmitter P C, *How to Democratize the European Union…and Why Bother?* (Rowman & Littlefield 2000)

Schneider M P A, Kinsella S and Godin A, 'Redistribution in the Age of Austerity: Evidence from Europe 2006–2013' (2017) 24(1) *Applied Economics Letters* 672

Scholten M and van Rijsbergen M, 'The *ESMA-Short Selling* Case: Erecting a New Delegation Doctrine in the EU upon the *Meroni-Romano* Remnants' (2014) 41 (4) *Legal Issues of Economic Integration* 389

Schwarz M, 'A Memorandum of Misunderstanding – The Doomed Road of the European Stability Mechanism and a Possible Way Out: Enhanced Cooperation' (2014) 51 *Common Market Law Review* 389

van der Schyff G, 'Constitutional Review by the Judiciary in the Netherlands: A Bridge too Far?' (2010) 11 *German Law Journal* 175

Scott C, 'Accountability in the Regulatory State' (2000) 27(1) *Journal of Law and Society* 38

Scott J and Sturm S, 'Courts as Catalysts: Rethinking the Judicial Role in New Governance' (2007) 13 *Columbia Journal of European Law* 565

Segoin D, 'The Investigation Powers, Including On-Site Inspections, of the ECB, and Their Judicial Control' in C Zilioli and K-P Wojcik (eds), *Judicial Review in the European Banking Union* (Edward Elgar 2021)

Shaw J, 'Process and Constitutional Discourse in the European Union' (2000) 27 *Journal of Law and Society* 4

Simoncini M, 'Different Shades of Legal Standing and the Right to Judicial Protection of Private Parties in the Banking Union: *Trasta Komercbanka*' (2020) 57 *Common Market Law Review* 1867

Snyder F, 'The Effectiveness of Community Law: Institutions, Processes, Tools and Techniques' (1993) 56 *Modern Law Review* 19

Spaventa E, 'From Gebhard to Carpenter: Towards a (Non-)Economic Constitution' (2004) 41(3) *Common Market Law Review* 743

Spieker L D, 'Framing and Managing Constitutional Identity Conflicts: How to Stabilize the Modus Vivendi between the Court of Justice and National Constitutional Courts' (2020) 57(2) *Common Market Law Review* 361

Steinbach A, 'All's Well That Ends Well? Crisis Policy after the German Constitutional Court's Ruling in *Gauweiler*' (2017) 24(1) *Maastricht Journal of European and Comparative Law* 140

'Effect-Based Analysis in the Court's Jurisprudence on the Euro Crisis' (2017) 42(2) *European Law Review* 254

Steinvorth U, 'Applying the Idea of Solidarity to Europe' in A Grimmel and S My Giang (eds), *Solidarity in the European Union: A Fundamental Value in Crisis* (Springer 2017)

Stigler G J, 'The Theory of Economic Regulation' (1971) 6(2) *Bell Journal of Economics and Management Science* 114

Terpan F, 'Soft Law in the European Union – The Changing Nature of EU Law' (2015) 21(1) *European Law Journal* 68

Teubner G, *Constitutional Fragments: Societal Constitutionalism and Globalization* (Oxford University Press 2012)

Transparency International, 'From Crisis to Stability: How to Make the European Stability Mechanism Transparent and Accountable' (2017) <https://transparency.eu/wp-content/uploads/2017/03/ESM_Report_DIGITAL-version.pdf>

Tridimas T, 'The Constitutional Dimension of Banking Union' in S Grundmann and H-W Micklitz, *The European Banking Union and Constitution–Beacon for Advanced Integration or Death-Knell for Democracy* (Hart 2019)

Tridimas T and Xanthoulis N, 'A Legal Analysis of the Gauweiler Case: Between Monetary Policy and Constitutional Conflict' (2016) 23(1) *Maastricht Journal of European and Comparative Law* 17

Tuori Kaarlo, *European Constitutionalism* (Cambridge University Press 2015)

Tuori Kaarlo and Tuori Klaus, *The Eurozone Crisis: A Constitutional Analysis* (Cambridge University Press 2014)

Tuori Klaus, 'The ECB's Quantitative Easing Programme as a Constitutional Game Changer' (2019) 26(1) *Maastricht Journal of European and Comparative Law* 94

Türk A H and Xanthoulis N, 'Legal Accountability of European Central Bank in Bank Supervision: A Case Study in Conceptualizing the Legal Effects of Union Acts' (2019) 26(1) *Maastricht Journal of European and Comparative Law* 151

Tushnet M, 'Darkness at the Edge of Town: The Contributions of John Hart Ely to Constitutional Theory' (1980) 89 *Yale Law Journal* 1037

'Policy Distortion and Democratic Debilitation: Comparative Illumination of the Counter Majoritarian Difficulty' (1995) 94(2) *Michigan Law Review* 245

Valutytė R, 'Legal Consequences for the Infringement of the Obligation to Make a Reference for a Preliminary Ruling under Constitutional Law' (2012) 19(3) *Jurisprudencija/Jurisprudence* 1171

Violante T, 'Bring Back the Politics: The PSPP Ruling in Its Institutional Context' (2020) 21 *German Law Journal* 1045

Waldron J, 'The Core of the Case against Judicial Review' (2006) 115 *Yale Law Journal* 1346

Law and Disagreement (Oxford University Press 1999)

Walker N, 'Late Sovereignty in the European Union' in N Walker (ed), *Sovereignty in Transition* (Hart 2003)

Warren M, 'Liberal Constitutionalism as Ideology: Marx and Habermas' (1989) 17 *Political Theory* 511

Weiler J H H, *The Constitution of Europe: 'Do the New Clothes Have an Emperor?' and Other Essays on European Integration* (Cambridge University Press 1999)

'Prologue: Global and Pluralist Constitutionalism – Some Doubts' in G de Búrca and J H H Weiler (eds), *The Worlds of European Constitutionalism* (Cambridge University Press 2012)

'Van Gend en Loos: The Individual as Subject and Object and the Dilemma of European Legitimacy' (2014) 12(1) *International Journal of Constitutional law* 93

Wendel M, 'Paradoxes of Ultra-Vires Review: A Critical Review of the PSPP Decision and Its Initial Reception' (2020) 21 *German Law Journal* 979

White J, 'Constitutionalizing the EU in an Age of Emergencies' (2022) *Journal of Common Market Studies* 1

Wissink L, Duijkersloot T and Widdershoven R, 'Shifts in Competences between Member States and the EU in the New Supervisory System for Credit Institutions and Their Consequences for Judicial Protection' (2014) 10(5) *Utrecht Law Review* 92

Witte A, 'The Application of National Banking Supervision Law by the ECB: Three Parallel Modes of Executing EU Law?' (2014) 21 *Maastricht Journal of European and Comparative Law* 89

de Witte B, 'The European Union's COVID-19 Recovery Plan: The Legal Engineering of an Economic Policy Shift' (2021) 58(3) *Common Market Law Review* 635

'Guest Editorial: EU Emergency Law and Its Impact on the EU Legal Order' (2022) 59(1) *Common Market Law Review* 3

de Witte B and Beukers T, 'The Court of Justice Approves the Creation of the European Stability Mechanism outside the EU Legal Order: *Pringle*' (2013) 50 *Common Market Law Review* 805

de Witte F, 'Emancipation through Law?' in L Azoulai, S Barbou des Places and E Pataut (eds), *Constructing the Person in EU Law: Rights, Roles, Identities* (Hart 2016)

Justice in the EU: The Emergence of Transnational Solidarity (Oxford University Press 2015)

'Sex, Drugs and EU Law: The Recognition of Moral and Ethical Diversity in EU Law' (2013) 50(6) *Common Market Law Review* 1545

Wolfers B and Voland T, 'Level the Playing Field: The New Supervision of Credit Institutions by the European Central Bank' (2014) 51(5) *Common Market Law Review* 1463

Woodhouse A, 'Process Review as Panacea: A Critique of Process Review Advocacy in the European Union' (2020) 45(3) *European Law Review* 373

Yein Ng G, 'Judicialisation and the End of Parliamentary Supremacy: Shifting Paradigms in the Protection of the Rule of Law and Human Rights in the UK, France and the Netherlands' (2014) 3 *Global Journal of Comparative Law* 50

Ypi L, *Free: Coming of Age at the End of History* (Penguin Books 2022)

Index

www.ingramcontent.com/pod-product-compliance
Lightning Source LLC
LaVergne TN
LVHW011812200926
848484LV00005B/1163